HUNTING CARIBOU

Hunting Caribou

Subsistence Hunting along the Northern Edge of the Boreal Forest

HENRY S. SHARP &
KARYN SHARP

University of Nebraska Press
Lincoln & London

Library of Congress Cataloging-in-Publication Data

Sharp, Henry S.
Hunting caribou: subsistence hunting along the northern
edge of the boreal forest / Henry S. Sharp and Karyn Sharp.
pages   cm
Summary: "Participant ethnography of the subsistence
hunting practices of a band of Denésuliné in the
Northwestern Territories"—Provided by publisher.
Includes bibliographical references and index.
ISBN 978-0-8032-7446-4 (cloth: alk. paper)
ISBN 978-0-8032-7735-9 (epub)
ISBN 978-0-8032-7736-6 (mobi)
ISBN 978-0-8032-7737-3 (pdf)
1. Chipewyan Indians—Hunting—Northwest Territories.
2. Caribou hunting—Northwest Territories. 3. Subsistence hunting—Northwest Territories. 4. Chipewyan
Indians—Northwest Territories—Social life and customs.
5. Hunting and gathering societies—Northwest Territories.
6. Ethnology—Northwest Territories. 7. Human ecology—
Northwest Territories. 8. Northwest Territories—Social
life and customs. 9. Northwest Territories—Environmental
conditions. I. Sharp, Karyn. II. Title.
E99.C59S53 2015
304.209719'3—dc23
2015002778

Set in Sabon by M. Scheer.

For
Caribou, Wolf, and Loon

In Memoriam
Catharine M. Sharp
Alphonse Disain
Boniface Disain
Paul D. Miller
Ernest S. Burch Jr.

Contents

List of Illustrations . . xi
Acknowledgments . . xiii
Introduction . . xxiii

HUNT 1. Caribou . . 1

TEXT 1. Hunting and Predation . . 11
Small Game. Native Mammals. Scale, Guns, and Freedom.
Denésuliné Conceptualization of Hunting. Biology of Women as
Hunters. Trust. Hunting Is the Easy Part.

HUNT 2. Moose . . 28

TEXT 2. Food Storage . . 32
Meat Distribution. In the Village. Food Storage in the Bush:
Freezing, Drying, Smoking, Natural Refrigeration. Protecting
Dried Meat. Drying Caribou Meat. Marrow and Boiling Bones
for Grease.

HUNT 3. Caribou: Pursuit and Risk . . 51

TEXT 3. Persistence in Hunting . . 56
The Dangers of Moving through the Bush. Walking the Land.
Dog Teams. Boats, Opportunistic Contact in Hunting.

HUNT 4. Caribou: Waiting for Prey . . 64

TEXT 4. Weapons . . 73
Muskets and Rifles. Accuracy. How Weapons Technology Altered
Denésuliné Hunting. Women and Rifles. Social Changes from Changed
Hunting Methods. Pursuit Hunting and Following Wounded Game.

HUNT 5. Caribou: Walking, Kill Locations, and Spoilage . . 90

TEXT 5. Carrion and Scavengers . . 94
The African Model. Consequences of Human Scavenging. An
Anthropological Gender War. Eating the Dead. Snow Probes.

HUNT 6. Wolf . . 108

TEXT 6. Camp Formation . . 112
Pitching a Camp. Work Areas and Dog Beds. Area a Camp
Occupies. Range of Day Trips. Marking the Land. Average Area
Exploited by a Camp. Human Influence upon the Land.

HUNT 7. Moose: Hunting by Habitat . . 128

TEXT 7. Summer Doldrums . . 132
Inactivity. Problems with Making and Storing Dry Meat. Fish and
Other Things. Choosing a Camp Location. Scars on the Land.

HUNT 8. Caribou: Long-Distance Hunting . . 142

TEXT 8. Transporting Meat . . 145
Walking the Land. Storing Meat in Lakes.

INTERLUDE 1. Land Use and the Terrain at Foxholm Lake . . 152

HUNT 9. Bear: Failed Hunt . . 164

TEXT 9. Looking for Game . . 166
The Use of High Ground. The Scale of Distance in Hunting.
Time and Distance.

HUNT 10. Caribou: Calves . . 170

TEXT 10. Hides . . 174
Characteristics of Caribou Hide and Leather. Making and
Working Caribou Hide. Time Window for Taking Caribou Hide.
Parasites and Seasonality. Uses of Caribou Hide. The Need for
Hides Modifies Hunting Priorities. Hunting the Megafauna.

HUNT 11. Jackfish . . 190

TEXT 11. Women's Labor . . 193
Flexibility in the Sexual Division of Labor. Women's Work and
Social Status. Women's Tasks and Shared Work. Raw Materials
vs. Finished Products. The Balance of Temperaments.

HUNT 12. Bear: Stalking Prey . . 201

TEXT 12. Prey Choice . . 205
The Failure of Economic Analysis

HUNT 13. Missing Hunts . . 209

TEXT 13. Shadows of the Past . . 232
Geology, Rock, Ice, and Ground Cover. Permafrost, Drainage,
and Ice Action. Change. How Long Is the Memory of Unused
Technology? Clothing. The Generational Transmission of
Knowledge.

INTERLUDE 2. Wolves, Caribou, and Approaching Prey . . 240

HUNT 14. Caribou: Caching in the Fall . . 248

TEXT 14. Hunting from High Ground . . 257
Prey Selection. Hunting with Spears.

HUNT 15. Caribou: Failed Hunt . . 270

TEXT 15. A Puzzle . . 277
How Past Hunters Hunted the Land. Conclusion.

Selected Bibliography . . 283
Index . . 289

Illustrations

Photos

Following page 104

1. Tundra at Damant Lake
2. Rock Desert tundra
3. Half a dozen caribou close by the location of Hunt 5
4. Parts of two caribou being prepared for dry meat
5. The leg meat of the two caribou cut into separate muscles
6. The muscles being cut into sheathes
7. Finished dry meat hanging on a dry meat rack
8. Eddy and Phil with caribou meat waiting for a float plane
9. Wellington packing caribou meat up to the summer camp
10. The north-south bay, sand hill, narrows, and north shore of Foxholm Lake
11. Snow changes things
12. The winter camp of 1975 on the small lake

Maps

1. Northwest End of Foxholm Lake . . xx
2. Smalltree Lake . . xxi

Figure

Modified kinship diagram . . xix

Acknowledgments

Above all, we wish to thank the people of Mission and Discha for allowing us to live among them and share in the experiences of their lives. For the elder of us, who began this as an adult, those years were ones of trying to understand the operation of a complex and subtle culture seeking to survive in the face of the demanding climactic and environmental conditions of the Subarctic during a period of rapid—and profound—change in physical, economic, and social conditions. Personally it was a time of establishing and sharing relationships; the occasion to try to know and understand many of the most competent, delightful, decent, and complex human beings encountered in the course of a now somewhat lengthy lifetime. For the younger of us, it began as the opportunity to grow up among the Denésuliné. Experience of the social context in which the hunts recounted in this work occurred was among the circumstances of her childhood. She grew to adulthood with the bush life of the Denésuliné as part of the very fabric of her own life. This has given to the intellectual curiosity and understanding of her adult life an added dimension that few will ever be able to replicate. The Denésuliné willingness to share experiences with us has become one of the defining features of our lives and one for which we are eternally grateful.

We have chosen, out of respect and with thanks, to use the real names of the late Abraham Artchie and Ben Adam. We have also used the name of the late Fred Riddle. He has no descendants. There is no longer any reason to disguise his identity. The Subarctic is a harsh and demanding place, and life there is hard on people. Unfortunately, few of the individuals discussed in the text are still among the living. Other than those already mentioned, the names used in the text are pseudonyms. They are consistent with those used in earlier works. We discussed this with the surviving family and, largely to ensure their privacy, it was their preference that we continue this practice.

There are simply too many people at Mission and Discha to whom we owe our thanks and gratitude for us to mention them all. Special thanks, however, go to Joe Bigeye, not only for all the assistance he has given but for the decades of friendship we have shared.

We have used the real names of lakes and locations away from the village that are no longer in active use by the surviving individuals mentioned in the text or by their descendants. This means that because of changes in land usage in the last few years, only Foxholm Lake is disguised. We have continued to use the terms Discha and Mission, again largely for reasons of privacy.

The way animal names are spelled, capitalized, or pluralized may sometimes seem confusing. The topic of this work is quite different from that of *Loon,* but some of the issues involved in writing about the various cultural conceptualizations of the nature of animals dealt with there also apply here (Sharp 2001: xv–xvi). Essentially, where animals are written of in a western sense, western conventions of naming species and pluralizing them are followed. The Denésuliné conceptualization of animals is very different from the western conceptualization of animals. It is at times necessary to distinguish between animals as natural beings, as simultaneously natural and spiritual beings, and as categories.

We offer special thanks to Catherine L. Sharp. She is an artist rather than a social scientist, but she had a sustained interest in this work as it developed. She more than once took the time and trouble to read the manuscript as it grew and spent many hours discussing it with us. We thank her for her insights and advice.

Thanks to Jim Barger and Robert Kirkpatrick for their assistance in converting some of the draft into electronic form. Thanks from Henry go to Margaret Williamson Huber and Peter B. Huber. In the course of a pleasant visit at the home of two old friends a decade ago there ensued a long discussion about the nature of the approach to prey animals and the issue of prey selection that provided an invaluable prod to the preparation of this book.

We wish to thank Bryan Gordon for his comments to us on what the text said about the caribou herd following debate. Taking a manuscript from a draft to a publishable form is an intricate and complex process. We wish to thank the University of Nebraska Press for guiding us through the process. Working with them was interesting, informative, and pleasant. We particularly wish to note the efforts of Matt Bokovoy, the senior acquisitions editor, and Heather Stauffer, the editorial assistant. Sally Antrobus deserves thanks for taking on the task of copy editing the manuscript.

This study is based upon our experience among a specific extended family network: Karyn's mother's family. Karyn grew up from birth with this extended family network as one side of her family (her mother, a daughter of Paul and May, does not wish to be named). Karyn's mother and Henry were married in 1970 and remained married for a decade.

The extended family network, technically a bilateral kindred based upon the separate kindreds of Paul and May, at its maximum extension encompassed roughly 17 percent of the population of the Mission Denésuliné. The kindred was far larger than the number of individuals who spent time in the bush with Paul and May. Denésuliné winter camps are typically constructed from the wide membership of the extended kindreds by individuals (and their households) opting to join particular individuals (and their households) to form a bush camp.

The camp discussed in this text began to form with the marriage of Paul and May. As they began to establish their identity as a separate group, they frequently shared winter camps with relatives and affines. As they aged and their children grew older, they began to prefer to camp apart from other Denésuliné camps.

Each came to the marriage with a number of siblings. Those siblings who survived had in turn married and had children of their own. Over the years Paul and May sometimes camped with their siblings and their families. Paul had two sisters, married with large families three generations deep, who live in Discha. May came from a large family living around English River but had two surviving sisters, without living descendants, in the area around Mission. She also had a surviving brother, Abraham Artchie of Hunt 2. Paul's elderly father, who had become blind, lived in Discha at the home of one of his daughters. His own bush life was spent in the area that Paul came to favor and was used throughout his life. The attachment of the men of this descent line to this area was at least several generations deep.

Three of Paul's and May's surviving sons frequently wintered with them in the study area. Wellington, married with a single child at the start of the study, was the eldest of the brothers to winter with his parents. George, unmarried at the start of the study, became married during the course of it. The families of both brothers grew steadily over the course of the study. The youngest of the brothers, Phil, was in his early teens when the study began.

At times members of the extended kin network would spend time in the bush with Paul and May. Their second eldest daughter, married, widowed, and remarried, and her second husband Eddy came north for short periods several times during the study. Wellington's mother-in-law, widowed and living by herself in the village, came to Smalltree Lake for several months in 1975. Her daughter Ann, Wellington's wife, had two unmarried brothers who, at various times, either wintered with Wellington and Ann at Smalltree Lake or came up for shorter summer visits. George's father-in-law and his family came to Foxholm Lake to winter with his daughter and son-in-law during the winter of 1975.

Mortality strikes hard among people who live active lives in the bush. There were several deaths of young adults before and during the study. As a result of these deaths, and for other reasons, there were near a half-dozen children of various ages who at one time or another spent part of the year out in the bush in the company of their grandparents. Any given camp, in any given year, would have a variable number of children or visitors living with it for various periods of the year.

The relationships among the individuals named in the text are represented on the following diagram.

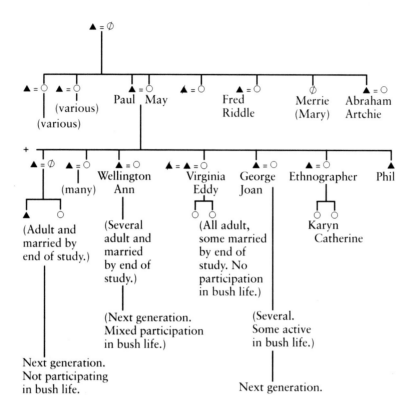

Modified kinship diagram

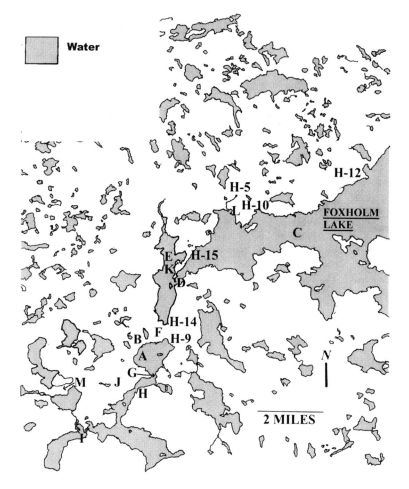

1. Northwest End of Foxholm Lake

A. small lake

B. winter camp

C. Foxholm Lake

D. narrows on Foxholm Lake

E. North-south bay of Foxholm Lake

F. portage

G. exit stream out of small lake

H. shallows

I. intersection of three creeks

J. highlands

K. lithic debris field

L. 1970 summer camp

M. creek used by George's father-in-law for his trap line

H-5. Hunt 5, caribou in summer

H-9. Hunt 9, failed bear hunt

H-10. Hunt 10, caribou calves

H-12. Hunt 12, bear

H-14. Hunt 14, caribou in fall

H-15. Hunt 15, caribou and landscape

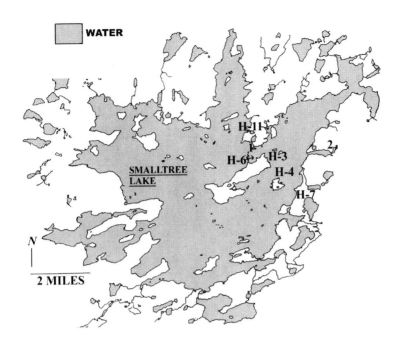

2. Smalltree Lake

H-3. starting point for Hunt 3, caribou

H-4. Hunt 4, caribou

H-6. Hunt 6, wolf

H-7. Hunt 7, moose

H-11. Hunt 11, jackfish

I. summer camp

Introduction

The primary purpose of this work is to present observational material about subsistence hunting among the Denésuliné of the northern Canadian Subarctic. There is surprisingly little observational material on subsistence hunting in the professional literature. With luck, this work will stimulate others to publish detailed accounts of aboriginal hunting and other subsistence activities before that knowledge vanishes. As it is unlikely that many readers will have any direct experience of subsistence hunting, we have attempted to present our material in sufficient detail to provide a solid sense of what subsistence hunting involves and how it is accomplished as well as to show how it connects to other aspects of Denésuliné life.

This work developed out of the attempts of a father and daughter to communicate with each other about their experience and understanding of the Denésuliné as the daughter progressed through school. Henry is a social anthropologist and ethnologist. Karyn is Denésuliné and an archaeologist who has developed a speciality in First Nations Studies. Over the years, as her interests and expertise developed, it became increasingly clear to us just how greatly our disciplinary specializations affected how we saw and understood our experiences of the Denésuliné and created difficulties in communicating past our specialized disciplinary knowledge.

We think that what is true for us is true for others in our disciplines. Archaeologists, paleoanthropologists, and ethnographers have always had difficulties understanding each other, but it increasingly seems that they simply do not talk to each other very much now. Whether we did so in the past is an open question, but all of us seem to hold to the belief that we used to talk to each other more than we do now.

As time passed, our separate attempts to understand each other's interests better and the questions that came from our disciplinary backgrounds developed into a joint project to examine the nature of Denésuliné subsistence hunting. This book is the result. Because we see the world differently and because our experiences of the Denésuliné have been very different, there are differences in how we see the material presented in it. It should be noted, especially because of the family relationship between us, that our agreeing that something is worth including in the text does not necessarily mean we agree on its interpretation or importance. This applies especially to the separate questions and issues arising from the frameworks of our separate disciplinary backgrounds.

We share an interest in trying to understand human hunting behavior both as it is manifested in the Denésuliné and as a factor in human evolution. We also share the belief that although the concerns and methodologies of ethnological research differ substantially from those of archaeology and paleoanthropology, ethnological data and ethnological interpretation are a necessary part of the attempt to understand the behavior and ecology of both past and present hunting societies. The book is ethnographic in nature. It is based upon participant observation fieldwork spread over a period of several decades. Being based upon participant observation research has affected the nature of the topics and questions that are examined within it. Many of the questions and issues of most interest to archaeology or paleoanthropology are not examined within this book because the focus of ethnological research is not directed toward developing data suitable to address those questions.

Denésuliné hunting is normally a male activity. Hunting by women occurs only under special and restricted circumstances (Sharp 1981, 1988a, 1988b, 1994, 2001). As a child, Karyn was able to go hunting with her grandfather (Paul). The gender restriction was applied to her by the Denésuliné after she passed childhood. As an adult, she was only able to participate in a single hunt. That hunt, in the company of her father and her uncle Phil, occurred in 1992. The circumstances surrounding that hunt were essentially duplicates of the circumstances presented in Hunt 1, save that Karyn was the first to spot caribou.

Although I (Karyn) was only allowed to attend a single hunt as an adult I do remember going on at least one hunt with my maternal grandfather as a child. As an adult I have fond memories of participating, even briefly, on the hunt with my uncle; he even said at one point I was good luck for hunting. However, this view is not common among the Denésuliné. In later years when I was working with my family on my PhD research, addressing questions of food storage among hunters and gatherers, I was unable to participate in any active hunting events. I didn't view the exclusion in a negative manner; it was frustrating but not malicious. In those years of conducting my research I believe the men, my cousins and uncle, didn't think to include me—it just didn't occur to them that I might want to join. Admittedly I didn't make any overt or clearly stated requests to join in the hunt, so I am not sure if I would have been brought along if I had asked, but for them it was just normal to head off without thinking to ask me if I wanted to join them.

Participant observation is based upon both observation and participation in the life of the peoples being studied. It is one thing to accompany the Denésuliné on a hunt and then assist in butchering the game and transporting it back to camp. It is quite another actually to participate in the approach to the prey, the killing of the prey, the butchering and transportation of the kill, and the disposition of the kill. Participation generates a different understanding of the phenomena being examined than does simply observing it. This has effectively shifted the hunts presented to those Henry experienced before Karyn became an archaeologist.

Ultimately, the book is but a single case study; a time-bounded study of one band-sized extended kin group under a specific set of environmental, social, and technological circumstances over a single temporal interval. There are limits to what can be drawn from a single case study. We have pushed those limits as far as we think is legitimately feasible. The fieldwork experience does, however, tend to raise questions that go beyond what the data it generates can answer. We have tried to explore some of those questions that have arisen from the fieldwork.

Beyond the nature of what the research experience and the data it generates tell us about the Denésuliné, there is the issue of other cultures of subsistence hunters who lived elsewhere in time and space. A single case study of subsistence hunting among a contemporary First Nation society cannot answer the questions we have about those cultures of humans and human ancestors. It can, however, raise questions that may or may not be applicable to understanding how some of those cultures made their living. This provides a third purpose for the book. We hope that some of the discussion engendered by it will be of use to specialists working on those cultures.

The conditions under which the research was conducted were often so harsh, trying, and isolated that it was not possible to live without a constant awareness of just how easily things could have gone wrong. These circumstances led to a more or less constant interest in how it would have been possible to maintain life without the technology of modern times. In particular, how would it be possible to keep everyone fed in the absence of a modern repeating rifle? In turn, this concern led to a series of questions about the nature of subsistence hunting and survival at other times and places. Some of these—necessarily more speculative—issues are examined at various points.

Mode of Argument

The manner in which this book is organized is slightly unconventional as there is no single narrative to unite the book. It is divided into two types of chapters: those labeled Hunt and those labeled Text. There are fifteen chapters of each kind. In addition, there are two chapters (Interludes) that break from the Hunt-Text pattern to take up different issues. The Hunt and Text chapters are of a very different nature. The Hunt chapters generally present a direct ethnographic account of a specific hunt. The essential aspects of these hunts can range from a sentence to several pages. Because of the specificity of their ethnological material, narrating the material in the Hunt chapters requires considerable use of the first person.

The Text chapters are more analytical and interpretive. Each develops or further explores aspects of material presented in the preceding Hunt chapter. These chapters are presented in a more conventional ethnographic manner. One purpose of the Text chapters in the first part of the book is to build a basic understanding of hunting as part of a complex subsistence system. Hunting is like a link in a chain. The chain is useless without that link, but without the entire chain, hunting is just a link. Unless the entire chain functions, everyone dies. The separate links are inadequate in and of themselves. The effect is to give the book a feel somewhat like that of the alternating chapter style found in Hugh Brody's *Maps and Dreams* (1981).

The order in which the material in this book is presented is determined by the contents of the Text chapters. With the exception of Hunt chapters 1, 13, 14, and 15, the Hunt chapters are placed where they are because they allow a reasoned segue into the discussion contained in the following Text chapter. With the exceptions indicated above, the order or sequence in which any given hunt appears in the book is of no particular consequence. If so inclined, readers should feel free to read the Hunt chapters separately from the Text chapters and to read them in any order that suits their interests. It is the cumulative effect of the material contained within the Hunt chapters that is of significance. Collectively, the Hunt chapters present a comprehensive picture (particularly when the chapter Hunt 13 is factored in) of the variety of kinds of hunts this particular group of Denésuliné engaged in over the time period covered in the work.

As indicated earlier, we presume that few readers will have had any firsthand experience of subsistence hunting. We have taken it as an obligation of this book to try and create a reasonably complete understanding of the nature of Denésuliné subsistence hunting. Hunt 1 is a basic introduction to the nature of Denésuliné hunting and the actions that follow a successful hunt.

We were particular in our choice of hunts to present. As an example, in the summer of 1975 Henry and George (Sharp 1988a: 21) were traveling northward about fifty yards off the eastern shore of the north-south arm of Foxholm Lake (map 1) when we saw several caribou bulls standing along the shore. George directed that the motor of the canoe be cut and the canoe turned eastward and allowed to drift toward the shore. What made this hunt so interesting was the concentration George displayed in focusing upon the caribou. It was not until the seventh mosquito that had landed on the top and back of his right ear actually began to bite that they attracted his attention sufficiently to cause him to raise his right hand and shoo them away. This hunt was not chosen for a hunt chapter for a number of reasons: the field notes about it do not include information about how many bulls were killed, the butchering, and the disposition of the meat, or whether we returned directly to camp. The hunt would have provided a useful segue into discussion of the intensity and concentration displayed by Denésuliné hunters as they approach game, but we felt that topic was covered adequately elsewhere and there was no reason to include this particular hunt.

Between us, we participated in several hundred hunts—in a substantial majority of which game was never encountered.

The hunts themselves were never a primary research focus during the fieldwork. Other issues always had higher priority. The hunts recounted were selected from some thirty or forty for which adequately detailed field notes could be coupled with specific recollection of the events and circumstances of each.

When human beings—and presumably ancestral human beings and related species—choose to live under climatic and ecological conditions as harsh as those found in the northern Canadian Subarctic, their survival depends upon the interconnectivity and mutual support provided by the division of labor within their society. Human beings are social animals. Their survival depends upon their mutual interdependence. Even though this is a book about subsistence hunting, it makes a basic point about human hunting societies: hunting cannot be understood if it is treated as an isolated phenomenon that stands outside the social context within which it exists.

The emphasis upon individual self-sufficiency and the concomitant abhorrence of dependency has long been recognized in the literature on Northern Athapaskan cultures (e.g., Solobodin 1960, 1962; Cohen and VanStone 1963; VanStone 1965). In practice, this is an indisputably useful approach to subsistence under the conditions faced by these cultures. Nevertheless, the fact remains that human survival under the physical conditions the Dene cultures face is only possible through the interdependency that culture provides to a social species. Exploring that interdependency as it relates to hunting and subsistence in an extant society is one of the fundamental things ethnology is able to offer to archaeology and paleoanthropology.

We have already indicated that one of the consequences of the way we have chosen to separate the material presented in this book into separate Hunt and Text chapters is the lack of a single narrative to order and structure the material within it. Presenting the material this way instead of attempting a series of exhausting discussions of each separate topic leads to a series of discrete bits of data and argument scattered throughout the work. This places more of a burden upon readers as it becomes incumbent upon them to link together the separate arguments within the book. There are a number of ways we have tried to address what may be a potential problem and make the linking of the separate arguments within the book somewhat easier on the reader.

There are a number of discrete chains of argument within the book. These arguments, although each centers around a separate topic, are interconnected. The consequences of one thread of argument have consequences for how one sees the topics considered in other threads of argument. We think it best to approach the book as one that is built around a series of threads or themes. This approach should serve to link the separate bits of data and argument to create a clearer picture of the nature of Denésuliné subsistence hunting and subsistence. Some of the more conspicuous themes are:

1. Gender.
The book is based upon the premise that the labor of Denésuliné females is the determining factor in the success and survival of individual Denésuliné social groups. This premise is embodied in separate discussions about the tasks women perform. It is incumbent upon the reader to imagine the consequences that would come from attempting to live in this environment without the objects produced by women's labor. It is the cumulative picture of women's labor that emerges from considering each of these separate activities that will or will not affirm of the validity of the premise. We are of the opinion that women's labor is an under-researched topic in hunting societies. We have tried to develop a fuller picture of just how significant the labor of Denésuliné women is and how their needs for material can alter the timing, nature, and focus of Denésuliné hunting.

2. Insects.
The harshness of the environment of the Canadian Subarctic and the coldness of its climate are widely known and

understood by outside investigators. The consequences of its insect populations are less well known or less well understood. Discussions of the sheer volume of the insect populations of the Canadian Subarctic and tundra are scattered throughout the book. When seen together, these serve to establish that the insect populations in fact pose a substantial threat to the health and safety of the human (and animal) populations. When these discussions are fit together, it becomes apparent that the insect populations affect everything from how humans clothe themselves to where they place their camps; from how, when, and where their children are able to play to how they care for their animals. It should be obvious that they affect how the Denésuliné hunt and how they conduct their work. A single account of the biting insects of the boreal forest and tundra may make them seem to be no more than a nuisance. The collective picture that emerges is something else.

3. Wolves and caribou behavior.

The Denésuliné exist as partners within a triadic relationship between themselves, the wolf, and the caribou. None of the three can be understood without understanding the other two (Sharp 1976, 1978, 1982). A disruption to any one of the three has consequences for the survival of the other two. There is information at various places within the book about the behavior of both wolves and caribou. It is there to develop certain aspects of the relationship between the three species, particularly as related to hunting, and reflect how the means of Denésuliné hunting depend upon their ability to approach caribou closely. One thread of argument shows that the ability to approach caribou closely is in fact dependent upon the absence of sustained contact between caribou and Denésuliné.

4. Scale.

Ethnographic writing tends to ignore the issue of scale. We focus on it repeatedly, particularly as it is manifested in the sheer size of the land and the sparseness of its animal populations. Understanding this, along with the migratory nature of the caribou, is fundamental to understanding how, where, and when the Denésuliné hunt as they do.

5. Mobility and Transportation.

Mobility is the primary way to ensure survival within the vast and harsh homeland of the Denésuliné. The ability to move—at any time of the year—from locations where there are inadequate resources to locations where there are adequate resources is the most basic survival technique known to both the Denésuliné and the populations of large animals of the tundra and the borderline forest areas of the Canadian Subarctic. The thread of argument about mobility is largely expressed through a focus upon the transportation of meat after game has been killed. The issue of whether one moves the meat to the people or the people to the meat, with all the consequences that flow from either choice, was one of the most basic recurring decisions of Denésuliné traditional life.

There are other themes in the work. For example, we address a wider range of gender issues than indicated in the preceding list of themes. We invite and encourage readers to search out other connections between the data and the arguments to build a greater understanding of Denésuliné subsistence hunting. Two major issues that are interconnected with almost everything else are developed in a more concentrated form of argument. These are the changes in hunting technology, particularly changes in weaponry (Text 3), and how changes in technology have altered where the Denésuliné hunt their land as well as how they hunt the land (Text 13, Text15). Analysis of camp formation (Text 6) and land use, with its illustration of how even a small camp can exert human influence over an enormous area of land, is basic to understanding the nature of Denésuliné subsistence hunting. This is especially the case if one thinks about human influence on the land and its animal populations during the times when all the Denésuliné lived dispersed in the bush.

Specificity

Because this work is an ethnographic case study that may be of some comparative or heuristic use to those interested in the subsistence behavior of human and related species elsewhere in time and space, we think it advisable to describe the study conditions in some detail.

This land, but a small part of the Denésuliné homeland, is a land of paradox and uncertainty. This land is ancient. The hunts examined here took place upon the Rae and the Hearne Cratons. These two cratons, once separate microcontinents (Wilson and Clowes 2009: 84–145), are among the oldest surviving continental rocks upon the planet. Indeed, their fusion with the Slave Craton may have provided the impetus for the formation not only of what became the North American continent but for the formation of many of the continental cratons upon the planet.

Paradoxically, this land is among the newest on the planet. Some 12,000 years ago, when humans first settled far to the south in what was to become Saskatchewan, glaciers still covered this part of the Denésuliné homeland. The glaciers kept this place buried in ice until 6,000 to 8,000 BCE. The oldest artifact we ever encountered in the vicinity of Foxholm Lake was a microblade core (identified for us by Herb Alexander, then of Simon Fraser University) indicating that humans were exploiting the environs of the lake before the glaciers had entirely vanished from the area.

Glaciers are not easy upon the land. If the passage of one glacier is hard upon the land's surface, the repetitive passage of many dozens of glacial advances and retreats is far harder upon it. Passage of a glacier rips up the land's surface and carries away vast quantities of it. On a granite surface, the passage and retreat of a glacier can shear away up to three hundred feet of it. After the dozens of glacial passages this place has endured, its surface is scoured down to granite bedrock covered only by debris left from the last glacial melting. With each glacial advance the land sinks toward the mantle of the earth. With each glacial retreat the land rises (isostatic rebound) upward toward its former position. At the present time the land is still undergoing isostatic rebound and still rising.

The bulk of the hunts recounted here occurred within a 500- to 600-square-mile area in the Northwest Territories of Canada. Located in the northernmost part of the transitional zone of the boreal forest on the Precambrian Shield, it ranges from twenty to thirty miles within the forest to twenty or so miles out onto the tundra. Caribou are often within parts of this area for most or all of the summer. The study area itself lies at the base or slightly south of a 5,000-square-mile patch of tundra at the southern junction between the high tundra and the transitional boreal forest. This 5,000-square-mile area is somewhat higher and drier than the full tundra to both the north and the east of it. As a consequence, it acts as a holding area for caribou moving off the high tundra and heading toward their wintering grounds in the forest.

Mean January temperature at Foxholm Lake during the 1970s was -30°F. Mean January temperature farther south at the village in Saskatchewan was -20°F during the same period. Rainfall along the southern margin of the tundra averages between ten and eleven inches a year. It increases toward the south but remains sparse. South of the tundra, paradoxically for a land where rainfall should only support dry scrubland, the surface of the land is up to 70 percent standing water in some form or other. This is part of the legacy of the permafrost that dominates the landscape of the region. So little time has passed since the glaciers last covered the country that, as the land continues its isostatic rebound, its drainage systems have not yet matured. The land is covered by lakes. There are many small streams but few rivers, and these run mostly short distances as connectors between the lakes. Off the sand hills and eskers, the ground surfaces are generally wet or rock covered and are difficult to move over.

The vegetation of the transition from the southern tundra to the northern edge of the transitional zone of the boreal forest is limited. This is an area of parkland forest and rock desert tundra. Throughout the region, grasses are scarce and shrub growth is sparse and scattered. The predominant ground cover is reindeer moss. The forest itself is of a curious nature. Though apparently continuous when seen from a distance, it is in fact patchy and discontinuous. Mature forest, especially near the tundra and close to Foxholm Lake, is very open. Trees are often thirty to fifty feet apart and there is no intervening undergrowth. Sheltered wet areas support denser growth of trees and generally have a wider variety of species than are found in drier areas. Within the wetter areas, there are small patches of "drunken forest"—trees tilting from the presence of ice blocks buried beneath the soil surface.

As the forest edges toward its limits in places more exposed to the wind or where the permafrost rises closer to the land's surface, the trees become unable to reproduce sexually. Those that have managed to gain a foothold are reduced to asexual reproduction. Where conditions have become too harsh for sexual reproduction, one encounters small trees surrounded by a circle of sprouting shoots. These are offshoots of their own roots and tend to create a variety of fairy circles upon the ground as the last trees fade into the openness of the tundra. Growth here is slow. We once took down a small tree, about two inches in diameter and about eight feet high, for a pole. Its trunk had more than one hundred growth rings.

Curiously, the harshness of the conditions along the tundra boundaries that creates the wide spacing between the trees also allows them unhindered growth. The forest within a half-mile of the tundra often contains the largest and tallest trees to be seen in the country. This spacing also provides some protection from forest fire. The boreal forest far to the south has evolved to burn roughly every century. By two hundred years of age the largely jack pine forests near the village are becoming ragged, and the individual trees within it are generally aged and in ill health. By as far north as Smalltree Lake, forest fires are far less frequent and, because of the patchy nature of the forest, do not burn with near the size or intensity of their more southerly counterparts. By the time one nears the tundra, the individual stands of forest are sufficiently patchy that forest fires are quite rare.

In all the discussion of the harshness of this land, there is an aspect of it that can easily be overlooked: the sheer beauty of it. Animal life is so sparse in this place that trackways and trails in the snow are scarce. From the time the first snow falls and throughout the ensuing winter, the land retains its fairyland aspect. When approached from the air during times of no snow cover, the land is a patchwork of rock, sand, and water. It is hard to decide whether it is a lake full of islands or a land full of lakes. The land is dominated by patches of green and gray, spiced with the brightness of the bare sand. Between the strands of earth tones are the intense patches of the varying blues that mark the unimaginable profusion of lakes. Only on the ground does the subtle beauty of the place come alive (Sharp 1996). Within this land of immense distances, it often takes movement of but a few yards to go from one microenvironment to another; to move from mature forest into the scrub of a hillside along a creek or from the dryness of the reindeer moss to a sheltered gully rife with struggling vegetation or onto the softness of a moss meadow. Each kind of place has its different small life and its different sounds, smells, and colors. Over and over, mile after mile, this variation extends in infinite complexity. The same is true even on the lakes. It can be but a distance of a few hundred feet to go from the tens of miles of deep, open blue water on Foxholm Lake around a point into a sheltered inlet where the water becomes a kelp forest.

It is one thing to speak of reindeer moss as the predominant ground cover. It is quite another to realize that the reindeer moss flows across the land like an immaculately manicured blanket. Formed of muted grays, greens, and pale yellows, the moss is interspersed with the glossy dark greens of the ground-hugging berries and the contrasting shades of their fruits. The land is open and above all gives the impression of deliberate cleanness. It is not cluttered with the debris of death, decay, and change. For mile after uncountable mile, the reindeer moss covers the land. Come fall, the ground transforms into a brilliant panoply of color. The shimmering arrogance of the blood reds, scarlets, and crimsons of the leaves of the berry plants contrast with the less flamboyant reds of the shrubs and the deep verdant greens of the spruces. All this is offset by the intense scattered brilliance of the yellows of the willows and hardwoods; a yellow so intense it edges into the painful. Every rock, boulder, or stone outcrop among the moss or lining the lake shores seems as carefully placed and as immaculately manicured as if it were part of a Japanese garden crafted and maintained by a thousand gods.

The Denésuliné walk this land. They live among its colors and textures. They are surrounded by a silence that can become so intense that the sound of a gentle but heavy snowfall of large fluffy flakes can become a roar so intense that it causes actual pain. The sheer beauty of a place is often the deciding factor in determining where to pitch a camp or build cabins for the winter. Everyday Denésuliné bush life is bombarded by a low key beauty of an intensity that shapes their entire perception of their land and transforms the very harshness of it.

On the tundra and within the contiguous forest, animal and plant resources are limited. The variety and numbers of animal life found here are far less than were found in the Mammoth-Steppe tundra (Guthrie 1990) or the forested areas of Pleistocene Europe. Indeed, farther south along the several hundred miles of the Saskatchewan–Northwest Territories border, Acton and colleagues (1998: 25, 36) report the presence of as few as fifteen to no more than thirty-seven mammal species.

Non-migratory large animal life is particularly limited, and that life is spread over an immense area of land. The crucial resource for human life is the caribou. There are no alternative populations of large animals capable of sustaining human life. Fish are abundant and provide a valuable dietary supplement, but with traditional Denésuliné fishing technology they are incapable of providing an adequately reliable nutritional and caloric intake to support a human population.

The period covered by this study was the end of the Dené-suliné transition from bush life to village life. Henry's field-work began in December 1969. Karyn's fieldwork began in the first decade of the twenty-first century and still continues. During the first decade of the study Henry acted as a member of Paul's household (Sharp 1988a: 47–49), and the results of all hunting went to Paul's household. After the 1977 field season Henry accompanied the hunters but did not hunt; a situation reflected in the choice of hunts presented in the text.

The Mission Band is a composite one. One segment of its membership is formed by people whose experience or family ties are oriented toward the people of the Churchill River drainage farther south in Saskatchewan. These Denésuliné are specialists in the exploitation of the full boreal forest. Some of these, until recently, trapped and hunted as far south as Cree Lake, some 430 miles south of Dubawnt Lake in the Northwest Territories. Scale is a factor not just in terms of the quantity of meat it takes to feed a small group of human beings for months at a time in a harsh and demanding climate; it is also a factor in the sheer size of the land and the distances that have to be traversed. The Denésuliné of Mission, as of about 1970, numbered just over 500 souls. If the areas of the tundra that had been used by the previous two generations are included, the area of exclusive exploitation rises near to 70,000 square miles.

The other component of the Mission Band is derived from Denésuliné whose ancestry comes from peoples who hunted and trapped farther north and to the northeast. These are Hearne's Caribou Eaters (J.G.E. Smith 1976). These Dené-suliné were specialists in the exploitation of the transitional zone of the boreal forest and the high tundra to the north of it. Individual members of the group examined in this work regularly lived, hunted, and trapped as far out onto the tundra as Dubawnt Lake.

The twentieth century has been a time of great transition for the Denésuliné of the Mission Band. Through the 1920s their lives were much as were those of their ancestors of the preceding century. They lived a life that was based in the bush. Supported by subsistence hunting with a cash/credit income from trapping, life alternated between periods spent dispersed in the bush in small extended family groups and periods spent in all native communities (Helm and Damas 1963). Visits to the trading posts in Saskatchewan (primarily Discha) were infrequent. Those visits were generally seasonal and normally centered around times when church activities and holidays could be combined with the sale of fur.

The process of concentration of the Denésuliné population into Saskatchewan and around the trading posts continued throughout the 1950s and into the 1960s. The local population received a full-time resident priest in the early 1950s. In 1953 the priest ceased full-time services at the native community church near Discha and moved to Mission to found a village there. From then on, Mission became the focal point of settlement for Denésuliné establishing residence near the trading posts. By the time this study began, the process of aggregating into permanent settlements was at its end. During the 1970s progressively fewer and fewer families made the trip into the bush for the hunting and trapping season. More and more hunters and trappers went out to their trap lines without taking their families with them. At the beginning of the decade more than 170 people, out of a total population approaching 600 people, made the trip into the Northwest Territories.

By the start of the 1990s there were but thirty to forty individuals who made the same seasonal excursion into the Northwest Territories. The demography of those who still went north had changed. Only a few families made the seasonal trip. Most of those who ventured out were adult males who, following the pattern that had developed among the boreal forest specialists in Saskatchewan, left their families behind in the village.

It was a great deal easier to exercise governmental control over the Denésuliné who lived in Saskatchewan than it was to exercise control over the Denésuliné who were based in the Northwest Territories. Yellowknife is far from Discha. The bush areas in the NWT where the Mission Denésuliné lived and trapped were far from the areas where the native population of the NWT was concentrated. In effect, this was a rump area largely ignored by the government of the Northwest Territories. All administrative functions involving the Denésuliné who were based in Mission but who trapped, hunted, and lived in the NWT were delegated to the Royal Canadian Mounted Police (RCMP) at Discha and the Saskatchewan Department of Natural Resources (DNR) agent based there.

It was a different time, one that lasted through the 1970s; a time in which there was no effective regulation of the bush life of the Denésuliné who went into the NWT. They had to have trapping licenses—which were free—in order to sell their fur. There were a few animals, such as grizzly bear, that were protected; killing those could cause complications. The only means the RCMP or DNR had to patrol the northern areas was by float or ski plane. The cost of chartering a plane was so great that neither of their budgets allowed them to justify the expense for anything short of reported violence or unexpected death. The Denésuliné of the NWT lived so far from white administrative control that they were effectively free of it.

For those Denésuliné who hunted and trapped in the Northwest Territories, the combination of the remoteness of this area and the location of the boundaries between the political subdivisions of Canada—coupled with the widespread North American belief in so underfunding government agencies that they are unable to function properly—allowed the continuation of a degree of freedom probably unparalleled anywhere else in the United States or Canada.

One of the differences that did affect the local Denésuliné was that in Saskatchewan all traplines had to be registered, and their placement was regulated by the DNR agent at Discha. The government of the NWT did not require that traplines be registered. This meant that the Denésuliné of the NWT were free to regulate their placement upon the ground and their use of the land. They were free to regulate their own behavior and manage disputes among themselves.

By the beginning of the 1990s, the conditions of Denésuliné life had changed greatly (Sharp 1998). In terms of subsistence hunting, the Mission Denésuliné were no longer a bush-dwelling people dependent upon the land for their survival. They had become village dwellers far more heavily integrated into the wider Canadian economy. Life in the bush had become an excursion rather than the normal condition of daily life. There had been changes in hunting technology as well. Snowmobiles were by then commonplace, and all terrain vehicles were becoming so.

Both kinds of vehicles greatly extended the range that hunters based in the village could reach quickly on their hunting excursions. Going out to hunt was still an important part of the lives of many Mission Denésuliné, but going out to hunt is simply not the same kind of activity as is living in the bush among what it is that one goes out to hunt. Hunting still provided a substantial part of their diet, but improved transportation and the greater incomes available to people had shifted basic subsistence from the yield of the hunt to the yield of the store.

HUNTING CARIBOU

Hunt 1
Caribou

There had been no recent sign of caribou (*Rangifer taran-dus tarandus*) where we were camped near Foxholm Lake. It was a time of active searching for caribou. The hunters had already searched for several miles along the shores of the lake. They had gone up the north-south bay at the east end of the lake to its end and had then gone on foot northward for several miles out onto the muskeg meadows heading toward the next big lake to the north (Knowles Lake, locally called Spider Lake). George had later searched by himself farther west along the south shores of Spider Lake. They had searched the high sand plateau to the west of the north-south bay. The creek out of the south end of the small lake across the portage—where our winter camp was located— had been explored southward for several miles to where a lake/creek chain joined it from the east (see Interlude 1, following Hunt 8, for more about the terrain). The two creeks were joined by a short deep stream that flowed from a lake and river chain to the west. The men had gone up that creek, across the lake that was its source, and searched the wetlands to its north and northwest.

The camp's hunters later determined that the caribou were five or six miles north of where we had looked off the north shore of Foxholm Lake and that they had been missed by only a few miles. There had been no sign of caribou within the areas searched. The only tracks found in all that searching were those of moose (*Alces alces andersoni*).

George and I decided to take the canoe that I had at camp and search northeastward toward Joe's Camp, some twelve or fifteen miles away. The first time I had done this was with Wellington and Paul in 1970. Caribou were then plentiful at Foxholm Lake, and Paul was using the trip to show me the country and an old camp he had used some twenty years before. I was to make the trip again in 1977, this time with George in a search for caribou at a period when they were absent from the part of Foxholm we were using and we needed to find food for our camp. In 1992 Karyn, Phil, and I again started the trip at a time when caribou were absent from the part of Foxholm Lake where we were camped, and it was Karyn who first spotted them. The trip took us east along the north shore of Foxholm Lake and across the large northward-projecting arm of the lake. We crossed this wide arm and entered a large stream that drained a series of lakes to the northeast.

The land north of Foxholm Lake, although it contains a series of large lakes—each of which would be a major feature in any of the states east of the Mississippi River—is part of an extensive stretch of relatively dry, flat, land some 5,000 square miles in area. This stretch of land, dozens of miles wide (west-east) and deep (north-south), parallels tree line from the northwest to the southeast. This area is rich in browse. When caribou move out of the high tundra in late summer, it is this stretch of land that holds them until they are ready to move into the forest when the snow comes and the small lakes begin to freeze. It is almost as if the caribou herds are waves that, instead of breaking on the forest, form a rough chop zone just north of the forest until the onset of snow, ice, and cold weather leads them to break through the barrier and flow into the forest. The northern shore of the west end of Foxholm Lake is but a few miles south of this caribou holding zone. Caribou often enter the northern end of this stretch of relatively dry ground by early July and may be there as early as June. In most years, some bull caribou choose to remain in this zone close to the forest edge for nearly the entire winter.

In "normal" years—if there is any such thing as normal with caribou movements—the zone has provided earlier access to the caribou for those Denésuliné who lived at the edge of the boreal forest as well as providing a last access to caribou for those Denésuliné who were moving southward off the tundra and into the forest. It has, for hundreds of years, provided the Denésuliné with a crucial early summer and often mid- to late winter food reservoir (see Text 13, Shadows of the Past).

The trip to Joe's camp in a small sport canoe with but a two-horsepower motor to push it was long and slow. The little canoe was vulnerable to waves on the open lake, while the river route off Foxholm Lake toward Joe's Camp was often nearly blocked by shallow stretches. The deeper parts of the river were riven with rocks and boulders that could easily puncture the bottom of a canoe or an aluminum boat. It did, however, take us northeast of the area where we were camped and exposed us to a more northerly section of the high, dry upland. It was a proven area to look for caribou when they were expected to be nearby but were not in evidence at the northwest end of Foxholm Lake itself.

As it happened, we found caribou after we had crossed the far northern bay on Foxholm Lake and started up the rocky river passage. Well before we reached Joe's Camp we saw a small bunch of caribou bulls on the north shore of the river. They were along the shore between the bouldered shoreline and the tree growth just inland. We cut the motor and turned the canoe toward shore. When the caribou noticed us heading toward them, they calmly walked into the trees and vanished. The land just inside the trees was a series of ridges (thirty to fifty feet in elevation) and narrow gullies. The ground was difficult to move over, both for the caribou and for us, although the caribou seemed to manage it more comfortably than we were able to do. The ridges were not terribly high but they were difficult to climb. Much of the ground surface was littered with cobble-sized stones and small boulders and there were many cracks and holes in the exposed bedrock. It was difficult to get firm footing when walking, and when carrying a heavy load there was the constant risk of a broken foot or leg.

The caribou we had seen from the boat had moved away and were out of sight by the time we reached the shore. We found a place to beach the canoe and quickly moved inland toward where we had seen them vanish into the timber. George knew to head toward the crest of the first ridge within the timber and, quietly but quickly, led the way. Several hundred feet inland, the forest vanished. We saw caribou moving among the ridges inland, and moved in their direction. As we crested the first ridge, we saw the now scattered bunch of caribou. They had moved inland to the ridge crest, crossed it, and dispersed over the low ground between the first and second ridges. The ridges were less than a hundred feet apart. Widely scattered trees grew over the ridges and in the gully between the ridges. The caribou had spread out in the gully. As soon as they saw us crest the ridge, they began to run in several directions. We were about two yards apart as we approached the caribou, and each of us was able to get off one shot. Each of us knocked down one of the bulls before the rest of them vanished into cover and moved out of sight.

Killing is not an end in itself. It is the start of a process of utilization of the animal that has been killed. Butchering the animal is the next step.

The land surface in this area is essentially devoid of topsoil. The ground surface that is not bare rock or some form of water is normally sand, covered only by fragile and often thin moss and lichen growth. Butchering a large animal on such a surface requires skill as well as considerable practice and some forethought. Fresh meat, often in the hundreds of pounds, is quite vulnerable to contamination from debris found on the ground surface, and sand is particularly noxious and difficult to remove. If one is fortunate in the place where the caribou dies, there will be dwarf birch (*Betula* spp.), willows (likely including dwarfed sandbar willows, *Salix interior*), and other bush-sized vegetation (various species including *Salix bebbi-*

ana) that can be used to keep fat and other body parts elevated above the ground surface while the butchering proceeds.

Butchery practice varies with the seasons as a function of outside conditions and air temperature as well as the physical condition of the animals that have been killed. We followed normal butchering practice for this time of the year. It was late enough in the summer that many of the bulls had begun to build up fat to prepare themselves for the ensuing fall rut. At this time of the year, when hunters first approached a downed caribou bull it was not uncommon for them to make a small (inch or less), shallow cut at the base of the sternum to see if the animals had begun to build up a subcutaneous fat layer. Once this has been done, the first step in field butchering a caribou is to remove its head.

The head is removed by slicing the throat and cutting upward through the spine. The primary concern is gaining access to the tongue so that it can be removed. The head is a delicacy—particularly for the women of the camp—but it is rarely taken back unless the camp is close by or there are few or no restrictions on the ability to transport the meat. The heads of yearlings or animals without antlers (caribou cows also grow antlers) are more likely to be taken back for consumption. The antlers of bull caribou are extremely large. The head is difficult to transport if the antlers are not removed, but they are difficult to remove from the skull without damaging it. Removing the head has a pragmatic aspect, as its removal makes skinning and butchering easier, but it is also done out of respect for the spirit of the animal. The head of the animal is a focus of communication between its spirit and the humans who have killed it. It must be treated with respect even if it is to be taken back to camp and consumed. Who handles it and how it is handled are key to determining future relations between the hunter and others of its kind.

If the head is to be left in the bush, as was the case here, it is carefully set aside from the rest of the carcass to form the first pile separate from the carcass. The heads are moved away and turned over so that they rest on their antlers. Each head is routinely covered by the skin removed from its body unless the hide is to be transported back to camp. The tongue, which is a favored Denésuliné delicacy, is always removed and taken back to camp. This practice varies from kin group to kin group. The tongue is always taken for consumption, but it has been observed in other kin groups that the hunters sometimes cook and eat the tongue where the animal has been killed and butchered.

If the season and weather allow, the animal is then skinned. The hide, which has been ringed by the knife cut where the head has been taken off, is cut down the center of the neck, thorax, and abdomen and then out along the center of the inside of each leg. The hide is ringed at the end of each leg, normally just above the knee. If the entire leg is to be removed and transported back to camp, the hide is still ringed above the knee but is left on the lower part of the leg. The hide on the lower legs is a favored material for sewing baskets to store dried caribou meat. The genitalia of male caribou are cut off and tossed (usually with the left hand while bending over to make the cut) into the bush away from the rest of the carcass. Depending on the individual preference of the person doing the butchering, the female genital opening may either be ringed or split as the hide is pulled off. The anus is normally split, although a few individuals prefer to ring the hide around it.

Skinning a caribou requires little knife work. Experienced hunters remove the skin largely by pushing their fists between the skin and the flesh. Removing the skin this way does a much better job of separating the hide from the fat, flesh, blood vessels, and supporting tissues that connect the hide to the animal. This allows the hide to dry more quickly and largely eliminates the need to scrape the hide if it is to be worked or tanned. Once the cuts have been made and the fist thrusts used to separate it from the flesh, the hide is simply pulled off the animal.

The fat is carefully removed from the back of the animals. In late summer, bull caribou build up a large sheaf of fat that runs from their mid-back to their genitals. This sheaf of fat is even more desired than the tongue, and it is handled more carefully than any other part of the carcass. It is carefully set aside so that it is exposed to the air while the butchering proceeds, and it is very carefully kept from contact with the sand or the ground vegetation. If any bush-sized vegetation is in the area of the butchering, the sheaf of fat is carefully draped over it.

Once our two bulls were skinned and the external fat was removed, each carcass had its legs removed. Removing the front legs is an easy matter of a few long cuts. Removing the back legs requires more skill. The knife cuts have to be made deep into the muscle tissue of the rump to keep as much meat as possible attached to the leg, and the deep ligament connections of the femur make access difficult as they are recessed near the acetabulum. It takes some care to avoid cutting the relatively thin abdominal wall and opening it. One leg is often left attached to the animal to provide a hold for maneuvering the body during butchering. The tenderloin is removed from both sides of the backbone and set aside.

After the animal has had its head removed, has been skinned, and has had its legs removed, its abdomen is opened and the guts are removed. At this time of the year, this is done by carefully opening the abdominal wall and rolling the carcass to one side. Someone skilled at field butchery is able to detach the abdominal contents with a few knife strokes so that when the carcass is turned onto its side the intestines and other abdominal organs will roll out onto the ground. During this process the diaphragm is cut, and the hunter reaches into the chest cavity to sever the windpipe, esophagus, and blood vessels so that the lungs spill out beside the intestines and the other internal organs. The lungs of many caribou are heavily parasitized. *Echinococcus granulosis* can form large cysts in their lungs and the parasites, which are primarily parasites of canids, can infect humans. There is considerable variation among the Denésuliné as to whether or not they will handle caribou lungs or use them for dog (*Canis familiaris*) food. The way this kin group butchered caribou, the entire carcass was carefully cut away from the lung tissue to avoid any contact between it and humans.

Any internal organs or portions of intestinal fat the hunter intends to take are removed from the carcass either before it is rolled over to allow the organs to spill out or afterward as the guts are exposed on the ground. The spillage of these internal organs creates a separate pile of remains.

Once the guts have been taken out, the carcass is rolled back onto its back. If a leg has been left on the animal as a handle, it is removed at this point. The ribs are separated into three pieces—left and right ribs and the sternum. Separating the ribs from the carcass is the first point in the butchering process where a heavy blade—usually a heavy kitchen knife or butcher knife—is necessary. A smaller blade can be used, but it makes taking the ribs a much slower process and it is hard on the blade. In the absence of a heavy knife blade, an ax or hatchet can be used. The ribs are a favored part of the caribou. If the hunters of this extended kin group chose to eat while they were butchering or before they began to transport the meat back to camp, a rack of ribs was their preferred part of the carcass.

The normal practice of this kin group of Denésuliné is to separate the remaining part of the carcass into sections. An ax or hatchet is extremely useful for this but not always available. The pelvic section is separated from the spinal column. The spinal column is cut into two pieces. The neck, which has already been separated from the head, is now separated from the torso. These heavy, bonier parts of the carcass are taken back to camp if transport allows. When transport is restricted, the meatier parts of the carcass that are suitable for making into dry meat—legs, ribs, tenderloin—as well as selected internal organs, the external and internal (mostly intestinal) fat deposits, and the tongue all have priority for transport.

Transport of the meat back to the camp is the next and in many ways the most crucial step. All that can be transported is separated for transport. What cannot be taken away is carefully stacked and covered to keep scavengers off it. In late summer the primary concern is birds, especially seagulls (*Larus argentatus, L. philadelphia*) and ravens (*Corvus corax*). Unfortunately for humans, larger scavengers such as bear (*Ursus americanus, U. arctos*), wolf (*Canis lupus*), or wolverine (*Gulo gulo*) are perfectly capable of tearing apart any attempt to stack and cover the meat. If they find it, it is gone.

This creates a characteristic tripartite set of piles where each caribou has been butchered. One contains the head, one the stored and covered meat. The last is the offal remaining from the butchering process. The head and gut pile are normally within five to ten feet of each other. The stacked and covered meat will be placed where it seems safest and may, depending upon local topography, be some distance away from the other two. The meat pile is covered and concealed. The head is often covered by the hide of the animal that has been killed. The gut piles are left uncovered. The parts of the animal that are left behind uncovered—the guts and lungs as well as any offal that spills out if the intestines are ruptured either during butchering or from the gunshot that killed the animal—are far more nutritious than the head or the meat that has been stacked. These are the parts of the carcass that are most attractive to passing scavengers. Their attractiveness-as well as their smell tend to draw scavengers to them and provide some protection for the meat that has been stacked and covered.

Walking here, as is usually the case where caribou choose to be when they die, was difficult and posed the risk of a fall as we hauled the meat back to the canoe. It required a number of trips, each heavily laden. It was necessary to move slowly on the rough ground. We packed all the fat and meat the canoe would hold over the ridges and down to the shore. Because the rocks and boulders along the shore line posed a real risk of puncturing the sides or bottom of the canoe and because we were filling the canoe to its limits—something that seems to be the normal state when hunting and transporting meat by boat—we were particularly careful about how we loaded the canoe. Heavily loading the boat allowed us to get almost everything that was suitable for making dry meat into the boat, but we were not able to take the spinal sections, hips, heads, necks or hides. What was left was stacked—as always—

and covered in case we did get back into the area. The meat of each caribou was in a separate pile covered by leaves and brush. Each head was left a short distance away from the carcass from which it came. Each still rested on its antlers with the hide of the animal draped upside down over it. The uncovered guts, offal, and lungs made a third pile for each caribou.

In a situation like this the implicit understanding is that the meat would cease to be fit for human consumption long before we were likely to get back into the area, but if it were not scavenged by wolves, it might be usable for dog food. If a bear or wolverine found it or if sea gulls got to it, the meat would be so fouled that anything that survived would not be usable even as dog food.

Text 1

Hunting and Predation

The focus of this work is the hunting of large game by Denésuliné who live along the tundra fringes in the Northwest Territories of Canada. This is an area of tundra and parkland tundra; an area of the tundra that is sparsely forested and transitional to the more heavily forested transitional zone of the Boreal Forest that lies five to fifteen miles south of tree line. This is a permafrost area—one in which the ground is permanently frozen—with surface thawing during summer rarely extending more than a few inches below the ground surface. In terms of rainfall it is an area of transition between the near desert conditions of the southern tundra and the scrub subdesert conditions of the forest to the south. It is but one of many different ecological zones exploited by Denésuliné now based in the village of Mission (Sharp 2001) in Saskatchewan.

The Denésuliné were subsistence hunters. Their survival required a balanced usage of all of the large animal species that were available in the areas where they lived. They also made use of fish, birds, and small game native to the area. The balance in their usage of these species was partially determined by how differences between the various habitats they occupied were reflected in differences in the numbers and distribution of the animal species with which they shared the land.

The ancestors of these Denésuliné were self-determined specialists in hunting large game—large by post–megafaunal extinction standards—as their primary means for survival. The species upon which they chose to specialize was caribou. The cast of large animals among which they could have chosen was quite small. The primary large animals historically characteristic of this area are moose, caribou, musk ox (*Ovibos moschatus*), black bear, grizzly bear, and wolf.

Something that must be made crystal clear if there is to be any hope of understanding Denésuliné hunting and subsistence is the scale of distance on which life plays out here. The aboriginal Denésuliné populated this land at only about 1 person for every 100 square miles. Large animals are scarce within this land, and they are widely scattered throughout it. For most days of the year, any given plot of ground will be empty of large animals. Mobility, perhaps even more than strength, endurance, or knowledge, is crucial to survival in this land. All of the large animals that live here are capable of rapidly covering large distances and routinely do so. The humans who exploited those animals also had to be highly mobile.

This work does not focus on the usage the Denésuliné made of small game and fish even though these can be significant resources. During the height of a snowshoe hare (*Lepus americanus*) population cycle in the boreal forest, they can exceed five hundred animals per square mile. At times such as at the apex of a snowshoe hare cycle, it is possible to survive in this land by focusing only upon small game and fish, but these times are infrequent. Small game is mostly used as a seasonal bridging device and as a source of variety in the diet. The farther south one goes into the forest, the more important small game becomes in Denésuliné subsistence, as clearly demonstrated in Robert Jarvenpa's and Hetty Jo Brumbach's work among Denésuliné living some four hundred miles south of the tundra edge (2008: 70–78).

The lack of reliance upon small game by these Denésuliné is an adaptation to the ecological characteristics of the area in which they live. The land they exploit forms the transition between forest and tundra. The variety of small game species found here is higher than is the case either farther north or south. It contains species characteristic of both ecological zones, but the number of individual animals is less than is found either to the north or to the south. Of particular importance is that snowshoe hares, though present, are always scarce, while the species that replaces them to the north—the arctic hare (*Lepus arcticus*)—is at the limit of its range and is always rare.

Musk oxen became an item of interest to the Hudson's Bay Company in 1823 and were quickly hunted to near extinction (Burch 1977). They are slowly recovering and are now beginning to make occasional appearances near tree line. Moose are more characteristic of the forest than the tundra fringes, but moose are mobile animals—possibly even migratory in some places—that respond quickly to the effects of fire and changes in browse and forest conditions. During the period covered here—for the first time in the memory of the eldest of the Denésuliné who lived here—moose were becoming abundant around Smalltree Lake, and we saw their tracks and heard them along the tundra fringes at Foxholm Lake (Sharp 1988a).

Grizzly bear and black bear both inhabit the area. Grizzly bear were beginning to recover from a far more recent overhunting and by 1975 had moved at least as far south into the forest as Smalltree Lake. They remain scarce and few are encountered by the Denésuliné. Killing one is a rare event that, judging from stories and gossip, occurs only once every few years. When available, they are taken for fat, food, and hide. Black bear are relatively common. They are routinely hunted and are used for food. Their fat is highly valued, as are their hides.

In 2002 my (Karyn's) first field season was cut short due to the presence of a large grizzly bear. Our camp consisted of myself, my aunt, my uncle, his wife, his adopted son, one of their sons, and a pilot. The pilot and Wellington's son left within forty-eight hours of arrival along with several of my uncle and aunt's granddaughters. With the departure of his adult son and the pilot, my uncle was the only fully armed adult in the camp. Watching over six others who were not armed against a potential grizzly encounter was too stressful, and he decided that we should break camp rather than staying for the full four weeks.

Whitetail deer (*Odocoileus virginianus*) and mule deer (*O. hemonius*) are characteristic of forests far to the south in Saskatchewan. Their northward range expands and contracts according to the conditions of the forest. When accessible, they are taken for food. The stories and experiences of the hunters of Mission indicate that deer were common around the village in the early 1950s. By the end of the 1960s they were essentially unknown there. By the 1980s they were again in the area but were scarce. They do not exist near tree line. Buffalo (*Bison bison bison, B. b. athabascae*) do not extend into the area. Their meat is known only from memories of an earlier meat and pemmican trade conducted through the trading posts. There is no indication that cougar (*Puma concolor*) ever inhabited the area.

In 2002 during Karyn's stay in the community there was much upheaval and concern over cougar sightings in the area. According to the understanding of locals, two cougars had been released by Parks Canada in a conservation project, and there was heightened concern given the unknown nature of cougar. Regular sightings updates were provided on the regional radio station and people were encouraged to avoid these animals. Why Parks Canada tried to introduce animals not endemic to the region I will never understand. The fate of these two cougars is unknown at this time.

Wolves are common. They are taken (often quite reluctantly) because their hides have become so valuable. They are considered an edible animal but in practice they are not eaten. Beaver (*Castor canadensis*) are quite scarce near the tree line. They can become quite large (approaching ninety pounds) and are routinely eaten. Beaver are not terribly mobile animals. Because they are largely restricted to the area around their dens and houses, they were one of the few large animals for which locations could be known and would remain constant. Before the fur trade, they were a staple fallback prey item when other food was scarce.

The emphasis here upon caribou hunting reflects that among the species available to exploit, caribou were the primary prey for the Denésuliné who lived along and near the tree line. Caribou are a migratory species. Their migratory route is among the longest of any land mammal. Indeed, caribou are so mobile that they are constantly in motion. They are so continuously in motion that the concept of migration—with its implication of a destination, of going from point A to point B and back again—is a bit of hindrance to understanding them. The key to understanding them is to recognize that they are in constant motion and that from the perspective of any given spot on the ground, they never remain in one place for long.

Always they come and go, and always they are more likely not to be on any given spot of ground than they are to be on it. Anything that serves to reduce uncertainty about caribou movements, at a large scale and even more so at the local scale at which hunting occurs, is of enormous advantage to humans living as predators of caribou.

Predation is simple. It is the taking of the life of a living being in order to use its body for sustenance. Sometimes this is accomplished by killing the prey and consuming it. More often than not it is accomplished by overpowering the prey and beginning to consume it, incidentally killing it in the process of consuming it.

Predation was the basis of life on land for our earliest quadruped ancestors. When they came out of the water and onto the land, they came as predators (Kemp 2012: 3–4). Herbivory—the consumption of living plant tissue—by quadrupeds did not appear until the late Carboniferous or early Permian era and did not become established as the basis of the energy flow between plant and animal until the mid-Permian (Ray et al. 2012: 120–22; Steyer 2012: 118–20). Until then, the basis of the energy transfer between plant and animal was the consumption of dead plant material by detritus feeders. The appearance of herbivory fostered a massive increase in the quantity of energy that could be involved in an ecological system and led to the emergence of ecological systems of far greater variety and diversity.

Predation, though it has lost its role as the dominant source of energy within ecological systems involving quadrupeds, has remained a critical aspect of those systems.

Hunting, one of the forms of predation practiced by humans, is a difficult subject to write about (Tanner 1979). George Frison's *Survival by Hunting* (2004), with its attempt to introduce the hunter's experience and perspective into the analysis of hunting by *Homo sapiens,* is a path-breaking step in the analysis of human hunting practices. Still, the actual experience of subsistence hunting is hard to come by. The lack of that experience shows markedly in the analysis of the hunting behavior and practices of contemporary and recent humans. Given the importance assigned to hunting in our understanding of human evolution, that lack of practical experience shows even more markedly in the analysis of the hunting behavior and practices of our ancestral species and near relatives than it does in the analysis of living humans. This is perhaps more pertinent for the interpretation and reconstruction of Neanderthal (*Homo neanderthalensis*) behavior than for that of any other species.

The role and nature of hunting are confused by the last forty years of anthropological gender politics concerning the relationship between hunting and scavenging, but this is a lesser issue. We will return to it. The real problem in attempting to understand human hunting and specifically to understand the hunting behavior of the Denésuliné is the unexamined cultural baggage that we as Westerners bring to the analysis. Much of our cultural heritage has to be unlearned before we can begin to understand the Denésuliné. This is far too large a topic for the present book to examine, but we must address some aspects of the issue if we are to accomplish what we intend to accomplish here.

Our presumption is that the current set of beliefs, practices, and values surrounding hunting in North America—the context most of us bring to understanding Denésuliné hunting—originates in the beliefs and practices of English society, as delineated in Keith Thomas's *Man and the Natural World* (1984). For hundreds of years—at least since the end of Roman times—access to game and access to bladed metal weapons were tightly controlled in English society. That access was intimately embedded within the English system of class and power. It is likely that this has been true since the Iron Age and probably since the preceding Bronze Age. It well may have been true since the first appearance of bladed metal weapons in the British Isles.

It was from this context of intense social control of access to weapons and game, and its concomitant political and economic expressions, that the first successful English immigrants settled in North America. From the beginning of that settlement, there sat the forest with its strange and abundant wildlife (and native peoples). On the edge of daily life sat escape from the restrictions of the English social order. The presence of the forest was coupled with the lesser degree of social control and fewer mechanisms for enforcing the social order that characterized colonization.

If the very things that made colonization desirable—that vast forest with its unsettled land and the animal and mineral resources within it—were to be harvested, the forest had to be penetrated (see Curtin et al. 2001). This not only meant a loosening of the degree of social control exercised by English society; it also meant weapons had to be freely available and that game was there for anyone with a weapon to go and take it.

American culture evolved its attitudes toward guns and hunting from this break in an ancient context in which access to guns and game became the very symbols of individual rights and freedom as well as of the individual's escape from the restrictions of governmental control and social class.

This entire political context of what possessing weapons and engaging in hunting means is missing from Denésuliné culture. They are prepared to defend—and have defended—

their right to hunt, but hunting is not a traditional expression of individual freedom from a class structure and a political system. Its basis instead lies in a traditional conceptualization of themselves as a people and the relationship that exists between themselves, as a people and as individuals, and the moral universe manifested in the spiritual beings that embody themselves in the physical forms we see as animals.

The American culture that has developed over the last few centuries has, at least within the last few generations, applied the notion of the "fair fight" to hunting. It can readily be discerned in the public discourse featured in hunting magazines and is prevalent in other media representations of hunting as well as in cable television shows and statements from various political entities that support hunting. The key issue in this fair fight aspect of hunting—with its emphasis upon the clean kill, dropping the game animal with a single shot, and the wholesomeness of hunting (especially as a family activity)—is viewing the hunt as a sporting activity with its undertones of hunting as a contest between the hunter and the prey animal.

The critical aspect of this is the conceptualization of the hunt as a contest between the hunter and the animal.

In the Denésuliné universe, hunting is not a contest between human and animal. Their conceptualization of animals and the relationships that exist between individual Denésuliné and the Denésuliné people have been dealt with elsewhere (Sharp 1976, 1978, 1981, 1987, 1988a, 1988b, 1994a, 2001). It will be dealt with here as needed and is discussed at various points later. What is crucial is their lack of conceptualization of the hunt as a contest between human and animal.

Subsistence hunting is not a sport. It is not a business. Neither concept provides an adequate basis for understanding Denésuliné hunting. Hunting is an activity that embodies the moral and spiritual values of the Denésuliné. It is also a bloody, tiring, dangerous, and physically demanding activity. The nature and consequences of these characteristics do not fit with mainstream American conceptualization of hunting and are troublesome in the intellectual analysis of the hunting behavior of humans, human ancestors, and related species.

As a first point, the subarctic is not Africa. This is a point that speaks more to Western intellectual efforts to understand hunting than to the concerns of the public at large, although with the success of paleontological, archaeological, and nature shows on television, that may be changing. At stake is the attempt to understand human (both *Homo sapiens* and Neanderthal) behavior in Europe during the ice ages. That the physical conditions of the subarctic are grossly different from those of sub-Saharan Africa may be obvious, but the crucial role that environmental conditions in Africa played in our evolution, as well as the presence there of so many of our ancestral species and other species that affected our evolution, has given those conditions (then and now) a powerful role as "the" model for understanding human hunting. Unfortunately, the conditions found in sub-Saharan Africa—both now and for the last few million years—are so different from those of the subarctic that the hunting behavior of peoples adapted to those conditions provide a poor model for understanding the hunting behavior of humans and Neanderthals adapted to ice age Europe or the contemporary North American subarctic.

Throughout the world and, as far as we know, throughout human and prehuman history, hunting has been a predominately male activity (Washburn 1961; Lee and DeVore 1969). This is the case among the Denésuliné (Sharp 1977a; 1977b; 1981; 1988a; 1988b; 1994a; 1995; 2001). It has now been an active subject of investigation for more than fifty years, but the reasons for it are as elusive and uncertain as they were half a century ago.

Hearne's journal demonstrates clearly that Denésuliné women were capable of going off by themselves into the bush and surviving there for sustained periods of time (Hearne 1958: 168–72). There are and probably always have been far too many skilled and successful female hunters among the Denésuliné and among other cultures elsewhere in time and space to seek in human biology explanation for the gender disparity evinced in hunting. After observing and participating in Denésuliné hunts for several decades and watching a genera- tion and a half of girls come to adulthood, we are flatly pre- pared to state that there is no physical difference between the sexes that would prevent women from hunting. Denésuliné men have on average—but only on average—greater upper arm strength than do Denésuliné women. Denésuliné men are on average—but only on average—taller than Denésuliné women. However, Denésuliné women are big enough, strong enough, and quick enough and have sufficient endurance to hunt as effectively as do Denésuliné men.

Through archaeological research on hunting and gathering societies we see many examples of women not participating in large game hunting (Hawkes et al. 1991, 2010), and many take it as a near universal that women do not participate in the hunt. However, this is not always the case. As in the Hearne example provided, we do find references to women hunting, although it is often viewed as ephemeral or anecdotal evi- dence. Yet if one were to consider the length of time women are often left alone when the males are away on hunts or tend- ing trap lines, we can quickly determine that subsistence on small game snared in close proximity to a camp will not suf- fice as a consistent food resource as the small game will be rapidly depleted.

In recent years, through my (Karyn's) work with the Dakelh (Carrier) People of British Columbia—also Dene—I have found increasing reference to and have encountered female hunters. Estimates indicate that at least a fifth of the female Dakelh population are hunters and have been hunting for at least the past seventy years (which could be a result of colonial- ism, but the basis for this interpretation also applies to the Dakelh of central British Columbia). Admittedly they are not hunting in the same sustained manner as male hunters are, away for weeks at a time, but their time spent on the land in search of plant materials, often alone, provides them with occasions to participate in opportunistic hunting on a fairly regular basis.

There is no built-in physical or mental difference between the human sexes that is capable of explaining why hunting is a predominantly male activity. The explanation, if there is an explanation, is most probably somehow deeply rooted in the history, origin, and evolution of the division of labor in human and ancestral human culture. Hunting requires that hunters get away from the group and out into the bush a great deal. It is often a solitary activity. The bush is a dangerous place. No matter how effective humans may be as hunters, they are potential prey to a great many species of animals. Isolated humans or small groups of humans are far more vulnerable to death or injury at the hands of other humans than are entire camps or large groups of humans. And the nature of the bush itself produces an increased exposure to risk simply from being and traveling in the bush. There is always an increased risk to survival that comes with movement away from the group. If there is a functional aspect to the explanation, it is probably derived from recognition that females of reproductive age are of greater value to the survival of a group than are males of reproductive age, and the survival benefit that comes from restricting the exposure of females of reproductive age to the increased risk that comes from the necessary wandering that successful hunting requires.

The scale of Denésuliné hunting has consequences that are likely alien to most of us. The Denésuliné hunt to feed themselves and those who reside with them in the bush. This normally means that they are hunting to provide for a group of between two and twenty people. As the traditional Denésuliné bush diet was meat based, their hunting had to involve a sufficient number of animals killed to provide for the needs of those in the camp. The customary way of thinking about hunting is in terms of the pursuit and killing of an animal. This is now the way North Americans hunt, and it is also the way scholars tend to think of hunting by aboriginal peoples. Academics are well aware of mass hunting, be it Native American buffalo hunts or the drives of buffalo off cliffs, but we have no actual experience of the conduct of these things. We also lack experience of the mass game drives of our colonial ancestors or the immense scale of the market hunting of our all too recent past. By default, we think in terms of what is familiar to us: the North American sport hunter out hunting for an individual of a particular prey species.

The quantity of flesh that humans need to sustain themselves in a subarctic environment is quite similar to the amount of flesh that the large wolves of the tundra and boreal forest need to sustain themselves within their shared environment. Humans, however, have needs that wolves do not. The most obvious extra need of the traditional Denésuliné was the requirement for caribou hides to make clothing, shelter, blankets, ground cloths, nets, snares, and a host of other things. The demands of the contemporary Denésuliné are not as great as were those of their ancestors, but they are still considerably greater than are those of an equal number of wolves.

Denésuliné survival is not about the brave and noble hunter of Western ideology resolutely going off into the trackless wilderness to find, pursue, and kill a single animal. It is about feeding families, and it must be conducted on a scale that produces meat in the hundreds of pounds and often by the ton.

Throughout the Denésuliné homeland humans on the ground are few and far between, and the distances between their camps are considerable. Life in the bush for the Denésuliné is one in which support and aid in times of trouble are far away. This forces the group to rely upon its own resources and efforts in a way that is difficult for those raised in more densely populated southern regions to understand.

What is true on the larger scale of the society is also true in the daily lives of Denésuliné living in the bush. Of concern here are the distances involved in the hunting and killing of game. Game dead in the bush is of no value unless it can be brought to the people who need to process the meat and prepare it for use or storage. Hunters, particularly when they are engaged in solitary hunting, can range a great deal farther afield in their search for game than the distance from which they can carry back any game they might kill. This issue of transporting meat to where it can be processed and used is one of the crucial factors in understanding how, where, and why the Denésuliné hunt as they do.

Perhaps the most difficult thing for a Westerner trying to understand Denésuliné hunting comes from the shared religious background we bring to that task. We are not interested in the nature—or truth—of religion here. Our focus instead is upon something far more specific. At least since the beginning of the collapse of the Roman Empire as marked by the withdrawal of its legions from England, Christianity spread through England and Europe without interference from established states. As an aspect of that spread and rise to dominance, Christianity brought with it a particular view of nature and animals and of the relationships between human and animal and between human and nature (see Thomas 1984: 17–50; Brody 2000). We wish to state again that we are not interested here in the nature—or truth—of religion. Our concern here is the perception of animals and nature and the relationships that exist between them and human beings. To be blunt, the traditional Christian conceptualization of nature, animals, and the relationships that exist between them are so bizarre and destructive that they have to be set aside in order to gain any understanding of Denésuliné hunting and of their relationship to the universe within which they exist.

In Denésuliné thought, animals are simultaneously spiritual and physical beings who consensually sacrifice their physical forms to human hunters to enable them to survive (Sharp 1988a, 1988b, 1994a, 2001). The power that exists in this relationship rests entirely with the animals. The concept of a contest between human and animal/spirit would simply be without meaning and probably beyond comprehension. It is far closer to the reality of Denésuliné thought to try and understand the hunt as a ritual sacrifice of the god (Hubert and Mauss 1964: 77–94; Robertson Smith 1901) that occurs only because the actions and state of the hunter elicit the consent of the animal (Sharp 1994a). The hunt is a cooperative mutual performance between Denésuliné and animal.

Since the publication of Rodney Needham's *Belief, Language, and Experience* in 1972, it has been clear that the concept of "belief" is a Western cultural form rather than a human universal, although it is almost impossible to write in the English language without using the word. It is not valid to speak of Denésuliné conceptualizations of animals and the relations between humans and animals in terms of belief. The concept of belief does not provide a valid explanatory mechanism; but this does not mean that Denésuliné ideas about the nature of animals and their relationship with human beings does not permeate their culture, their daily lives, and how they practice subsistence hunting.

One consequence of this Denésuliné conceptualization of the universe they live in is of particular importance in understanding the nature of how they engage in subsistence hunting. A cultural thought system such as this one is such a fundamental and pervasive aspect of life as a cultural being that not only is it inescapable—it becomes reality (Sharp 2001: 117–24). Regardless of individual differences in ability or reflexivity, and regardless of individual differences in interest, comprehension, or understanding; regardless of any individual differences, the framework such a comprehensive thought system provides is simply how individuals understand their world and how they interact with it.

This Denésuliné framework is of particular significance to the outsider's understanding of their subsistence hunting when it comes to considering the erratic nature of the animate resources that live within their homeland. Until well into the twentieth century the Denésuliné lived in small groups scattered over a vast area. They were normally far removed from the assistance of other Denésuliné. The animate resources of their vast homeland were mobile, often widely scattered, and often unpredictable in their movement. The locations where camps were placed were often within areas that came to be devoid of the animate resources that were necessary to feed their residents. Certainty was hard to come by.

The consequences of these conditions become immediately apparent if one imagines oneself as the person responsible for obtaining the food to keep a camp fed, even a small camp, with its elderly or dependent individuals, infants, and women who are pregnant, lactating, or caring for small children. What is it that keeps driving the hunters to get out into the bush to search for game in times of scarcity, or when conditions are rough, or when their experience tells them there is nothing for them to find? The Denésuliné have long experience of life in the bush. They know well the variability in food supply that exists within it. They recognize when all the usable game has left an area and they must move on—regardless of the conditions or temperatures outside—to a more productive place. What their culture and the reality it creates provide them is a fundamental trust in their relationship with the animal/spirits. The relationship between them is one in which the animal/spirits have assumed the responsibility to help the Denésuliné to survive by exposing themselves to contact with the Denésuliné and allowing themselves to be killed by them. This relationship engenders a trust within the Denésuliné: a trust that holds that if they behave as they should, if they show the respect to the animal/spirits that they should, then the animal/spirits will provide them with the opportunity to survive.

The existence of their trust in this relationship is fundamental to understanding how the Denésuliné persevere and thrive in the harshness and uncertainty of the conditions under which they live. It is this trust that generates the effort to hunt regardless of how adverse the immediate conditions of life are and how unlikely the prospects for success may seem.

The Denésuliné do not kill animals for sport or trophies.

For the Denésuliné, killing is not an end in itself but a step in a process of utilization of the body of the animal that has been killed. Always, the animal and the use to which its remains are to be put are the center of the process of hunting.

Our cultural view of aboriginal hunters, whether in literature, the media, or in ordinary conversation, is clouded by a series of muzzy Romantic and other strange notions. Of particular interest here is the image of the noble hunter going off into the dangerous wilderness to find food for his family. This image takes on other characteristics in the harsh conditions of the Canadian context (Atwood 1972), but the core misperception of the image remains: the focus upon the hunter. Reality is rather different. Finding and killing the prey are the easy part. Our Romantic misperception of the process of hunting with its attendant visualization of all the other persons involved as inactive dependents passively awaiting the hunter to save them from certain starvation is something we will return to later in the work. At the moment, we want to focus on the idea that killing is the easy part.

We can argue about whether or not animals are sentient and self-aware until the cows come home, but this is really a rather purposeless argument that owes more to the view of the nature of animals embedded in Christian thought than it does to observation of how animals behave. Animals are sufficiently sentient and self-aware that they seek to avoid threats to their well-being. They try to avoid or evade predators. They are not particularly fond of being killed. When they do encounter predators, they flee or resist them. If they are wounded, they try to escape, often enduring intense pain and discomfort to do so. In spite of this, the fact remains that animals are easy to kill.

The point of hunting is not to produce a clean kill but to get the animal down so that it can be killed, butchered, and converted to food. Any wound that immobilizes the animal is effective at this. What the hunter brings to the situation is the ability to follow the animal after it has been wounded. Time becomes the hunter's ally, and wounds that only injure the animal will eventually bring it to a stop, where the pursuing hunter can close with and dispatch it.

A final point needs to be made here. It is a point to which we will return later. It is also the most critical aspect of Denésuliné survival as subsistence hunters. If hunting is the easy part, it should be apparent that transport of the meat and processing it into a form that allows it to be consumed or stored is the hard part. Hunting, particularly when the prey is migratory, is erratic. When hunters can generate meat, it often comes in a boom or bust pattern. There is either not enough or there is far too much. There are times, at any given location, when there simply are no animals available. The Denésuliné have great experience of these times and have developed effective methods for dealing with them, the most basic one being relocation to a different area. At virtually all other times, hunters can generate more meat than the members of their camp can consume.

There is a crucial consequence to the erratic nature of the hunters' ability to generate meat. The buffer between want and plenty is the ability of the women of the camp to prepare and process the meat into forms that can be stored. It is women's labor and the products of their labor that determine the quality of life and the long-term survival of Denésuliné bush camps.

Hunt 2

Moose

The field session of September 1972 and January 1973 was spent at Mission in Saskatchewan rather than in the bush in the Northwest Territories. My truck had been shipped to Discha by barge. In early October the first heavy snows of September had melted off and the bush was largely clear of snow cover. There was a rough road, really more of a trail but wide enough for a vehicle, that ran from just outside Discha south to Riou Lake. Abraham Artchie, then in his early sixties, had come to me to ask if I would drive him down the road toward Riou Lake, as he wanted to look for bear. It was the time of the year that black bears were taking to their dens (grizzly bears did not come this far south). He wanted to travel down the road to look for tracks, which he would then follow to the bear's den. He felt the ground was still soft enough in places and there were just enough scattered patches of snow to hold tracks so that he had a reasonable chance of following them. He said he did not care how old the tracks were— "even weeks"—as he was confident that once he found them he would be able to track the bear to its den.

We set out in late morning a few days later, driving from the village toward Discha and then south on the Riou Lake road. We had not gone more than a hundred and fifty yards when we saw a lynx bound onto the road. Abraham yelled at me to stop the truck. As soon as I did, he jumped out of the cab and began to chase the lynx down the road while waving his arms and shouting loudly at it. The lynx, now at the edge of the woods, reacted by breaking into a run and vanished into the woods at high speed. I knew the Denésuliné ate lynx and that lynx fur was valuable (then about forty dollars a pelt), but I was utterly perplexed by his actions. Once back in the truck he explained that if they were chased, lynx would sometimes climb a tree. He had been trying to tree the lynx.

The road to Riou Lake was within the full boreal forest rather than being part of the transitional zone of the boreal forest. The area was dominated by jack pine forest (*Pinus banksiana*) but there was a far wider variety of trees—including paper birch (*Betula papyrifera*), quaking aspen (*Populus tremuloides*), and balsam poplar (*Populus balsamifera*)—than were found just a dozen or so miles to the north. The ground cover was still reindeer moss (*Cladonia* spp.). The only time I ever saw actual grass, as that term is understood by those who live farther south, was in the bed of a drained and abandoned beaver pond along the south shore of Lake Athabasca. Scattered throughout the area along the road were stands of hardwood trees. Undergrowth, while virtually absent from almost all the forest areas, did exist in places.

We continued along the road for five or six miles, traveling slowly so that Abraham could scan the road and roadsides for bear tracks. Eventually he called for me to stop as he had seen a set of tracks from the truck. They turned out to be fresh moose tracks. We parked the truck, gathered our gear, and set off at a walk. The moose had crossed the road and turned up an animal trail within the woods that headed to the northwest. It diverged from the course the road followed, heading deeper into the forest. The ground was still soft from the recently melted snow. Patches of shallow snow covered it in places. Abraham was carefully following the tracks, watching for changes in their freshness that would indicate that we were approaching the moose.

The day was seasonally warm. Temperature was in the forties and there were broken clouds. It was a breezy day. The breeze helped with noise we (mostly me) made while walking after the moose. After about a mile and a half of tracking, the tracks became so fresh that they indicated to Abraham that the moose should be close by. I was wearing a parka with a synthetic cloth cover while Abraham was wearing one with a natural cloth cover. He asked me to stop and wait while he continued ahead, as he thought we were now close enough to the moose that he feared it might hear the noise of the branches scraping against the synthetic fabric of my coat. Moose do have incredibly sensitive hearing, but I thought it was a remarkably polite way of asking me to stay put because I was making too much noise.

Abraham continued after the moose while I waited. He was gone about an hour and a half before he returned. He was puzzled that I had not come up to join him as he had caught up with the moose and killed it at the edge of a small moss-covered, boulder-filled wet area. He was sure that I had heard the two shots he had fired and was uncertain why I had not come forward to join him. Unfortunately, between my impaired hearing and the wind, I had not heard his rifle shots. When he approached the moose, he came upon it from the south—the downwind direction—and was able to approach to within two hundred feet of it. The animal, a cow that had no calf, had been standing by a stand of evergreens on the north side of an oblong-shaped boulder field roughly a quarter of an acre in extent. The trees were old enough to have thinned out considerably and had grown tall enough to have lost their lower branches to a height above the moose's shoulders. In this thinned-out patch of young growth, he had been able to see the moose clearly from his concealment in the hardwood growth on the south side of the boulder field.

I went with him to where it lay on the ground. He decided that he only wanted to gut it, as it was now getting toward dark and the moose had fallen a considerable distance from the truck. Between his age and health, and the fact that I had never field butchered a moose before, he felt skinning the moose and dismembering it was more than he could manage in the time we had before dark set in. He was concerned that if he did skin the moose when we could not haul all of it out from where it lay, it would be more likely to attract animals that would consume or foul the carcass. He was confident he could get his nephew to return with us the following day to help complete skinning and butchering the carcass and then haul it to the truck.

His nephew was quite willing to come and help, so we returned the following day. The moose had been undisturbed overnight. We were able to park the truck somewhat closer to where the moose lay. When it had been skinned and butchered we packed everything to the truck and took it back to the village.

Text 2
Food Storage

Abraham was of the generation of elders in 1972. His approach to killing a large animal reflected the practice of times when the Denésuliné lived in the bush and only occasionally came into the settlements that surrounded the trading posts, rather than the practices that had become customary among those who lived in the new permanent and far larger village. He was more concerned with the proper distribution of the moose meat among his kin, affines, and friends than he was in storing meat for his own use during the coming winter.

The practice of widely distributing the meat of a large kill had largely vanished among the then contemporary Denésuliné. Some meat was still distributed along lines of kinship and affinality if those kin and affines happened to reside (and were present) in the village and if relations between the people involved were positive, but the portion of the meat of a kill that was distributed was rapidly declining. There were even instances in which small portions of meat from a large kill were being sold to non-kin. Among the reasons for these changes were necessary adaptations to village life. The village at that time numbered somewhat more than five hundred souls. A pattern of distribution based upon residence within a small bush camp composed of kin, affines, or close friends simply did not work in the context of so many people living together. Distributing the meat of a moose among twenty or thirty people is a very different thing from trying to distribute the meat of a moose among five hundred people. Moose are large animals, but they are not large enough to be distributed meaningfully among residents of a settlement that large.

The Denésuliné do make dry meat from moose. The taste of moose dry meat is not as valued as is the taste of caribou dry meat, and it does not have the emotional value that caribou dry meat does. The Denésuliné devote less effort to drying moose than they do to drying caribou and prepare it in significantly lesser quantities. Unfortunately, the village conditions—the crowding and the sanitation problems, the large population of sled dogs with their defecation and urination, and the trash buildup that comes from human occupancy on that scale in the absence of any systematic system of trash collection—all combined to make it difficult to make dry meat there. The Denésuliné insist upon clean surroundings for making dry meat, for pragmatic reasons as well as out of a sense of respect for the remains of the animal/spirit that is being processed. The crowding and dirt of the village made it difficult to find a suitable spot within it. A few individuals did put up smoke tents (canvas tipis) or construct small log buildings that could be used for drying meat, but there were few of these.

The village was fortunate to have an Indian Affairs–operated community freezer. Electric service had not arrived until the summer of 1970. Prior to this the community freezer was powered by a separate generator. Its maintenance was not a high priority for the local Indian Affairs agent—who resided in Discha a dozen miles away—and it was not well kept up. Subject to frequent stoppages, it was not a terribly reliable place for a family to keep its food supply. It was also a small freezer for the use of five hundred people. There were problems with the allocation of space within it and with providing security for meat stored there.

Because the village had so recently received electric service and because of the high cost of electric appliances, the village had few home refrigerators or freezers in 1972. When the weather was cold enough to freeze meat, if a dwelling had an unheated area or adjunct outbuilding that offered secure storage, it was possible to keep meat for use throughout the winter.

Most of the meat from the moose Abraham killed that fall was distributed along his social networks. The rest was placed in the community freezer for later use by his family. None of it was dried or smoked.

Food storage in the bush is rather different. Away from the demands of the crowded village and the use of electric freezers, the Denésuliné are forced to rely upon traditional methods of food storage. There is variation in food storage practice between those Denésuliné whose lives in the bush are spent in Saskatchewan, especially among those who trap and hunt to the south of the village, and those who spend their bush lives north of the village. The basis for this distinction, aside from the greater access to caribou that those who live toward the tundra have and the seasonal variation in when caribou appear in the different regions, is the distribution of permafrost.

Circumstances of life in the subarctic of the Canadian Shield are always demanding. They are also often quixotic if not downright strange. For dozens of generations individual Denésuliné have found themselves in unusual circumstances (e.g., illness, sudden death, or an accident) in which their ability to store meat or other goods has been a factor in their survival. Their culture has provided them with a basic repertoire of techniques to which they have applied the full range of human creativity to solve the individual problems they have faced. From hiding meat under cairns of rock to hanging it in trees to suspending it under the ice of a lake, the Denésuliné are creative and practical in their approach to storing meat.

The basis for the bulk of Denésuliné food storage is freezing. The temperatures of the subarctic are cold enough that, in normal years, it is possible to freeze meat between October and April by exposing it to the outside cold. The most common manner of freezing meat in the bush is to place it on a "stage." A stage is simply a log platform. Normally rectangular, it is made by sinking four corner posts deeply enough into the ground to provide solid support for a simple platform of logs constructed near the top of the vertical supports. Stages are usually not constructed just for meat. They serve as all-purpose storage for items that can be exposed to the air and outside temperatures. They are usually made so that the platform is just above the head height of the person constructing the stage. The platform, the storage area, needs to be high enough to be above the reach of any sled dogs that might escape their tethers and get loose in the camp. This height is sufficient to protect what is stored on the stage from foxes (*Vulpes vulpes* and sometimes *V. lagopus* in winter) or other small animals that might get into meat stored there.

Stages used for meat storage offer no protection from wolverine or bear, which are easily able to climb onto the stage or tear it down. Some protection from bears is provided by the fact that the Denésuliné do not begin to store meat upon stages until the weather is cold enough for it to freeze. By that time bears have normally taken to their dens for the winter. For wolverines and late roaming bears, protection of the meat on stages depends upon the activity and presence of humans and dogs in the camp.

Small animals represent a potential threat to meat stored on the stages. Mice do not seem to pose much of a problem; gaining access to the stage may so expose them to predators that they are reluctant to take the risk. A greater threat comes from birds. Ravens are potential scavengers upon the meat stored on a stage, but the primary culprit, certainly the one that most upsets the Denésuliné, is the whiskey jack (northern or gray jay, *Perisoreus canadensis*). These birds are virtually fearless and have a high tolerance of the presence of humans. They will come to the meat even when people are walking around the camp or sitting and working right by the stage. Whiskey jacks are particularly drawn to animal fat.

Denésuliné prefer to hang the fat from caribou to dry before putting it away for winter storage, particularly the large sheaths of fat that build up on the backs of the bulls. Winter storage of fat is normally inside the dwelling, suspended from the roof or rafters or placed inside a separate unheated outbuilding if one has been constructed. The whiskey jack's predilection for fat is a constant annoyance while the fat is drying. Whiskey jacks peck at the fat or meat in such a way that they drill conical holes into it as they eat.

Fat is rarely stored on a stage after it has undergone its initial drying. It is so valuable and fragile that it is moved into more secure storage. When winter comes, Denésuliné field butchering switches from always skinning the caribou that are taken to often leaving the hide on the caribou—both as parts of dismembered caribou or over the whole carcass if it is not dismembered. The hide provides the meat with some protection against freezer burn—surface dehydration of the meat in the extreme cold—as well as some protection from whiskey jacks and ravens. Meat on a stage is often covered, usually with plastic sheeting or a tarp, to provide additional protection and to keep moisture, wind-blown sand, or other contaminants away from it.

Meat stored on the stages is either cut into sections for ease of later preparation or left as an entire carcass. The Denésuliné do not bring entire carcasses into the dwelling for thawing and preparation for cooking. The preference is to bring in a smaller section, such as a leg or a neck. If meat is left on the stage as an entire carcass it is far more difficult later to cut sections from it for cooking. There is a tradeoff between doing the butchering under unpleasant outside conditions at the time of the field processing and the inconvenience of later having to separate off a portion of suitable size to be brought into the dwelling and thawed for cooking. Bow saws, which are normally used for cutting firewood, are a remarkably effective and widely used means of cutting usable-sized portions off a frozen caribou carcass. Somewhat surprisingly, chain saws have their proponents for this task.

As the weather cools in the fall, particularly after the fall snow accumulation has begun, Denésuliné men living near the tundra often build up meat piles in the bush. Space on the stages in the camp is almost always at a premium. Meat piles in the bush are convenient and disperse the hunter's winter meat supply over a number of locations within a larger area rather than gathering it into a single location with the attending risk of losing it all in a single incident. The risk is that bush meat piles are unattended and more vulnerable to scavenging by other species.

We have never wintered in the bush within the full boreal forest—with its higher concentration of life and its wider variety of species—and are not sure how the practice of making meat piles works there or even if it is attempted. We do know that hunters there do make meat caches and that hanging meat from trees is more common. Denésuliné along the tundra edge accept that rodents, rabbits, foxes, squirrels, birds, weasels (*Mustela nivalis, M. erminea*), and other small species will scavenge meat they have stored in the bush. When they pile meat in the bush, they take considerable effort to stack the meat carefully and cover it with brush and other locally available material. They attempt to ensure that the meat is not exposed to the air in such a way as to give access to other species, and they construct a covering that is heavy enough to prevent small animals from displacing it or digging through it. Some animals are capable of reaching the meat no matter how well it is protected. Rabbits and foxes will tunnel under the meat and come up to it from below, a method that utilizes their digging skills and provides a way for them to access the stored meat without being visually exposed to their own predators. Denésuliné watch to see what has been trying to gain access to their meat piles and often use their meat piles as bait and set traps around them.

The primary protection for a covered meat pile is the fact that it will freeze into a solid mass, one that is too heavy for small animals to dislodge and spread around. They can gnaw at the edges, as it were, but they cannot cause serious damage to the stored meat. With larger predators, primarily wolf and wolverine once bear have denned for the winter, there is less possible protection for the meat. Wolves are remarkably shy animals, even this far into wilderness, and are reluctant to approach or tear apart things that smell of humans. This provides some protection to the stored meat. Wolverine are a different issue. Nothing the Denésuliné can do can protect a meat cache from a wolverine. One year George used fifty-five-gallon metal drums sealed by metal bands with locking clamps to store goods within his cabin, as he had been having problems with them getting in and destroying his supplies while he was gone. There is no way to be sure, but the wolverine that got into the cabin and opened the clamps on the barrels and destroyed their contents or scattered them all about the cabin was either frustrated by the effort it had had to spend figuring out how to work the clamps or was particularly playful after having figured out how to work them. If a wolverine discovers the meat cache, it is gone. The only real protection from them is their scarcity.

The Denésuliné in this area do not dig pits into the permafrost to act as natural freezers.

Freezing is not the only method the Denésuliné practice to store meat, although it is the primary long-term storage method. There are a variety of short-term storage methods, some of which still receive occasional and sporadic use. Presumably they made greater use of these methods in the past, but only presumably, as we have no real data on this. Essentially, all the methods that do not involve preparation of the meat are forms of refrigeration based on the presence of permafrost. In those areas where the permafrost is continuous, it lies close to the ground surface. Most all of the land that is not solid rock or sand has permafrost within a few inches of the ground surface. In sand deposits the sand may thaw to a depth of several feet during the summer. Fred Riddle commented that the deepest he had ever seen sand thaw during his more than thirty-year experience of the area was to a depth of four feet. Unfrozen sand more than a foot down is cool but not cool enough to preserve food.

Use of permafrost as a means of storing food generally involves lifting away the surface cover until a frozen surface is reached. The food can be placed there and then covered by the surface cover. This works best under heavy moss growth—to insulate the top of the covered food—or within muskegs (the colloquial term applied to almost all northern bogs, swamps, or wetlands). Storing food within a muskeg is essentially the same process as storing it under moss. A place is prepared so that the food rests on the frozen permafrost, and it is then covered by the vegetation of the muskeg. Storage in a muskeg adds two things that are lacking in storage under moss. The water of the muskeg is cold and acts to cool the food placed under it. And it is harder for passing scavengers, all of which rely at least to some extent upon scent to locate their food, to detect meat that has been stored under water than it is for them to detect food that has been stored under moss.

The water of the lakes is sometimes used for short-term food storage, but it is not a favored method. Lake water remains quite cold throughout the year, but it does warm significantly in shallow areas and at the top surface of the lakes. Most areas along the shores are shallow enough at the lake margins to warm during the summer. This reduces the effectiveness of the lakes as a place to store meat. Placing meat in the lakes is normally done only as a temporary measure to protect meat that is awaiting shipment south to the village or processing into dry meat. Putting meat in the lake is better than letting it sit in the warmth and sun on land, but it begins to deteriorate quite quickly underwater. Even if it does not spoil, its texture changes and its taste deteriorates.

It is difficult to imagine immersion in the cold water of a pond as an effective way to store the carcass of one of the megafaunal animals, as has been postulated for mammoth remains. Even if the meat did not decompose so badly that it could not be consumed, it would rapidly deteriorate in taste, texture, and quality. It would take exceptional circumstances to draw a human group back to such a stored carcass rather than seeking out alternate and fresher sources of meat.

Cooking meat often serves as a means of short-term storage. Temperatures in the subarctic are often cool enough, even in midsummer, that the temperatures inside dwellings can preserve portions of boiled meat for a week. This is less a deliberate strategy of food preservation than an accidental but useful byproduct of cooking food for consumption. Boiled meat is normally consumed long before it risks going bad. The labor and effort involved in building a fire and enduring its heat during the summer tend to limit summer cooking, especially inside the village where cooking occurs indoors. This is less of an issue in bush camps. The crowding and dirt of the village inhibit cooking outside, but these conditions are not applicable to the bush camps. These all have a specific area for an outside cooking fire, and the area is kept clean of litter. Cooking outside also disperses the heat of the fire so that it does not warm the dwelling. With cooler weather, a fire is normally kept burning when people are awake. It is common to keep a pot of food on or by the stove so that it is available on demand throughout the times people are awake. Much cold weather cooking is less an issue of making a specific meal than one of adding to the existing pot.

For several hundred years the Denésuliné have used Western foods in their diet. Transportation from the points of trade to the bush camps was so limited that their primary concern was with basic staples such as flour and lard. They made more limited use of other kinds of consumables, such as tea, tobacco, and treats for the children. These are items that have been shipped in to the points of trade from long distances away, and they are generally well packaged to survive that shipping. Storing these items in the bush normally means keeping them where they will stay dry and can be kept away from animals. If the primary camp dwelling is a cabin, they are normally kept in the cabin. If the camp lasts long enough, a separate log storage building may be put up. If the camp is in tents, as is often the case from the late spring to early fall, storage of these goods is more of a problem. If a stage has been constructed, it can be used if the goods are wrapped sufficiently well to protect them. Otherwise, it is necessary to keep them inside the tents.

Preparing meat for storage can increase the length of time it can be stored. It can reduce the vulnerability that comes from depending upon extremely cold weather for its preservation. It can also significantly reduce the bulk and weight of the stored meat, which greatly increases the ability to transport the meat that has been prepared. Of all the ways that humans have developed to allow meat to be stored for long periods of time—for example, salting, pickling, or smoking—the Denésuliné have settled upon air drying as their favored method of preservation. Fresh meat is virtually always their preference for consumption. Frozen meat is never preferred over fresh meat. At times dry meat may be preferred over fresh meat. Dry meat, particularly dried caribou meat, is emotionally and symbolically loaded in ways that frozen meat is not; it has qualities of meaning that the Denésuliné value above its taste. When they are first able to make it in a season, it is often preferred to fresh meat. It is also highly desired when they want variety in their diet.

If fresh meat is their preference for consumption, freezing is their basic method of meat storage. They freeze far more meat than they dry, and they consume far more frozen meat than dried meat. Air drying is their secondary method of meat preservation. In principle, it should be possible to dry the meat of any animal found within the lands the Denésuliné occupy. Air drying is exactly what it sounds like. The meat is prepared (as described later) and exposed to air. The exposure dehydrates the meat, at once reducing its weight by more than 50 percent and also reducing its moisture content such that the growth of bacteria is seriously retarded. Once dried, the meat can be stored for periods of longer than a year provided it is kept dry and receives adequate ventilation.

The presence of fat in or on the surface of the meat is one of the difficulties that must be addressed in preparing meat for drying. Fat obviously increases the energy content of the dried meat and does wonders to improve its taste, but it is difficult to dry animal fat well enough to preserve it. Wild animals rarely build up fat within their muscle tissue the way domestic animals (many of which have been specifically bred to do so) do. When wild animals do accumulate fat, it tends to form either internally around their organs or in deposits between their skin and their muscle tissue. This makes it easier to separate it from the muscle tissue and consequently makes their meat easier to dry. Few of the animals the Denésuliné kill have fat throughout their tissue, and those that do are not made into dry meat. Some, such as porcupine or beaver, which can have areas with dispersed fat deposits, may be smoked rather than air-dried, but this is more or less a side activity done for variety in the diet rather than a basic means of meat storage.

At the present time the Mission Denésuliné dry caribou, moose, and fish on a regular basis. Other animals can be and are made into dry meat but on a far more irregular basis. Animal fat, once separated from muscle tissue or the internal organs, can be air-dried. Bear fat can be dried or cooked down into grease, and bear are routinely taken for this purpose. We have little indication that bear meat, which can carry trichinosis, is made into dry meat, although in 2001 during Karyn's field season, the community was being treated for a wide outbreak of trichinosis from bear meat that had been dried and shared widely within the community.

There are indications from very limited comments informants have made that in the past there was a trade in pemmican and buffalo meat that passed between the southern part of Denésuliné range in Saskatchewan and Fort Chipewyan in Alberta. Because the individuals who talked about this trade had a family ancestry among the Denésuliné of English River along the Churchill drainage, it was not possible to determine when or if this trade passed through the Discha area or if it was directly between the Churchill River drainage and Fort Chipewyan. What is interesting about the comments is the fact that they specifically described the trade as involving two different kinds of buffalo. This raises the possibility that musk ox was one of the species called buffalo, implying a meat trade running from the tundra to the prairie, rather than indicating a distinction between two subspecies of buffalo—wood buffalo (*Bison bison athabascae*) and plains buffalo (*B. b. bison*). Musk ox is no longer found within the area used by this band of Denésuliné, and this was the only reference to their possible use as food that we encountered. During Karyn's more recent fieldwork, however, she witnessed an encounter between Denésuliné hunters and musk ox. Although they chose not to pursue it, it was clearly within the range of animals they considered suitable for consumption.

The Denésuliné do dry fish for human consumption. This practice, which involves splitting the fish and hanging it, is to be differentiated from the practice of hanging fish for dog food. Drying fish is more an activity of the forest, where fish make up a larger part of the Denésuliné diet than for the Denésuliné who live near the tundra edges. They dry a variety of fish species, and the product is quite tasty but does not last long. It is normally prepared during the late winter or early spring spawning runs and is usually consumed within a few weeks of being made.

Caribou dry meat is exactly that: dried meat. It is not cooked. To dry the meat, the Denésuliné construct a drying platform on which the cut meat is exposed to the air. There is no consistent pattern to the shape or size of platforms. That is a function of individual preference combined with the local topography and the placement of dwellings around the camp. The amount of meat to be dried is a major factor in determining the size of the dry meat rack. Dry meat racks are placed in an area that is clean and dry. The people cutting the dry meat and attending to it while it is drying have to spend hours around the dry meat rack. It is therefore desirable to build the rack where it is protected from wind and blowing sand.

The two most common shapes of drying racks are rectangular and A-framed. The rectangular racks look like smaller and narrower versions of the stage that is constructed for storage. But there is no platform on the top of a dry meat rack. Instead poles are laid across its narrow width. Dry wood is used for the construction of the rack. The willow that grows near the tundra does not grow large enough to be used for any but the smallest drying racks. This forces the Denésuliné to use spruce or other woods. It would be possible to use green wood for the corner support poles, but the poles that hold the meat while it is drying must be dry wood. Green spruce wood contains too many chemicals that would retard the drying process as well as imparting an unpleasant taste to the dry meat. The A-frames look much like a wide household ladder, with the poles for holding the drying meat on both sides of the A-frame, replacing the steps.

In drying racks of either shape, the cut meat is draped over the cross poles. Nothing is used to hold the meat to the racks. Hanging it this way allows the cut meat to hang downward to expose the maximum surface area to the air. The poles supporting the meat must be high enough to ensure that the hanging meat does not come in contact with the ground. The higher the meat is above the ground after it is hung, the safer it is from dogs that have escaped their tethers or from the depredations of small children who do not want to wait for the drying process to be completed. Rectangular dry meat racks are normally constructed when it is anticipated that larger quantities of meat will have to be processed. A-frames are normally used if smaller amounts of meat are anticipated.

Cut meat in the process of drying has to be watched and attended. It is turned periodically to promote more uniform drying. It has to be protected from moisture and is brought inside if it starts to rain. It is brought inside each evening as the day begins to cool and darken and is kept inside overnight. It is not placed back on the racks until any morning dampness or fog has dissipated.

There is variation in practice in determining how long the meat has to hang before it is ready to pack away. Assuming reasonable conditions—no rain or dampness, moderate temperatures, etc.—the meat needs to hang for three days to reduce its weight by roughly 50 percent. It can be consumed by the second day before it is completely dried, but at that point it cannot be stored except by freezing it. There is variation in Denésuliné practice—as well as the opinions of the authors—about hanging the meat for a fourth day. Unless conditions have been ideal, meat packed away on the third day is more vulnerable to damage while stored and will not last as long as meat hung for a fourth day. The fourth day of hanging further reduces its moisture content, making it better suited for long-term storage. It also makes the meat harder and more brittle—whether this is desirable is a matter of individual preference—and better preserves any fat within the meat. Obviously the length of time the meat needs to be hung depends upon the specific situation. Variations in temperature or humidity can lengthen or shorten the amount of time the meat needs to be hung before it reaches a state suitable for long-term storage. Variations in the skill of the person cutting the meat and the uniformity with which it has been prepared have similar effects upon the drying process.

Dry meat that is improperly dried is vulnerable to rapid spoilage. If the meat has been cut too thickly, the outside may appear to be properly dried while the inside still retains too much moisture for it to keep for lengthy periods. Spots on the improperly dried meat that have too high a moisture content are vulnerable to bacterial growth and can become fly blown. It is somewhat annoying to pull out a piece of dry meat, only to find parts of it covered with maggots or discolored by bacterial growth; it is far more serious an issue if the dry meat is the only food in camp. The skill of the person cutting the meat is a crucial factor in successfully preparing the meat to be dried. There is a premium on getting a rough uniformity of thickness in the raw meat if it is to attain a uniform state of dryness. Skill and effort play a similar role in the actual drying of the meat. If it is not turned regularly or if it is improperly turned, or if there are places where the meat has become folded, it will not dry to a uniform state. Successfully drying meat demands a great deal of skill, work, and experience.

The Denésuliné traditionally made a variety of containers to store dry meat. A favorite was to use the unprepared hide of the forelegs of caribou being butchered for dry meat as material to sew into a hassock-like sack. Gym bags and carryalls were quite commonly used during the 1970s and 1980s. The crucial aspect of whatever is used for storage is that dried caribou meat has to be exposed to adequate air circulation to prevent moisture from building up inside the container. Trapped moisture within the container rapidly leads to the growth of mold and bacteria that ruin the dry meat. Wrapping it in plastic or using air-tight plastic containers also leads to rapid mold and bacteria growth upon the dry meat and ruins it.

Caribou being processed for drying are normally stored in the form of skinned and sectioned portions of the carcass. When it is to be prepared, the preparer gathers together a sufficient supply of meat for the work session. The preference is to work through the available meat by doing one kind of cut at a time. Hind legs are usually the first part of the caribou that is prepared. The preparer gathers a sufficient number of legs for the session's work at a location by the rack where it is comfortable to sit down and there is a large enough flat area to work. This area is covered, either by plastic sheets (tablecloths were favored) or by spruce branches in the absence of plastic. The meat is removed from the bones and piled within easy reach. The long bones of the leg are set aside and saved if they are to be split for marrow and boiled down for grease.

The piled meat is cut piece by piece. There seems to be a preference to start with pieces of meat that are slightly smaller than an American football, although during Karyn's fieldwork she observed a preference for working with smaller pieces. Meat does not grow in rings the way trees that live in a seasonal climate do, and cutting dry meat almost seems a way to correct that condition. The meat is carefully cut with a sharp knife—simple carbon steel blades that can be sharpened with a file are preferred—almost like a section of tree trunk is peeled for making plywood. The idea is to generate a sheath of meat approximately six to eight inches wide by two and a half to three feet long, by roughly 3/8 of an inch thick. Obviously, the size of the sheath generated depends upon the size of the piece of meat being cut. The intent is to create a sheath that can be hung over the poles of the drying rack that is heavy enough to stay in place once it has been laid over the pole yet still expose the maximum surface area to the air. Once a quantity of meat has been cut into proper shapes, it is hung on the drying rack. Work normally continues until the prepared meat supply is gone or the drying rack is full.

Cutting meat is hard and tiring work. It involves very sharp knives. Cuts are common even among the most experienced preparers. Dry meat is prepared throughout the year if there is a sufficient supply of fresh caribou. It becomes an indoor activity only when temperatures outside become too cold to dry the meat rather than freeze it. The whole activity, including hanging the meat to dry, must then be moved inside. Dené-suliné bush cabins do not have high roofs or ceilings. Meat being dried inside must be hung from poles stretching across the cabin and has to hang down into the parts of the cabin where people walk and live. It can become a bit of an obstacle course to move around a twelve by fourteen-foot cabin that has hundreds of pounds of drying meat hanging down from just above head height inside the dwelling. Work that is tiring and demanding in the comfort of nice weather is far more demanding during the colder and harsher outside conditions that characterize most of the year in the subarctic. The meat is almost always cool or cold from how it has been stored before processing and the outside air temperatures are rarely ideal. This is work often done without wearing gloves. Hands become cold from the air and handling the meat. Even with ground cloths to sit on, the ground a few inches above the permafrost becomes cold to sit on and the outside air adds to the discomfort of the person cutting the meat. Denésuliné prefer to work at cutting meat in stints broken by doing other things or moving around to get a break, but it is often necessary to work more or less continuously for hours at a time in order to get the job done in the face of less than ideal weather conditions or the volume of meat to be processed.

Dry meat is sometimes smoked as well as air-dried. The use of smoke is not for purposes of preserving the meat. Small fires, almost smudge fires, are built under the drying rack. Again, wood choice is a critical factor. The wood must be dry and free of the sap that permeates so many of the spruce and pine trees of the area. Burning these to produce smoke causes the dry meat to take on a foul taste that essentially prevents it from being used for human consumption. Finding and hauling in an appropriate supply of wood for the fire is time-consuming and is a task passed to the children of the camp whenever possible. The smoke from the fire under the drying meat is never allowed to become too heavy or too abundant. The reason for the smoke fire is to keep flies away from the meat while it is hanging so that they do not lay eggs on it. Even if conditions are such that the fly eggs do not survive to hatch, the eggs have to be scraped off the meat; an avoidable demand on time and labor at a time when time and labor are in short supply. In practice, use of a smoke fire seems to have more to do with the taste of the finished dry meat than with anything else. Some people like the taste smoking adds to the dry meat and smoke their meat. Others do not like the taste of smoke on their dry meat and do not smoke it during its preparation.

As noted, a few Denésuliné built smoke houses in the village, but it was not possible to determine whether these were actually used for smoking meat to preserve it or simply combined smoking with air drying. Smoking and air drying are used in combination in the bush to preserve heavy cuts like shoulders, hips, necks, or ribs. With these thicker pieces, the meat is not dried all the way through. Instead, the outer surfaces are dried and smoked to a sufficient thickness to protect the inner portions of the meat from exposure to the air and to biotic contaminants. The undried interior meat changes in texture as it is treated, but it still remains raw. It is cooked before it is consumed. It takes far longer for these thick pieces of meat to air dry. They often have to hang for more than a week to reach a degree of dryness that will preserve them. When this is done, there is an effort to make sure that they are placed on the drying racks away from the thinly cut drying meat. Over the course of the time it takes the thicker pieces to dry thoroughly enough to be preserved, they receive a much heavier dose of smoking than does the thinner cut meat drying on the same rack.

It is possible to smoke or dry entire gutted small animals. We have seen them but we did not observe any being prepared.

Making grease from animal fat and bones is another way to preserve animal tissue. Rendering fat by boiling it is mostly used to extract a finer grease from bear fat. As far as we know, bear fat, unlike caribou fat, is not eaten without being processed. Caribou fat is used for cooking, although lard has become so readily available with the use of aircraft to enter and leave the bush that it has almost completely replaced the use of caribou fat for cooking or making bannock (the northern homemade bread prepared in a cast-iron skillet). Caribou fat is normally eaten directly to accompany either cooked caribou or caribou dry meat. Individual portions are cut from the air-dried fat taken from the backs of bull caribou in the late summer to early fall season.

Bones provide both marrow and grease. During our fieldwork we saw no preparation of marrow for storage. It is a highly desirable food, but there is very little of it in an animal carcass, especially if there is more than one person to feed. Marrow is normally consumed as soon as it is removed from the long bones of the caribou legs and is generally available only when the long bones collected during dry meat making are split to be boiled for grease. In all the food preparation and butchering we saw, marrow was never more than an incidental treat, mostly consumed by children. It was never separately processed or harvested. If it was not eaten on the spot it might have been boiled along with the bones, but we never saw this happen. We never saw a hunter extract marrow during field butchering or consider marrow as a factor in determining what portions of a carcass to bring back to camp.

Given the emphasis placed upon marrow as a food resource in the course of human evolution, we should perhaps stress these points. Marrow is a rich and nutritious food that is often available to be scavenged from kills made by predators of other species. Unfortunately, there is not very much of it in any given carcass. While there may be enough marrow in an animal carcass to make it a worthwhile food for a single animal to scavenge, there is not enough marrow to be found in a single carcass to make it a significant food for more than one human-sized scavenger. Whatever the role it played in the course of human evolution may be, it was never a worthwhile food source for groups of human ancestors.

Boiling bones is the last step in the dry meat making process and has become increasingly rare with the ready availability of lard. When grease is made, the bones are split or fractured. A hatchet is the preferred tool for breaking bone for boiling. Both the blade and the flat hammer portion of the hatchet are used to break the bone apart. The blade is used to split the bone lengthwise if there is marrow to be extracted; otherwise the hammer portion is preferred as it produces smaller pieces of bone, from which more of the grease can be extracted. The bone pieces are placed in a large pot partially filled with water over an outside fire and allowed to boil until the grease is extracted. Boiling bone requires a very hot fire and is a slow process. It is one of the few cooking or food preparation activities considered dangerous enough that small children are kept away from the area where it is being prepared.

During the time of our fieldwork, the only non-meat products of the bush that were preserved were berries. These were gathered in considerable quantities as they became available throughout the summer, but virtually all that were gathered were eaten fresh or made into jam. Winter storage of fresh berries was a thing of the past. Some were occasionally made into jam, but they generally had better uses for the sugar they could afford to haul into the bush than using it to preserve berries for winter consumption. Jam was regarded as a treat and did not last long before it was consumed.

Hunt 3

Caribou

Pursuit and Risk

On May 1, George, Wellington, and I set out to cross Smalltree Lake (map 2) to examine the site where Wellington had placed his summer camp for the past few years. We wanted to see if it was a suitable location for our own summer camp. The two of them were mostly interested in confirming that the location would allow Paul a good long distance view up and down the lake ice and that it would be high enough and sufficiently exposed to the wind to blow away the coming hordes of mosquitoes (thirty plus species) and black flies (twenty plus species). We traveled from the winter cabins on the side of a sand hill off a long, narrow lake joined to the eastern shore of Smalltree Lake. Our destination was the tip of a thirty-foot-high sand ridge on the west side of Smalltree Lake that formed a point projecting into the lake. We had to detour around a number of islands in the lake. The route was circuitous but was chosen partly in response to the deteriorating ice conditions of the main lake. We were traveling with a toboggan pulled by the Skidoo. Wellington was driving the Skidoo. George was standing at the back of the toboggan (where the driver of a dog team would normally stand) to steer it and control its lateral motions. I was stuck with riding in the toboggan.

A Skidoo, a toboggan, three people, and assorted rifles, axes, and other miscellaneous gear make up a fairly heavy load. The midwinter ice on these lakes is normally four to six feet thick, but by early May it was waning rapidly. It was still several weeks until break-up, but the ice was noisy to travel over as it was on the edge of "chandling" (or "candling," the choice seems to be a local dialectical preference throughout the north). It was beginning to move up and down when objects passed over it. There are times moving across the ice in the spring when a toboggan (and its passengers) sit at the center of a moving depression in the ice surface. If one looks outward from the toboggan across the lake, it is not possible to see the lake surface. All that is visible is the sky above and the moving edge of a circular depression in the ice centered upon the toboggan.

Currents in the lake water from springs, stream outlets, or the flow and movement of the lake water itself produce weak spots in the ice. Because the ice of the lake contracts and expands in response to temperature changes, cracks form in the ice surface. These cracks in the ice can separate the frozen lake surface into separate floating plates. Some of these plates of ice can "pancake" (flip over) when asymmetrically loaded. Denésuliné folklore is replete with stories of dog teams and toboggans (not to mention bush planes) vanishing beneath the ice as an ice sheet flips over. Wellington himself had twice had his dog team and toboggan break through the ice while traveling during the spring. Within two weeks he was to go through the ice yet again. He was making a trip from the new summer camp back to the winter camp. He had to stop near the north end of one of the islands in Smalltree Lake because one of his dogs had become tangled in its harness. When he stepped off the toboggan to go and untangle the dog, he instead went straight through the ice. The water was too deep for him to touch bottom, but he was able to grab hold of the ice at the sides of the hole he had just made, pull himself back onto the surface, and get on the toboggan. One May, while he was traveling by dog team on the ice near Mission with his wife and children riding in the toboggan, the entire toboggan went through the ice. It was only his dogs' desperate struggle to keep from being pulled into the water that allowed them to claw their way to solid ice and in the process drag the toboggan carrying him and his family onto solid ice. Fortunately someone happened by and helped help him get a fire started on shore.

Needless to say, with our heavy load and the ice conditions what they were, our route across the lake was chosen with some deliberation.

Unfortunately for the course of our deliberate passage, just as we reached the north end of an island, we saw a mixed group of eleven caribou cows and yearlings standing out on the lake ice some distance from the west shore of the lake (map 2, H-3). The caribou were about two and a half miles away (Wellington's estimate) and considerably south of the sand point for which we were heading. We stopped and looked at the caribou. There were about ten seconds of thought and discussion before Wellington announced that we would "try it."

The Skidoo was turned toward the caribou and accelerated to its maximum speed. The caribou immediately heard and saw us. In this country in past years, caribou would often stand and wait when they saw human activity. Apparently not recognizing humans as a danger or simply not recognizing what humans were, they would stand and watch until they were approached quite closely. These caribou may have been hunted from snowmobiles during the past winter, as they turned and ran toward the shore and the enveloping cover of the forest well before we reached them.

Upon reaching the shore they broke a path through the deep snow at the shoreline and continued into the forest. They kept moving into the forest for several hundred feet until, still on solid footing within the forest, they came near the shore of a small muskeg lake adjacent to the forest. Here they stopped moving away from the lake and milled around.

Wellington kept the Skidoo heading at high speed toward the spot where the caribou had gotten off the lake and onto shore. He then shortened the distance we had to travel by heading directly toward where he had seen the caribou moving into the woods. He drove the Skidoo and toboggan as far into the circling willow growth as it would go until it became hung up. At that point, he and George both headed directly into the woods. George, who was smaller, shorter, and at the back of the toboggan, had a more difficult time getting through the willows and deep snow than Wellington did and was slightly behind him as they entered the forest. I was sitting in the toboggan and got out of it only to sink to my waist in snow and willow branches. By the time I disentangled myself, all I could do was trail behind them. I did not arrive until they had fired, so I had to rely on their accounts of the kill rather than witnessing it.

Wellington arrived in sight of the caribou milling about in the woods just before George did. The effect was to place George and Wellington in line but at an acute angle to the animals, with Wellington closer to them than George was. Only Wellington opened fire on them (Sharp 1988a: 55–57). He was able to kill four. These were quickly skinned, butchered, piled, and covered. Because of the weight we were carrying we were able to take only a little of the meat with us.

After we had finished at the kill site we went on to inspect the sand point where we were planning to place the summer camp. When we had finished our tasks there, we began the return trip to the winter camp. While we were en route we encountered two caribou on the lake ice just beyond effective rifle range. We stopped and George and Wellington both took a shot at them. Both claimed to have hit one of them but the caribou seemed uninjured and both were able to run well. They rapidly fled and were not pursued.

May 2, 1975

The next day Wellington took his dog team out to pick up the rest of the meat from the four caribou he had killed the day before. His nephew and one of his young sons followed on a toy toboggan pulled by a sled dog. They returned to camp several hours later, telling that while Wellington was off his toboggan, his sled dogs had seen caribou passing on the lake and had run off after them. Wellington did not return to camp for some time. He had had to walk the five miles or so back to camp to get the Skidoo so he could go and run down his dog team. He found them tangled in the brush along the shore where they had tried to follow the caribou into the forest, some distance away from where they had taken off after the caribou. It took him so much time to recover and untangle his team that it was too late in the day for him to get back to the meat that had been piled after the kill.

May 3, 1975

It was not until the following day that Wellington was able to get back to recover the meat from those four caribou. By then wolves had found them and the meat had been lost.

Text 3

Persistence in Hunting

H unting is dangerous. It is something the Denésuliné take very seriously. Respect for animal/spirits
so thoroughly permeates Denésuliné culture that it
is very difficult for them to approach hunting in a casual or
haphazard manner. When the Denésuliné begin a hunt, they
follow it through to the point that weapons are used or the
prey escapes beyond the range of their weapons. To reach this
point, the Denésuliné will pursue a hunt to the point of putting their own safety at considerable risk. Wellington's hell-
bent-for-leather chase across Smalltree Lake in the Skidoo,
in spite of the deteriorating ice conditions of the lake and
pulling his brother and me behind, was neither a stunt nor a
game. It was a normal and quite typical Denésuliné response
to contact with an animal/spirit. This does not mean that a
decision to pursue is unthinking or that visual contact with
a prey animal will automatically generate a hunt. While we
were examining the site for the tents on the sand hill, two
caribou moving up the lake passed by where we were working. Both Wellington and George saw them, but they made
no effort to pursue them. However, once a decision to pursue
has been made—as it was when we stopped out on the lake
by the island—then the pursuit is going to be carried through
until the caribou either show their willingness to die for the

hunter(s) by allowing themselves to be killed or show their refusal to die by escaping.

Most of the danger in hunting comes not from contact with the prey or other animals encountered in the bush but from the very process of moving around in the bush. A helter-skelter pursuit is a vivid illustration of this, but it is simply that, a more dramatic instance than most. Short sprints to reach a firing position are common, but most hunts do not involve any such dramatic chase. Hunting tends to be more about the use of cover, awareness of wind direction, and the careful control of motion in a deliberate approach to the prey. The risk comes from the hunter's movement through the bush.

The bush is an inherently dangerous place. Movement through it amplifies that danger substantially. Basically, this part of the Canadian Shield is rock, sand, or some form of water. Where it is exposed rock, the issue is footing. Bare rock is slippery; wet bare rock is treacherous. It is also an unforgiving surface upon which to land if one falls. If the rock is in the form of cobbles, boulders, or smaller pieces, again the issue is footing. Boulders and boulder fields are mostly avoided. It is normally safer and easier—not to mention faster—to walk around them than it is to try and cross them. With smaller rocks there is the added problem of their movement. The rocks themselves can give way or move, throwing the hunter to the ground. Unless it is deep, snow cover does not exactly do anything positive toward alleviating this problem.

It is difficult to hunt, to be aware of the local environment, or even to walk quickly if all the walker's attention has to be directed toward watching where he has to place his feet. This is not good country to move through or try to accomplish something (like locating game) if you have to spend all your time watching where you put your feet.

Surfaces that offer easy walking—sand hills, eskers, frozen lakes, packed trails through the snow—provide the favored routes for travel through the country. Unfortunately, the places on the Canadian Shield that offer the most food to the animals of rarely coincide with such surfaces. Creeks and stream courses, low muskegs and swampy areas, lake shores, rapids, and open water in winter are all far more likely to hold small game and fur-bearing animals as well as to attract larger animals. Hunting and trapping consist largely of a process of traveling from one rough spot to another; a deliberate seeking out of places that are inherently dangerous and difficult to move through.

The difficulty of walking this land is one of the factors behind the Denésuliné use of other means of transportation in the bush. Throughout the time we are examining, the dog team was the favored means of winter travel used by the Denésuliné when deep in the bush and away from the village and its convenient gasoline supply. Dog teams have great advantages for those who travel through the bush in order to gain their subsistence. Aside from the obvious advantage of being able to be fed from the land, dog teams are quiet. They do not disturb wildlife with the noise of their passage, nor do they leave behind the smells of oil, gasoline, or combustion, none of which evoke a positive response from the area's wildlife. Dog teams are remarkably quick and can travel for long distances. They are extremely reliable. Their ability to travel over rough ground and under difficult conditions far exceeds that of snowmobiles or ATVs.

This is not to say that there are not problems with dog teams or with using them in the bush. They need continuous care. Dogs have to be fed all year round and watered in summer. They are of little functional value when the weather is too warm or when there is inadequate snow cover. With their absolute love of running and pulling, sled dogs probably qualify as insane. There is the problem of control. They will try to pursue caribou on sight regardless of circumstances. Many Denésuliné trail a heavy rope behind their toboggans. This allows the team to be tied when stopped in the bush, but on the frozen lakes there is nothing to which one can tie the dog team. Getting off the toboggan when it is not possible to tie the team risks having the dogs take off in pursuit of caribou or whatever else catches their interest. A dog team that has taken up a chase normally ends up in a tangled mess in the first patch of brush encountered. This can mean a considerable hike to find them. On the lakes it can mean miles of walking to catch up with them.

Movement through deep snow is so slow and so energy consuming that it is necessary for human hunters to establish a trail network to avoid having to break through deep snow whenever they attempt to go somewhere. These trail networks are largely derived from the movement of dog teams through the bush. Hunters follow the same trail networks over and over to keep the trails packed and clean. The existence of these trail networks constrains where the hunters can travel, but the increase in the speed of travel and reduction in the effort it takes to travel offset that restriction. If there are problems with food supply so that the hunters have to venture off their trail network to hunt new ground or get into different areas, winter travel becomes a far more dangerous and energy consuming process.

The Denésuliné make extensive use of boats once the ice begins to break up on the lakes. The advantages of ease of travel and increased carrying capacity are obvious. Boats also allow movement across the lakes when the ice is breaking up or has insufficient strength to support walking or the use of a dog team. Water is the great killer in this land. The large lakes are normally ice water from November to June. The smaller lakes freeze earlier in the fall and often remain frozen until May. Going through the ice, especially when alone, is usually fatal. Even putting a foot through thin ice on a small stream can produce soaked feet. A soaked foot and pants leg that would be but a nuisance in milder climes become a risk to life itself in the cold of winter. Fortunately, in extreme cold, wet footgear and pants legs freeze so quickly that there is usually time to deal with it, but the isolation of a single hunter, often days removed from assistance, amplifies the seriousness of these situations.

Even when the water is not frozen, its potential lethality remains. Lake water that spends nine months of the year as ice water does not reach temperatures comfortable for swimming in many places. In these frigid waters you do not casually swim to shore from a boat that has overturned. Travel by small boats and canoes in lakes filled with cold water is dangerous under the best of circumstances. The rockiness of the land is matched by the rockiness of the lake bottoms. There are rock piles scattered throughout the lakes and rivers, many reaching close enough to the water surface to sink a boat attempting to pass over them. Thunderstorms can quickly generate waves high enough to sink a boat, particularly an overloaded boat. Many of the lakes are tens of miles long or wide. Their expanse gives ordinary winds ample opportunity to build large waves. The temptation to continue a journey, to try to get home rather than putting ashore to wait out the waves, or the urge to meet a schedule all become temptations that claim Denésuliné lives.

Most Denésuliné hunting is what Frison and others have called "opportunistic" (2004: 41). It is based upon accidental contact with prey animals rather than a deliberate search for them. The Denésuliné do engage in deliberate hunts (e.g., Hunt 2) in which they set out after a particular kind of prey, seeking sign of that prey in order to follow it to a kill. Such hunts are much less common than hunts that depend upon accidental contact with prey; deliberate hunts are more common within the boreal forest, where prey species are more likely to have a specific home range.

We think the idea of deliberate hunts for a specific type of prey is part of a widespread misconception about the nature of subsistence hunting. The misconception is tied to another widespread set of misconceptions centering around the idea of "knowing the land." Both sets of misconceptions are based upon a common idea: that hunters know where the game is.

In certain specific circumstances this is not a bad idea. Knowing that in deep snow deer will "yard," and knowing where they are yarding or have yarded in past years, makes possible setting out deliberately to seek deer in those places. This approach to hunting—which is based upon knowing the land, knowing the behavior of the prey, and knowing the local history of the prey animals' use of the land—certainly does occur.

The flaw is in assuming that all hunting occurs like this. The case of deer yarding is obviously restricted to specific kinds of forest, to specific patterns of climate and snowfall, and to prey that is not migratory. Implicit in this set of conceptions is the notion that humans can "know" both the local terrain and the behavior of the local animals so well and that both are so constant that they can be known. There are times and places at the edge of the tundra where the primary prey is migratory and the land areas are so vast relative to the size of the human population, where this conceptualization of the Denésuliné approach to hunting might have some validity. The example of known water crossings springs to mind, although even in this case, the question of timing comes into play. Caribou migrations are so variable, and the vastness of the land gives the caribou so many choices as to where they go and when they go there, that basing human survival upon such knowledge would be risky.

Reality is simply more confusing than the conceptualization of hunting tactics that so much of the literature suggests. The simple fact is that all hunting, like all politics, is local. No matter how well the Denésuliné know the land—and they know it very well—know the behavior and recent history of migrations of their prey, "knowing" in the sense it appears in much of the anthropological literature is a fundamentally flawed concept.

It would be better to think of hunting as a chaotic process in which the Denésuliné have knowledge of some of the attractors than to think of hunting as a deterministic process.

Almost half a century ago at Duke, I got into a passing discussion with my dissertation supervisor, the late J. Christopher Crocker, about hunting. I was somewhat perplexed by what I had observed in the field and was trying to make sense of it. His own fieldwork was among the Bororo of South America. The environmental similarity between the circumstances of our separate experience of hunters was essentially nil, yet the fact remained that we had both worked with hunting peoples. He made an observation that I have always found central to my understanding of Denésuliné hunting. He commented that among the Bororo it seemed to him the key issue was "not in knowing where to find game but in knowing what to do when they did find game."

The reality of the world in which the Denésuliné live is that at a local level—the level that Denésuliné face on the ground—no one knows where the caribou will be and when they will be there. In a time before aircraft, radio tracking, satellite monitoring, and modern communications technology could be applied to determining where the caribou are, these were questions to which no human could know the answers. It is a problem to which the experience, observations, and understanding of thousands of individuals over uncounted generations of Denésuliné have been applied. The stakes in this "game" are their own survival and the survival of their families.

The Denésuliné have survived very well. They have dealt with the uncertainty as a people at the systemic level through the utilization of caribou throughout their migratory range (Gordon 1975, 1990, 1996; Burch 1972). They have dealt with it at a smaller scale through patterns of sharing and food distribution within kin groups. They have dealt with it through the pattern and manner by which they distribute social groups upon the ground (Sharp 1977a, 1978: 55–79). They have dealt with it through their systems of belief, religion, and folklore. They have dealt with it through the careful transmission of skills and knowledge from generation to generation through uncounted generations. In other words, they have developed a culture, with all the richness and complexity the term indicates, that enables them to survive by dealing with the uncertainty of caribou movement.

All that being given, the fact that every Denésuliné hunter who occupies a specific place on the ground and is tasked with keeping himself and his family alive must deal with is that no one knows where the caribou will be or when they will be there.

The phrases we have been using to describe Denésuliné hunting—opportunistic, accidental contact, or out and about—are accurate in describing the nature of contact between the hunter and the prey. Contact between humans and animals is accidental in the sense that it is not planned; and it is not known where, when, or if it will occur. Yet the terms may still be misleading. If it is not known where the caribou are, it is known that it is necessary to be out in the bush in order to be exposed to them. A large part of Denésuliné hunting involves engaging in activities that increase the chances of such a contact occurring. Whether going out deliberately to look for caribou or to engage in some other task, such as checking a trap line, the Denésuliné always carry their weapons with them and always carry the gear necessary to deal with any encounter between them and caribou or other animal/spirits. In effect, everything the Denésuliné do in the bush is hunting; the Denésuliné are always hunting.

The Denésuliné approach to survival is based upon treating every excursion into the bush as a hunting trip. Beyond this, the timing and the manner of completion of the other activities they have to undertake are arranged to ensure that they are steadily and consistently exposed to the bush and the animal life within it. The encounters that occur between the Denésuliné and the animal/spirits upon which they depend are accidental, but the opportunities that create those accidental encounters are deliberately constructed by the way Denésuliné culture determines how each hunter will act and approach the environment in which he lives.

Hunt 4

Caribou

Waiting for Prey

MAY 3, 1975

SMALLTREE LAKE, NORTHWEST TERRITORIES

The last week of April and first week of May 1975 were a busy time for the men of our camp. All of us had come to Smalltree Lake at least partly because Paul had expected caribou to be moving northward up the lakes toward the calving grounds and to be plentiful (Sharp 1988a). He was familiar with the area around Smalltree Lake and had wintered there in past years. He preferred the area one lake to the east, the northern part of Anaunethad Lake, where he had long had cabins by a river. His use of the Smalltree Lake area was an adjunct of his occupancy of Anaunethad Lake. Over the last decade he had made only limited use of the area. His son Wellington quite liked the Smalltree Lake area. As Wellington matured he had begun to center his own efforts there and for the past few years had spent the fall season on the lake.

The intent was to take a sufficient supply of caribou from the spring migration to ensure enough caribou dry meat to last into the fall and the arrival of the winter caribou migration. The dry meat taken would not be the primary item in the diet but a highly valued supplement to fish and other game taken over the summer. The focus of the spring hunt would be the caribou moving north up the lake ice on their way to the calving grounds far out on the tundra.

Hunting on the ice of the frozen lakes has its own difficulties and particular needs. The crucial issue is visibility upon the lakes. The atmospheric conditions present there now closely approximate those we associate with prehistoric or at least pre-industrial times. It may be difficult for people who have grown up in modern times in industrial nations to recognize just how different atmospheric conditions are in much of the north. This is even more so for those raised in the eastern and southern parts of the United States or near major urban centers elsewhere in the world. What aviation authorities refers to as CAVU (clouds absent, visibility unlimited) is frequent. Even when there is substantial cloud cover, visibility of more than a hundred miles is commonplace. The difference in air quality is such that it is only when weather-fog, rain, etc. creates restrictions on visibility or when there is smoke from forest fires or some other abnormal condition that one encounters visibility of less than one hundred miles. On low relief terrain like that found in this part of the Northwest Territories, one obviously cannot see that far, but the limiting factor is the curvature of the earth rather than the clarity of the air.

As a pragmatic measure, the clarity of the air and the extended visibility mean that when not looking over the glare of lake ice, it is possible to pick out, count, and identify individual caribou as to sex and size in groups of up to a hundred animals from distances of two or three miles away.

We later learned that the primary northern movement of the wintering caribou had been up other lakes both to the east and west of Smalltree Lake. Caribou turned out to be sparse where we were that spring. The men had been actively searching for them and were out hunting almost every day. Each man hunted on his own. Each would take his dog team out on the main lake. Wellington preferred to hunt the west side of the lake, while George preferred to hunt the east side. Each would travel southward down the lake. They traveled where they could see for long distances down the ice but stayed close enough to shore to be able to see the tracks made by any caribou leaving the lake to move into the bush. Paul stayed closer to camp.

Paul and I went out on the ice to hunt. We used the Skidoo to pull his toboggan. Access to the main lake was becoming difficult as the ice at the mouth of the ten-foot-wide junction connecting our side lake to the main lake was starting to break apart. The ice at the junction was barely a yard across. The water at the opening into Smalltree Lake had cut a small break in the sand banks that lay behind the rocks and boulders forming the shoreline of Smalltree Lake. The land surface was about five feet above the level of the water. The water at the opening was shallow, so the sun—not to mention the regular toboggan traffic—was working on it very quickly. Paul had not taken any caribou to make dry meat for the summer and was a bit concerned that the last of the caribou would pass before he could get any for his wife May to prepare.

With some difficulty we were able to get the Skidoo and toboggan through the passage and out onto the ice of Smalltree Lake. The ice on the big lake was not in good shape, but it was still several weeks from melting away from the shoreline around the lake. It would cease to be usable without extreme danger within two weeks, but not until June would it fully break up into individual sheets and melt.

Paul preferred to hunt by finding a place to wait upon the lake ice where he could see caribou moving up the ice from the south. He wanted to be where he could see a long way down the ice. Caribou, and most of the other large animals of the tundra and tundra fringes, have decent distance vision. If he could see them from his vantage point upon the ice, they could see him. He dealt with this by carefully choosing the spot where he waited upon the ice. The crucial issue for him was to use the local topography by placing himself where he could see and gain access to the caribou without placing himself where he became an obstacle to their movement. As he read the situation, this meant stopping the Skidoo and toboggan about one third of the way between the east shore of the lake and the shore of the first of the islands that occupied the middle of Smalltree Lake.

To get to the calving grounds, the caribou had to move north. They did not like to move overland. They were more vulnerable to wolves in the coarse and granular snow that still covered much of the inland area than they were on the lake ice. Not only could they see wolves on the ice much farther away than in the woods; they could run faster on the ice and expend less energy than they had to expend to run through the bush. Paul also knew that caribou moving up the lakes did not like to move off the lake ice onto the islands in the lake. He judged his place to sit and wait to be close enough to the east shore—and far enough away from the shore of the islands— for the caribou to feel they could safely pass between where he sat and the shore of the islands.

This also meant he could sit and wait for the caribou to come to him—no small thing for a man in his fifties who had had a heart attack. If he did kill any, the carcasses would be in a place from which they could easily be transported to the summer camp site on the west shore of Smalltree Lake where they were to be cut into dry meat. Once the Skidoo and toboggan reached the place where he wished to be, we stopped and settled in to wait (map 2, H-4).

Hunting caribou on lake ice is not quite as straightforward as it may sound. Aside from the fact that it is cold on the ice and that one takes the full effect of any wind, it is necessary to remain still and be reasonably quiet. It is possible to talk softly, at least when caribou are not in sight, but any unnecessary movement needs to be avoided.

The idea of ice is probably not exactly what folks raised in southern and urban places would expect it to be. If the lakes freeze quickly—they can freeze overnight in a cold snap—they form a crust of clear ice that is often toned with a slightly bluish tinge. It can reach a thickness of several inches in a matter of a few hours if extremely cold when the lake freezes over. This first crust of clear ice is often extremely strong. When water freezes, it expands in volume by roughly 10 percent. This expansion does not stop when the ice first forms but continues until the temperature of the ice drops below a certain point. As the ice continues to expand, it has nowhere to go. This causes it to develop cracks and causes the separate sheets of ice to rise or fall to relieve the pressure of their expansion. The ice of a lake surface soon becomes uneven, and it changes in texture and appearance, with bubbles often forming within it and giving it a clouded appearance.

As the ice continues to grow in thickness throughout the winter, it freezes at the bottom of the ice sheet and gains in thickness by growing downward. The undersurface of the ice is not smooth but forms a rough and jagged surface and often has projecting spikes of ice poking downward like icicles. As the ice moves up and down with changes of temperature or with changes of the lake's water level, the process of cracking continues. Each crack is a point where water from below the ice has access to the surface of the ice. In cold times this water rapidly freezes, often cementing the ice sheets together and "healing" the fractures in the ice surface. As the water warms with the sunlight and milder temperatures of late winter and spring, the water that flows onto the ice freezes more slowly and, eventually, does not freeze at all.

The cold surface of lake ice provides a perfect place to catch snow. It is normally cold enough for it to snow long before it is cold enough for the lakes to freeze. How the snow builds up on the ice depends upon air temperature and the strength of the sunlight. In most cases the snow falls upon the clear ice and sticks, only to be partially or completely melted off by warmer days or days with strong sunlight. The snowfall and its melting, something that can be repeated many times, serves to roughen the surface of the ice. Eventually, as the weather continues to get colder, the snow begins to build up upon the frozen lake surface. In autumns marked with alternating warm and cold spells, the water that flows up through the cracks in the lake ice onto the ice surface can freeze to form a sheet of ice that is then covered with snow. The snow on the lakes can become a layered concoction of snow that has become wet and frozen, then covered with water that has frozen into a layer of ice, only to be covered with snow again. The entire process can be repeated several times over.

As determined by rainfall, this area is technically a semi-desert. As a rule of thumb, the tundra is a frozen desert while the forest areas are semi-desert. The entire area is continuous permafrost, with the area of discontinuous permafrost beginning some distance to the south. Ice on the lakes near the tundra normally reaches four to six feet in depth by mid-January and at places can be noticeably thicker. The land around the village is in the full boreal forest in an area of discontinuous permafrost. There the lake ice is normally but around four feet thick by mid-January. From the late 1960s through the early 1990s (before the effects of climate change became so obvious on the ground), several feet snowfall quickly covered the ground; certainly by well before Christmas, even in a warm year. As the snow begins to build upon the lakes, it encounters one of the other major factors that affect life in this area: the wind.

The snow that falls here, particularly in the fall, is usually soft and fluffy. The area is so quiet, especially when it is cold, that the sound of a heavy, fluffy snowfall can be absolutely deafening. In the forest, protected from the wind by trees, and along the lake shores, where it builds up in the willow growth ringing the lakes, the snow can exceed six feet in depth, depending upon the local topography.

The snow on the lakes does not stay soft. The wind is an almost constant feature of the environment here, and it blows with full force across the lakes. It carries the snow away from the lake centers toward the shoreline, where it is trapped by the willow growth, and into the forest edges. The wind packs whatever snow remains upon the lakes, making it harder and grainier than when it fell. Indeed, the wind is so strong and so constant that much of the exposed tundra is snow free. Over much of it the snow is blown behind obstructions that block or deflect the wind. It gathers into drifts, as happens over much of the West where snow fences are so common. Sheltered gullies on the tundra or tundra fringes sometimes pack tens of feet deep with drifted snow.

With the strengthening sun of late winter, the snow upon the lakes continues to thin and harden. Its surface becomes increasingly granular. It generally provides sufficient traction to be easy to walk around on so long as it does not become wet. It was upon an ice surface like this that Paul and I waited for caribou. The day was overcast so it was not overly glaring, but ice is nevertheless ice, and it reflected what ambient light there was. The glare made it hard to locate the horizon against which caribou would first become visible as they moved up the lake. Glare also made it hard to judge distances to objects on the ice or along the edges of the shore or the islands.

After we had been out a few hours, Paul detected a band of fifteen to twenty caribou moving up the lake. They were coming directly up the ice, closer to the shores of the midlake islands than to the lake's east shore. As this particular arm of the migration flowed northward up Smalltree Lake, it was dominated by cows and yearlings. At this time of the year bulls and cows do not travel together. In fact, many of the bull caribou never make the journey to the calving grounds. A few bulls had passed by, but there were far fewer of them than there were cows and yearlings. The Denésuliné focus is upon taking the fattest caribou. At this time of the year the bulls had not recovered from the stresses of the fall rut and the ensuing winter. The preferred target was large yearling caribou followed by healthy pregnant cows. These were the animals that were in the best physical condition and most suited for human consumption.

We sat quietly, watching the band of caribou moving up the lake. They were well aware of our presence but did not seem sufficiently disturbed by it to alter their course up the lake. As well as we could project their course, it seemed they would stay to the west of us and pass through the gap between ourselves and the shore of the islands. Paul had picked his spot well. We remained still, watching the course of the caribou. It was not possible to close the gap between ourselves and where we thought the caribou were going. They were watching us as they came; any attempt to stand and walk toward them would have resulted in their fleeing. Neither of us considered using the Skidoo to close the gap to the caribou. All we could do was wait until the caribou got as close to us as they were going to come before we opened fire.

It is a central feature of Denésuliné belief that the power to determine if an animal is killed by a hunter rests with the animal. However, because animals allow themselves to be killed by Denésuliné hunters does not mean that they die easily or do not strive to stay alive. The caribou did not come close to where we sat, but Paul needed meat. When we did open fire upon them it was at a longer range (two hundred and fifty plus yards) than the Denésuliné normally choose to shoot at the animals they hunt.

Hunting is not a sport, and it is not a clean or romantic business. At that range, in the glare off the ice and with the confounding effect of the ice upon the judgment of range, it was necessary to be very deliberate in each shot that was taken. At that distance it is not possible to discriminate as finely individual differences between the caribou—sex, size, condition, position within the group, etc.—as it is at closer ranges. Not all the shots we made were as clean as we would have liked. The idea was simply to get the animals down.

Caribou value their own lives as much as we do our own lives. A number of the caribou took hits but were able to continue to run and managed to flee the lake. One animal took a shot that severed both front legs just above the knees so that its lower limbs were hanging from its upper legs only by bits of skin. Its lower legs were flailing in the air as it attempted to run away across the ice on the stumps of its upper legs until a further shot brought it down.

There were now eight caribou down on the lake. These quickly had the heads removed and the tongues taken out. They were then gutted and skinned but they were not dismembered. Paul wanted to take them over to the west side of Smalltree Lake to where the summer camp was to be. There they would be lined up on the ice by the shore to be processed into dry meat once he had made the move to the summer camp. He took care that the animals were lined up side by side, and their abdominal openings were carefully packed with snow. To protect the carcasses further, he carefully tore strips about two feet long by four inches wide out of plastic bags and tied them to the willows along the shoreline just in front of where the caribou were left. The strips would blow in the wind and keep away both bird and animal scavengers. His precautions worked.

Text 4
Weapons

The Denésuliné do not use automatic weapons. Large caliber semi-automatic rifles are exceedingly rare; I did not encounter any until the 1990s. The Denésuliné do experiment with new technology, and that experimentation includes weapons. The large caliber semi-automatic rifles that were available to them were either modern (military) small caliber high velocity or conventional smaller caliber (e.g., .243). None of these weapons- or the calibers in which they were available-had proved useful for hunting caribou. The military calibers produced too massive a wound to leave a carcass useful for processing into food. The .243 was too light for the broad range of prey sizes the Denésuliné are likely to encounter. Those firearms were now used for target practice, plinking, or shooting at nuisance animals that came near camp.

The Denésuliné have had access to firearms since the first third of the eighteenth century when they came in direct contact with the Hudson's Bay Company. They were familiar with firearms long before they had access to them, as the Cree had had access to them for several decades and had used them in raids against the Denésuliné. The weapons initially available were smoothbore flintlock muskets. These were slow to fire, cumbersome to load, and terribly loud. They had a considerable shock effect when used upon people who were not familiar with them or had none of their own. They fired a large projectile that did massive damage when it did hit a target. These weapons were greatly desired. They were valued as prestige items. Their primary utility lay in their use in warfare, raiding, or trade.

The flintlock muskets to which the Denésuliné had access were smoothbore. This means the weapon fires a ball-shaped lead projectile down a barrel that is not rifled. The shape of the projectile and the lack of rifling in the barrel make the weapons very inaccurate. They were not accurate at longer ranges and were often beyond usable accuracy at distances as short as a hundred feet away. The flintlock muskets made available by the Hudson's Bay Company could not be relied upon to hit caribou or other large game animals at any significant distance.

A flintlock musket relies upon contact between a piece of flint and a steel plate to generate sparks. The sparks from that contact fall upon an exposed platform that is filled with black powder. When the sparks ignite the powder on the platform, some of the flame from that ignition travels through a hole in the gun barrel to ignite the powder charge inside the barrel and propel the ball out of the muzzle. When the musket is put into its final preparation for firing, the black powder that rests on the platform is exposed to the wind. It can be spilled or blown away, which blocks the firing process. The black powder is likewise exposed to any moisture in the area where the weapon is used. The weapons are difficult to use when it is raining or when it is noticeably damp. They are also difficult to use in the cold. Winter temperatures where the Denésuliné live often drop below the point that even modern steel is weakened. The small parts of the muskets could become brittle and were subject to breakage. The cold temperatures could also impede the process of generating the sparks that came from the flint striking the contact plate, again rendering the weapon unreliable if not outright unusable.

The musket did have one advantage. The musket balls that were fired could be recovered. Once recovered, they could be melted and recast into new projectiles. One of the village elders,

Ben Adam, then in his seventies, asserted that "a good man could get by with twenty-five musket balls for an entire winter," using them over and over (field notes, January 17, 1970).

In addition to all these difficulties in using the musket as a hunting weapon, there was the problem of using them in the extreme cold. If it were carried outside, the weapon would become so cold that it would have to be handled with extreme care. Not only would it become fragile and subject to breakage, but bare human hands would freeze upon contact with the weapon and might well stick to exposed metal parts. While all these difficulties could be overcome, doing so was a slow and cumbersome process—not what a hunter wanted to be doing when preparing to fire on a prey animal he was close enough to shoot at.

There were circumstances in which the flintlock musket would have had value as a hunting weapon. In general, it would have been effective for occasions when the hunter could close to within fifty feet of his target. This would have made it a useful weapon for hunting moose in conditions of fairly close cover. It would have been an effective weapon for killing bear as they emerged from their dens, but the Dené-suliné have a number of other effective ways to drive bear from their dens and kill them. It is unlikely that a musket was ever a preferential choice for that use. Having a musket at the ready—that is, ready to fire—might well have been a preferred way of hunting bear when they were outside their dens. The shock effect and the massive tissue damage of a musket ball might have been preferable to having to close with the animal to use a spear. This may have been a seasonal use as the late summer to fall fat buildup in bears might have made it difficult for a musket ball to penetrate deeply enough to put the animal down.

Under the conditions where the musket could have been carried in a nearly ready to fire condition, it might have been a weapon of choice for men to carry as they traveled alone and faced the possibility of an unexpected encounter with a large animal like a bear or moose. The same might have applied in those circumstances when unexpected contact with hostile humans was of concern.

The most probable use of the musket as a weapon for hunting caribou would be as an ambush weapon fired at close range. This would be particularly likely at those times of the year when the hunters were focusing upon the kill of a single animal rather than on larger kills. This would include circumstances such as when the caribou were on the ice of the lakes and could not be approached by a hunter moving over the ice or when the caribou were off the lakes in winter or spring but deep snow restricted their movements to trails. If conditions allowed the hunter to approach unseen to within twenty-five to fifty feet, then the flintlock musket could become an effective weapon for the kill of a single animal.

In general, the flintlock musket had a variety of uses in Denésuliné culture but was of limited value as a hunting weapon. The older technology and tools of hunting—spears, snares, bows, etc.—would have been far more effective, both in the variety of conditions under which they could have been used and in the number of animals they could have brought down in any given encounter.

There were soon to be two technological changes in rifle design that affected the Denésuliné. Rifled muskets became increasingly common in the United States through the eighteenth century (e.g., the Kentucky Rifle of Appalachian mountain fame). Rifled muskets solved the accuracy problem of the smoothbore musket. The best of the rifled flintlock muskets achieved an accuracy that nearly equaled the best modern rifles. Many were capable of making kills at ranges of four hundred yards; some of the best were capable of consistently hitting a target at distances well beyond that. The drawbacks to rifled muskets were that they were very expensive and difficult to obtain. Their appearance in large numbers would have altered significantly the way the Denésuliné hunted.

The next technological change was the appearance of percussion cap rifles. The technology was widespread by the close of the first third of the nineteenth century. The percussion cap firing mechanism would have eliminated many of the difficulties involved in using the flintlock firing system in conditions of extreme cold, wind, and wet weather. Percussion cap weapons would have been easier to use, but unless they were coupled with a rifled barrel, they would not have resulted in any significant change in Denésuliné hunting practices.

The crucial change in rifle technology, the change that did alter how the Denésuliné hunted, came with the post–Civil War appearance of modern repeating rifles that used self-contained cartridges (what we now think of as a bullet). The first of these that is well remembered is the lever action style so familiar from Western movies. Its magazine was internal to the rifle and stock and carried a sufficient number of shells to give the hunter a number of shots without having to reload. It was relatively light, far shorter than its contemporary single shot muzzle-loading muskets, and had a rifled barrel that gave it considerable accuracy. It is considered one of the most effective designs ever created for use under demanding climatic circumstances and rough physical conditions. In .30-30 caliber the weapon was heavy enough to deal with the largest game, yet not so powerful as to damage overly the remains of animals taken for meat. It was a Denésuliné favorite for generations and is still widely used.

The appearance of the modern repeating rifle was a transforming technology for the Denésuliné. It completely altered the way they hunt. The ramifications of those changes in the way they hunt, which have not been and probably never will be documented or studied, were widespread. At minimum they affected the size, constitution, and distribution of Denésuliné residential groups in the bush. They have changed the way the Denésuliné use the land they occupy and where they choose to place themselves within their land. They are probably the greatest single factor in the Denésuliné abandonment of the tundra toward the close of the nineteenth century. They have changed the way young men came to maturity and established themselves as competent adults capable of supporting a family. They have changed the way the Denésuliné take and use caribou and the way they deal with animals that are wounded but not immediately killed in the course of hunting. The repeating rifle induced a profound set of changes. It is easier to deal with them by working backward from the present.

Contemporary Denésuliné hunting is based upon the modern repeating rifle. Most use bolt-action rifles, but the lever action .30-30 remains in common use. Rifles are complex pieces of machinery. They are expensive. Modern rifles are extremely durable and reliable, but they do need to be maintained if they are to remain durable and reliable. Denésuliné rifles are used under harsh conditions. They are subject to extremes of climate and suffer from the roughness of the ways in which they are transported in the bush. They often have to be stuck in boats or toboggans where they are subject to impact and vibration as well as being bounced around. To protect their rifles virtually all Denésuliné men keep and/or carry them inside a case, often one made within their family. Most are constructed out of canvas, but tanned hide is frequently used. Most are decorated with needlework or are beaded. If damage occurs that the owner cannot repair himself, the Denésuliné do not have reasonable access to the services of a gunsmith. Repair of a malfunctioning or damaged rifle is often not a practical option. The lifespan of a Denésuliné rifle tends to be short.

Rifles are complex in other than a mechanical sense. They are socially important elements of a hunter's gender identity as well as being an integral element in his relationship to the spiritual beings that are perceived in the mundane world as animals. The Denésuliné conceptualize the world in such a way that gender is a crucial aspect of how one relates to animals and the spiritual world. The Denésuliné conceive the nature of these relations between humans and animals such that contact between a rifle—an implement used to kill animals—and a post-pubescent female is offensive to the animal/spirits. In effect, contact between a woman and a rifle risks polluting the weapon and reduces or destroys its effectiveness. How rifles are stored within the dwelling and how they are handled and by whom they are handled are complex but low key reflections of the basic Denésuliné conceptualization of the universe within which they live and the nature of their relationship to that universe.

The Denésuliné prefer to approach their prey to within one hundred feet before they fire upon them. Caribou are herd animals, normally encountered in groups. Shooting at short range has enormous advantages for the hunter facing a group of animals. Among them are an increased ability to identify individual animals and the characteristics of each animal, to determine where to place their fire (see Text 14, Hunting from High Ground). This was also characteristic of Denésuliné hunting before the advent of firearms, although the use of bows and spears often required an even closer approach or actual contact with the animals. Repeating rifles give the hunter a greater ability to control the movements of the herd once it comes under fire, allowing him to increase the number of animals he is able to kill in any given encounter.

This was and remains the basic approach to Denésuliné hunting: a close approach and careful selection of the prey animal.

The modern repeating rifle with its self-contained cartridges added two crucial elements to the way the Denésuliné were able to engage their prey: accuracy at long range and speed of fire.

Accuracy at long range came with the first rifled muskets and remained with rifled percussion cap weapons. It became normal with the modern repeating rifle and enabled an entirely different type of encounter in Denésuliné hunting. For the first time, the Denésuliné were able to engage caribou at ranges far beyond those that could be reached with the bow, spear, or smoothbore musket.

As soon as the lakes freeze, caribou move out onto them and form into groups that spend much of the winter there. This is one of their central behavioral adaptations to the harsh winters of the subarctic. Caribou are well equipped to withstand the cold and the wind and only rarely need to seek shelter from cold and wind. Being on the lakes probably does increase the energy demands upon them, but this is offset by the savings in energy expenditure that come from the easier movement possible upon the ice of the lakes. Being on the lakes, particularly during daylight, also makes it much easier for them to spot approaching predators. In effect, this means that it is easier for the caribou to see approaching wolves. In conditions where both animals are able to move freely, caribou run faster than wolves. These conditions are far more likely to be found upon the snow-covered frozen lakes than in the deep snow of the forest. Both caribou and wolves are aware of this. Caribou have to run much lesser distances on the frozen lakes to avoid the path of approaching wolves or to convince the wolves that there are other caribou toward which they should direct their efforts. In a strange form of mutual cooperation, caribou and wolf jointly determine which should not be pursued; a joint decision that reduces energy demands and makes life a bit easier for each species.

Humans have little better success in approaching caribou on the frozen lakes than do wolves. Unlike wolves, humans are not capable of the bursts of speed that wolves can use to close with the caribou. Both wolves and humans are capable of endurance in pursuit that will outlast and exhaust caribou, but this is a high-energy approach to hunting caribou. For humans at least, if caribou leave the lake ice for the bush and the trail system they have most likely created to move back and forth to feeding areas, pursuit becomes a high-risk expenditure of energy that is likely to come to naught.

With the range and accuracy of the rifled musket and the (also rifled) modern repeating rifle, the Denésuliné, for the first time in their history, were able to exploit the caribou refuge upon the lakes without the risk or energy expenditure of a long distance pursuit designed to drive the caribou to exhaustion. If humans could not close with caribou on the lakes in the way that wolves could close with them—the way humans would have had to close with them to use a spear or bow—they could easily approach them to within the accurate firing range of a modern rifle.

If the lake upon which the caribou were spending their time was not too wide, or if they were not too far from shore, the range and accuracy of the modern repeating rifle allowed the Denésuliné to hunt caribou from concealment along the shoreline.

The new ability to kill caribou routinely at distances of three hundred plus yards rather than having to close with them or get close to them also affected Denésuliné hunting on land. The effectiveness of the single hunter was greatly improved. It became possible to make hunting an adjunct to being out and about for other reasons rather than its having to be a specifically dedicated activity.

The advantage of not having to close with the animal/spirit is obvious, particularly with large and dangerous animals like moose and bear. Denésuliné ability to exploit these species increased markedly. Caribou do not pose a real threat to the safety of the hunter the way moose, bear, and musk ox potentially do. However, caribou were often spotted on land at ranges beyond that traditional weapons could reach and under circumstances that would not allow the hunter to close to within a distance from which they could be killed. Animal/spirits sighted under these circumstances suddenly were available prey. Less obvious about this is the effect of seasonality upon this kind of hunting encounter. During the summer and early fall, when the snow cover is gone, caribou are far more confident in their ability to outrun predators than they are during times of the year when the land is snow covered. In July and August the bulls almost seem oblivious to anything other than themselves; we have seen them wander into Denésuliné camps in spite of the barking of tethered dog teams and ongoing human activity. They, particularly the mature bulls, are more likely to wander around by themselves than at other times of the year. They are also less bothered by the threat of predators and will wander closer to humans and human habitations. They will allow other species to approach them more closely than they will when there is snow cover.

It is not during this period of seasonal obliviousness that the extended range of a rifled firearm is so transformative for Denésuliné hunting. That occurs when snow covers the ground and the caribou return to their normal state of alertness. Far more of the caribou Denésuliné hunters encounter can be taken at the ranges a rifled firearm can accurately reach than can be taken at the ranges previous weapons could reach. The modern repeating rifle greatly increased the number of caribou that could be taken during those periods of the year when snow and ice cover the ground and the caribou are dispersed in their winter feeding areas. The ability of the Denésuliné to supply themselves with fresh meat during the winter, when caloric demands upon them were greatest, expanded enormously.

Increased ability to generate fresh meat throughout the winter, when food is at its scarcest, had nutritional benefits beyond the simple intake of calories. The primary means the Denésuliné had to combat vitamin deficiency during colder months came from the consumption of fresh rather than stored and prepared meat. In effect, the Denésuliné were increasingly able to rely upon a sustained yield approach to winter survival. With this new capability came a lessening of the need to venture onto the tundra during the summer to stockpile large quantities of dry meat for use into the winter season.

The manner in which the Denésuliné were able to meet the caloric and nutritional demands upon them during the coldest and harshest times of the year also changed. As the modern repeating rifle improved the effectiveness of the individual hunter in taking fresh meat throughout the winter, there was a concomitant effect of reducing the need for collective hunting and the use of snares and nets during the winter season.

The changes induced in Denésuliné hunting techniques and the attendant social consequences caused by exploiting the repeating rifle's accuracy at distance were amplified by the rate of fire that repeating rifles were capable of achieving. The bolt-action rifles of the last century are capable of remarkable rates of sustained, carefully aimed fire. The Denésuliné did not receive military training in marksmanship. Rifle shells were and are expensive, so practice tended to be slowly accumulated over the years rather than in short bouts of intensive activity.

Most Denésuliné men acquired their proficiency in the use of a rifle over their teen years. Individual competence varies widely. Few men would be able to achieve the eight rounds of aimed fire per minute demanded of their military counterparts, but the Denésuliné rarely needed to fire at such rapid rates.

The increased rate of fire that a repeating rifle provided, compared to a single shot weapon, allowed a single hunter who encountered a small group of caribou to knock down several of them during the encounter, rather than being able to take only a single animal at each encounter. Not only was the taking of caribou by a single hunter throughout the cold seasons of the year far more practical than it had been, but the caribou (the only large animal the Denésuliné normally take as other than single kills) could be taken in sufficient numbers to support the social group to which the hunter belonged.

Aside from making life in the bush far safer and more secure, the increased ability of individual Denésuliné to take caribou in the numbers they needed during the cold parts of the year acted to reduce the need for collective hunting, both during the summer on the tundra and during the fall and winter in the forest. As the shift from collective hunting toward individual hunting continued through the 1880s into the post–World War I era, some kinds of hunting vanished from Denésuliné practice: the construction of fences on the tundra, mass kills by spearing caribou from boats during water crossings, and setting winter nets and snares for caribou.

As hunting shifted from a collective effort to an individual one, it had ramifications for how young men were able to establish themselves as competent adults. The repeating rifle shifted the nature of caribou hunting such that individual men became far more capable of providing subsistence for themselves and for a family than they had been when they had to rely upon traditional weapons. As with so many cultures, Denésuliné men had to build up a certain material kit in order to function as an adult. It took time and the support of family to develop this kit. Denésuliné men often developed the basic hunting skills they needed well before they were able to own a dog team, rifle, or other gear required to function alone, so there remained social checks on the speed at which young men were able to establish their economic and social independence. With the repeating rifle, young men could much more readily demonstrate their ability to generate the subsistence needed to support a wife and family.

The Denésuliné lived in the bush with only occasional visits into the trading posts through the World War I period. Their only real individual access to cash came through trapping and selling furs. Trapping rarely put a great deal of cash in the trapper's hand, but it did allow the individual to enter into a credit relationship with the fur traders. Critical to being able to enter into a credit relationship with the traders (in this area, primarily the Hudson's Bay Company) was the establishment of a reputation for competence and performance. Demonstrated success as a hunter was a critical aspect of establishing such a reputation among the Denésuliné, and what other Denésuliné said to the traders was one basis upon which the traders determined whether or not they would extend credit to an individual.

There were other consequences to the improvement of the ability of an individual hunter to generate food that came with the repeating rifle. Not only were young men better able to achieve the ability to support a family—young married couples were better able to move off and winter by themselves in the bush. Living alone in the bush is risky. Bush life is physically demanding and a constant round of chores and activities have to be performed to keep away the harshness of the outside conditions. A simple thing like getting a bucket of water from the lake can be extremely demanding in weather of -30°F or -40°F when the water lies beneath a frozen-over hole in five feet of ice that can only be reached down a slippery path of packed snow leading to the lake shore and then out onto the ice. Things like a bout of flu or dysentery—that in and of themselves are distressing but only troublesome in the company of others—can quickly become life threatening in isolation. The cold does not go away because a human has become ill or incapacitated. Water still has to be brought in from the lake. The fire must still be kept burning. Wood still has to be brought in or gathered. Food still has to be brought in and prepared or gathered. Without the support of others, even a few days of illness or incapacity can quickly make life precarious.

Still, more young couples were able to move off by themselves. This allowed them to establish their economic and social maturity far more quickly than was the case when they remained within a residential group of senior kin, siblings, and in-laws.

The increased ability of the single hunter to generate more meat on the ground also changed the lives of those Denésuliné who were part of larger groups. The groups themselves, as with young couples and growing families, needed fewer adult males to draw upon for the labor necessary to ensure their own survival. Individual groups were able to become smaller and were able to place themselves farther apart from each other. With these changes came changes in the distribution pattern of the meat obtained from the bush. Smaller groups needed less meat for themselves, and increased distance between them reduced the need for surplus meat to flow between groups along lines of kinship and affinality.

There is one final change in the nature of Denésuliné hunting induced by the repeating rifle that needs to be considered here. Denésuliné caribou hunting is generally directed toward killing a number of animals at a single time. The reasons for this should be obvious. The customary figure is that 90 percent of the aboriginal Denésuliné diet was flesh. We have no idea how accurate an estimate that number is, but it is indicative of just how greatly the Denésuliné depended upon flesh for their survival. When meat is the primary item in the diet, it takes a lot of meat to feed even moderate numbers of humans.

With the traditional weapons and technology of the Denésuliné, killing a large number of caribou at a single time was largely seasonally determined. Caribou are vulnerable upon the tundra, where fences can be used to lead entire bands into pounds where all can be taken. When the caribou leave the barren grounds for the forest in winter, fences and pounds become useless. There is the further problem of transportation. It is one thing to kill lots of caribou and make dry meat from them. In good times it can be made in massive quantities. The problem was what to do with it. As the seasons turned and the Denésuliné had to leave the tundra for the forest, what dry meat they had made had to be taken with them or abandoned. Even if they used their dogs as pack animals and dragged toboggans after them, they did not have the ability to transport dry meat in anywhere near the quantity that they had the ability to make it.

No matter how successful their efforts at killing caribou and making dry meat upon the barrens were, Denésuliné wintering in the forest were forced to take caribou throughout the winter.

With their traditional weaponry, making mass kills of caribou within the forest or along its fringes was harder than in open country. Large numbers of caribou can sometimes be taken at water crossings, but these crossings are quite seasonal and the timing of caribou crossings is quite erratic. Places where caribou can reliably be taken in large numbers are few and far between.

Some of the techniques used on the tundra could be modified for use within the forest. Fences of brush and small trees could be placed upon the ice of the lakes to direct the movement of the caribou to a central area where they could be killed. (Wellington and George attempted to do this on Small-tree Lake in 1975, but no caribou moved up the side of the lake where they put the spruce fence.) Fences and pounds can be built on the tundra-covered expanses of higher ground that are found within the forest, but the movement of caribou over these areas is, again, terribly erratic.

When the caribou go to the lake ice in the winter, they have to leave the ice to feed and to move from lake to lake. Because it is so energy consuming and physically taxing to move through deep snow, the caribou make and follow trails through it. These trails into the bush can be seen from the ice and are a crucial key that tells Denésuliné moving along the lakes where the caribou are and where they have gone. They are also places where heavy posts could be driven into the ground to support the caribou hide nets the Denésuliné made to capture caribou. They were good places to set caribou hide snares. All of these were effective techniques for taking caribou, but the simple fact is that mass kills of caribou in the forest during the months the lakes are frozen and deep snow covers the ground are rare and erratic. It was not possible to base human survival entirely upon them.

The point of all this is simple. During the months of snow, ice, and cold, the Denésuliné had to depend upon their hunters' efforts in pursuit of individual caribou in order to generate the supply of fresh meat needed to survive the winter.

Given the limitations of the traditional weapons technology of the aboriginal Denésuliné, this was a taxing requirement. What the Denésuliné did have to accomplish this task was what wolves had to keep themselves alive during the winter: endurance. The crucial form of hunting, especially during hard times and times of scarce game, was based upon the ability of a hunter to follow the targeted game until it became so exhausted that the hunter was able to close with it and dispatch it.

Humans are not able to run, particularly in deep snow, at speeds remotely approaching those that caribou or wolves can reach. Pursuit hunting did not mean running the prey animal down but following it in a consistent pursuit that did not allow the animal to rest and recover from its efforts. Healthy animals, particularly when they can choose the paths they travel, cannot only run quite fast—they can run for long distances. Pursuit of a healthy caribou could often take more than a day and could sometimes stretch for several days. This type of hunting makes very different kinds of demands upon hunters (see Hunt 13). They not only have to only be willing and able to make the physical effort to pursue the animal, but they have to be willing to stick with the pursuit even when it means staying out in the bush overnight with only whatever they are carrying with them. This became a bit easier when the Denésuliné adopted the use of dog teams and could use them not only to follow the animal but as a supply base for staying out overnight.

Along with this emphasis upon pursuit hunting of healthy prey went an extreme emphasis upon following up prey that were wounded. Wounded animals, unlike healthy ones, tend to run fairly short distances and then lie down. How far and how long depends upon the health and condition of the animal and the nature and severity of its wound. Nevertheless, pursuit of a wounded animal is far more likely to be successful than is pursuit of a healthy unwounded animal.

The pursuit of wounded animals became a basic aspect of Denésuliné hunting. It was not only practiced—it became a recognized moral component in how Denésuliné should relate to the animal/spirits that allowed themselves to be killed to ensure Denésuliné survival. It was the right thing to do, and the virtue of doing it was important to the Denésuliné. In contemporary times this is shown mostly through tales and stories but also through the criticism directed at those who do not do it.

With the appearance of the repeating rifle, the Denésuliné emphasis on following wounded game began to vanish. In modern times it has almost vanished from Denésuliné hunting practice. This does not reflect some kind of moral deterioration or the degeneracy of generations younger than those of the speaker. It reflects a basic change in the nature of hunting caused by the accuracy and rate of fire of the modern repeating rifle.

Transportation of game that has been killed back to a point where it can be processed has always been the critical factor in hunting. With mass kills the Denésuliné were already at the point of the kill. With larger—but not mass—kills the Denésuliné would either move their camp to the location of the kill or establish a smaller temporary meat processing camp. Under modern conditions the repeating rifle often brings down more animals than the Denésuliné can immediately transport back to camp. When faced with this situation, it no longer pays to exert the time and effort to follow up on wounded animals that have escaped to cover. What is down at the spot of the kill needs to be field butchered and prepared for storage or transport. Time away from this risks the meat that is in hand, through not immediately butchering it but also by exposing it to scavengers and other predators. The Denésuliné recognize the moral value in pursuing wounded game, but the practical demands of dealing with what has been killed and is at hand outweigh that moral value.

Hunt 5

Caribou

Walking, Kill Locations, and Spoilage

C aribou remained plentiful as the summer of 1970 settled into a routine. The herds remained in the general area, drifting away only to return a few days later. We had remained on the hillside of the bay where the float plane had dropped us off for only a week before all the tents were relocated. Paul decided to move across the bay of the lake to a flatter location on a small triangular point formed by a bedrock outcrop into the lake. The location of the new camp was better for the hunters to walk out among the caribou, and it was considerably easier for them to pack the meat they had killed back to camp. We now had an adequate supply of meat for making dry meat, so their hunting was reduced to occasional excursions for fresh meat rather than stockpiling large numbers of animals for further processing. This allowed the men to become very selective about the kinds and numbers of animals they took as well as about where they hunted. This was before the advent of snowmobiles or all terrain vehicles. There was a seventeen-foot aluminum boat with a ten-horsepower motor at the camp, but it was too cumbersome to portage for any distance. The boat allowed the water transport of meat to the camp but only from locations along the main lake.

Any meat that was taken elsewhere than within reasonable packing distance to the shore had to be hauled back to camp on people's backs. The use of dog teams to transport the meat was not practicable at this time of year. The summer season can be quite warm and sometimes downright hot. The camp thermometer has registered 94°F in July and hit 100°F farther south at Smalltree Lake. The temperature, even when it was in the forties, was sufficiently high that trying to work the dogs would quickly cause them to become overheated. The ground surface was so rough and rocky that using a toboggan without snow cover would quickly ruin it. Toboggans were far too expensive to be abused this way. George did try to make a "rock sled" out of logs to use with his dogs, but the one he made proved to be too heavily constructed and did not work well enough to be put to use.

Meat spoils much faster in the summer heat. Until the nights begin to cool in August, blow flies and other insects rapidly find the stacked meat and, in spite of efforts to cover it, are able to gain access to it and damage it. The meat is also more vulnerable to discovery by other predators and scavengers. This made the location where caribou were killed almost as important as what was killed. Packing in large quantities of meat—a normal load would be a pack sack with any desired internal organs, the fat from the intestines and back, two sets of ribs, the sternum, the tongue, the tenderloin, and three legs carried over the shoulders along with the rifle—was a laborious process in the warm weather, with pestiferous insects and difficult footing. Many Denésuliné carry cord with them when they hunt so that if they kill caribou far from camp they can make pack frames to bring in the meat. Dragging meat, even on a travois, over the rough ground bruises it and the meat gets dirty. Caribou hides can be used to wrap the meat for hauling, but because of the bruising and the dirt, this is only done when snow covers the ground. If it is cold enough, the hide of the killed animal can be frozen into a rough toboggan, but we never saw this done. All the time spent packing the meat, recovering, preparing for the next trip, and returning to the meat was time in which it was vulnerable to degeneration or damage from heat or scavengers.

All this only increased the selectivity the hunters used in determining if any given sighting of caribou would be followed up. It also affected what parts of the caribou and how much of the caribou would be brought back to camp.

George, Wellington, and I departed the tent camp on the triangular point for an afternoon hunt (map 1, H-5). As we intended to hunt close to the camp, a number of the older children tagged along with us. The two men were at least as interested in getting out and looking around as they were in locating caribou, but they were willing to take a few animals for fresh meat if we encountered any not too far from camp to pack back comfortably. We went a few hundred yards north of the camp and turned east for several hundred more yards before we again turned north. The land over which we traveled was the normal mixture of vegetation-covered sand, bare rock, lichen-covered rock, and shallow wet areas and muskegs. One tries to stay on solid, dry ground when one travels like this. Staying dry—that is, keeping your feet from getting wet—is the first priority, with the smoothness of the ground and the ease of footing a close second. The wet areas were unavoidable, but in this area the muskegs were small and shallow and it was possible to go around them.

The land rises gently inland to the north of Foxholm Lake. As we turned north and headed inland (a quarter to half a mile), the surface of the ground soon became dominated by small ridges five to ten feet high and running east to west. Geological knowledge is not a family strong suit. It is unclear if these were remnants of intrusive dykes with their surface exposure shaped by the glacial advances and retreats or if they were just harder bedrock shaped by those same glacial advances and retreats. Whatever the case, they dominated the local landscape. The ridges themselves were not that high and were just wide enough for caribou to walk comfortably along them in single file. The ridges somewhat sheltered the spaces between them, usually about fifty to one hundred feet, from the north wind. This created low areas between them that were about one third covered by vegetated wet areas. The rest was mixed dryer areas of rock covered with sand and decayed vegetation that supported the normal moss and lichen ground cover. These mini-valleys also supported a considerable growth of scattered waist-high shrubs and dwarf birches that broke up the visual perspective of the area and provided cover for anything not taller than the bushes.

As we passed the low area after the first ridge, we saw a number of bull caribou walking along the third ridge and some moving in the low area between the second and third ridges. They were fairly scattered. George and Wellington were walking some distance apart and quickly separated even more once the caribou were seen. As they spread out, George and Wellington were able to close to within seventy-five to a hundred feet of the caribou and we quickly took several bulls. One of the bulls was gut shot. Instead of trying to follow the rest of the fleeing animals, it walked backwards in the opposite direction (I saw it walking backwards) before it lay down and died (I did not see it go down). The other shot caribou were considerably scattered as they fell but were quickly skinned, butchered, and stacked. What meat we could carry was packed into sacks or loaded on our shoulders and we headed back to camp.

Text 5

Carrion and Scavengers

The bull that had been gut shot is the instructive part of this routine hunt. The animal had walked far enough backward before it lay down to die that it went undetected during the butchering. The animal simply folded its legs and went down on its belly and chest before it died. This put it below the tops of the scrub bushes that covered the area and it was missed. I did not return to the area until three weeks after the hunt, and it was at that time that I found the caribou lying where it had died. The carcass was intact. The eyes were still in their sockets, and the skin of the animal had not been broken save for the entry wound of the rifle shot that had killed it. During the three weeks between its death and the time I found it, the weather had turned a bit cooler. Even before we had set off the mosquitoes and black flies were gone. The cooler nights had affected other kinds of insects as well. The blow flies were gone. The other kinds of flies that inhabit the area in the summer were greatly reduced in number although I cannot speak to how cooler weather had affected their variety. I inspected the carcass carefully but did not roll it over. There were no maggots on the carcass, and it did not smell particularly strongly. There was no indication of insect damage, and there was no indication of scavenging by fox, mice, wolf, bear, or other quadrupeds. The birds had not been on the carcass as it showed no sign of droppings on it and no indication of pecking.

For three weeks this dead caribou bull had lain upon the tundra in an area full of terrestrial and avian predators and scavengers—not to mention insects—without being damaged and apparently without being discovered.

Obviously the climate, soil, rainfall, and environmental conditions of a place as large as Africa vary immensely, and it is only at a rather extreme level of abstraction that one can talk about Africa or the Canadian subarctic as an entity. However, anthropology's historical problem of overusing African material as the model for understanding past and present hunting behavior is a real one. Evasion of discovery by a single dying caribou graphically illustrates the problem with using sub-Saharan Africa as a model for understanding the behavior of subarctic hunters in North America and prehistoric Europe. The African environment has (and had) a much larger, more diverse, and richer fauna than do the more southerly parts of post-megafaunal North America. The comparison is even starker in terms of animal populations and diversity of species between sub-Saharan Africa and the North American subarctic. While the contemporary and near contemporary North American subarctic cannot be the basis for a direct comparison with ice age Europe, it can provide a more realistic basis than can either contemporary or past sub-Saharan Africa for understanding the peoples of ancient Europe who survived by hunting its bird, fish, and mammal populations.

If nothing else, that this caribou carcass survived intact for three weeks indicates the differences in the nature and numbers of the guild of scavengers in the two places. Vultures do not range this far north. Aerial scavenging is primarily the domain of sea gulls and ravens. These birds are not as effective at finding dead animals as are vultures, and they are probably less effective—or at least slower—at communicating the presence of a carcass to others of their species than are vultures. With the possible exception of the wolverine (which routinely takes live prey), there are no specialized land scavengers in this place. Those animals that do scavenge are quite effective at it, and had they found the caribou, they would have made short work of it. The crucial point is that they did not find it. It seems almost unthinkable that a carcass the size of a caribou could have lain undetected and undisturbed for three weeks in sub-Saharan Africa.

The situation with this single caribou carcass serves as an indicator of other crucial differences between sub-Saharan Africa and the subarctic and of the risks in using Africa as a primary basis for understanding recent and contemporary human hunting behavior, both in general and specifically for interpreting the hunting behavior of the human species that have inhabited the European land mass over the last million or so years.

On this point we disagree to an extent on assessment of the roles scavengers play in the subarctic and in Africa. The Canadian Shield is approximately 3 million square miles, compared to Africa's savannah of 5 million square miles. The distances to traverse are potentially greater in the African savannah than in the subarctic. However, the impacts of scavengers are greater in the African savannah than in the subarctic. My (Karyn's) understanding is that the differences are attributable to Africa's far longer growing season. The overall biodiversity of flora and fauna is considerably higher in Africa than in the subarctic, maintaining a much denser assemblage of plant life, supporting greater herbivorous life and a higher diversity of predators and scavengers. In contrast, in the Canadian subarctic the growing season is greatly reduced and is concentrated into a window approximately four months long at its maximum. During those four months the density of species can increase exponentially for smaller animals such as ducks, rodents, and insects—those with high birth rates and rapid maturation rates. However, larger game and predators are not able to take full advantage of the short period of growth, and so their numbers are never able to match the density that small animals and insects can achieve. As a consequence their overall population density cannot become high enough to support a scavenger-focused subsistence strategy, although I cannot think of any large mammalian species that are solely scavengers.

As was pointed out by my father in this description of the hunt, the weather changed soon after the hunt and the number of flies had already decreased significantly, reducing their overall diversity and density on the landscape. In Africa, primary fluctuations in the insects would be due to rainfall and breeding seasons, but the near absence of bugs, as we see seasonally in the Canadian subarctic, is unlikely. Had this caribou been killed in late June or in July, the set of outcomes for the "forgotten" bull would have been a different.

I have to disagree with Karyn a bit here. It is not that the differences she cites between Africa and the subarctic are not true or that people did not then know about these differences. The issue is more the case that the literature on subsistence hunting is thin and was even more so three decades ago. Scholars turned to Africa because it was then one of the few sources of information on subsistence hunting. Unfortunately, subsistence hunting in Africa was and remains a poor guide to the behavior of subsistence hunters in subarctic or ice age conditions.

The crucial differences this single dead caribou indicates are not the differences in the guild of scavengers found in these various places but differences in the scale of the animal biomass, the variety of species, and the number of individual animals of each species.

The subarctic is sparsely populated. Because there are so few players, life in the subarctic is played out over a much wider scale—as it were, on a much larger playing board—than it is in the far richer situation found in sub-Saharan Africa. This means that animals that move have to move over greater distances than they do in warmer and richer climes. Animals that have home ranges have to have much larger home ranges than they do in warmer and richer climes. Because of the scale of the playing board and the much lesser number of players on that playing board, the pace and intensity of the game of life played upon that board is slower and less intense than it is in warmer and richer places. It is almost analogous to the difference in the pace of life between a modern urban area and a modern rural area. The consequences of life in both places are the same. Animals that are found by predators end up just as dead as they do in warmer and more comfortable climes. The contest between predator and prey is just as intense and violent in the subarctic as it is anywhere on the planet. Yet, somehow, the pace is still slower. Animals that are prey seem to encounter their predators less often. Many of the animals that live near tree line seem to wander around by themselves more than they do farther south. They seem to move about with less fear and anxiety than do animals in richer locales with higher population densities.

I (Karyn) attribute this to open sight lines and an ability to observe predators at a greater distance in the transitional tree line area compared to the densely wooded full boreal forest farther south.

The survival of this caribou carcass for such a long period of time does raise the issue of human scavenging. Scavenging has a checkered history in anthropological thought. There has been a great deal of serious thought (e.g. Gamble 1986)—as well as a great deal more non-serious thought—devoted to the subject and to its relationship with hunting. As I (Henry) have lived through the debates of the last near half century with an interest—but with an ethnologist's rather than a specialist's interest—in the topic, it may be useful to clarify how I see the issue. (Karyn has a rather different take on the subject!) This is hardly the place to try and present a half century of debate on the topic. As a non-specialist, my perspective on the issue is impressionistic and the interpretation here is simplistic, but it does affect how the material is presented so it needs to be made clear.

The presumption in the late 1950s, through the 1960s, at least since the Man the Hunter Conference, and well into the 1970s was that hunting played a crucial—if not *the* crucial— role in the evolutionary transition of our ancestors into modern humans (Washburn 1961; Lee and DeVore 1969). The 1960s were a time when Robert Ardrey, in a series of best sellers (1963, 1969), popularized Sir Arthur Keith's *A New Theory of Human Evolution* (1949); sometimes in an essentially verbatim popularization. This brought a formerly arcane debate within paleoanthropology into the public eye. This was also the time when the writings of Konrad Lorenz (1974) attracted great public attention. Questions and issues normally confined to scholarly debate became public issues that drew widespread attention, spreading beyond to the public at large. They became of interest in psychiatric and psychological writing and discussion. As interest and consideration spread into the wider public domain, the debates changed as other disciplines and interests brought their own perspectives and concerns to bear.

The late 1950s and the 1960s also brought a wealth of new fossils, scientific techniques, and other material to analyze. They came at a time when anthropology was expanding. With its increase in size and numbers came a fluorescence of talent. The emergence of so many skilled specialists in turn brought with it an explosion of ideas and interpretations.

There was a down side to this explosion of ideas and the apparently insatiable public interest in these topics. As was characteristic of the sensibilities of the times, hunting was seen as a male activity. As the view that hunting was the crucial step that led the transition from nonhuman to human gained wider public interest, that male-dominated aspect of its interpretation spawned a plethora of works (which continued for decades and may still continue; I have long since stopped paying attention) that carried the notion to extremes. Females essentially disappeared from consideration in the analysis of human evolution.

The 1960s were also a time of growth for the modern feminist movement. The male dominance that had come to characterize the analysis of the role of hunting in human evolution could not go unchallenged. The crucial blow was struck by Elaine Morgan in *The Descent of Woman* (1972). It was not that the arguments she raised were of special interpretive or analytical value. What was of value was the way in which she inverted the arguments of the male-dominated approach to the role of hunting in human evolution. By essentially turning the common arguments and assumptions of the time on their head, she exposed their weakness and forced their reevaluation.

There ensued a continuing gender war in anthropology and among a wider lay public by now more interested in other things. Scavenging became a casualty of this gender war. Scavenging became the feminist alternative to hunting; the alternate reality of human evolution. The long-term result was to create a view of hunting and scavenging in which the two were seen as opposites. A binary divide was created between them. The one male. The other female. Each was a champion for the superiority of a particular gender in human evolution. This consequence of the gender war remains.

What is produced by scavenging will always be a very limited part of the human diet. We, and presumably our ancestors, simply do not have the concentration of stomach acid that allows creatures like crocodilians or monitor lizards to devour almost anything they encounter. We cannot digest bone, horn, or teeth. The same lack of digestive power restricts our ability to consume decaying or bacteria-infested meat.

The human ability to consume harmful bacteria is probably wider than we recognize in our era of modern fresh foods. O'Connell recounts a time when a very smelly and rotten elephant was scavenged; its smell was so foul that approaching it made one gag severely (J. F. O'Connell; personal communication). I (Karyn) have experienced consumption of meat that has gone a bit rancid and would have been discarded in more urban areas. It was not badly contaminated and produced no food poisoning, even in someone who had undergone a renal transplant.

Nevertheless, the crucial factor is that hunting and scavenging are not binary opposites or fundamentally different activities. Scavenging and hunting are aspects of the same activity. (Obviously we are speaking about scavenging or hunting larger animals rather than smaller ones. An individual primate killing or picking up and eating something small like a squirrel is not at issue here.) The core of their identity lies in two things. The first is the fact that both scavenging and hunting require getting out and moving through wide areas of land in the search for food. Both require primates to be away from whatever safe areas they have and more exposed to predators or chances of accident and injury. Even the area around a carcass is a dangerous place. Whatever killed the prey is liable to be close by and inclined to defend its kill.

The second and most important thing is that the product of both scavenging and hunting—either found or killed—became something distributed within a group rather than being consumed by a solitary individual. The evolutionary power of both lies less in chemicals they add to the diet than in creating and reinforcing division of labor within the group that is coupled with food sharing. In both activities, it is the group that becomes the producer and the distributor of food. It is that step that is the crucial one in the establishment of the socialness that defines the creation of humanity.

What people will eat is at least partly determined by what is available to eat. There is little doubt that in the absence of other food, the Denésuliné would eat scavenged meat. In practice, the Denésuliné do not scavenge. We have never actually seen or heard about anyone scavenging over the more than thirty-five years that between us we have spent among them. In talking about the cleanness of particular species of wild animals, Denésuliné have indicated that there are conditions in which they would scavenge, but the only scenario that drew any consensus among them was that if they came upon a fresh wolf kill, they saw nothing wrong with shooing away the wolves and taking what they wanted of the untouched portions of the kill (Sharp 1976)—hardly an everyday occurrence. None of the people who talked about it had ever done it or known of anyone who had done it. The topic was aired more as an issue of the nature of Wolf as an animal/spirit than in terms of actual behavior. Aside from issues about the moral nature of particular species of animals, there are a number of practical reasons why the Denésuliné do not devote effort or thought to scavenging.

The most conspicuous reason has already come up several times: this is a vast land with a very small human and animal population. Living animals are widely distributed over the land's surface and are often (normally) very hard to find. Living animals do stand up. They do move around and leave tracks. This, in what is if not an essentially open country, is one in which it is normally possible to see long distances. Movement is what makes it possible to see living animals from long distances. The dead do not share this characteristic. Dead animals are down and do not move. They cannot be seen from long distances, and their lack of motion reduces the chances of their drawing the attention of scavengers. This situation is aggravated by snow cover. The effects of the wind are greatly reduced within the trees. The first snows of fall quickly bring a foot or so of snow cover. By midwinter the snowpack is usually several feet deep. In the absence of musk ox and buffalo, this depth of snow is more than enough to bury the carcasses of any animals that have died. Any intact carcass would be buried by snow and hidden from the view, certainly from the long distance view, of any predator or scavenger.

The simple reality is that the issue of scale removes scavenging from serious consideration as a human food resource in the subarctic. The land is simply too big, the conditions are too harsh, and the animal populations are far too low for their scattered and uneaten dead to provide a useful food source. How do you set out to scavenge in -40°F weather when faced with hundreds of square miles of land covered with several feet of snow?

Another aspect of that single dead caribou bull is relevant here. In all our years in the field, that bull was the only intact carcass either of us ever came upon, and we heard of few other such encounters. Animals do die, and animals are killed in circumstances that have nothing to do with human activity. However, just as the living are scarce and widely distributed over this land, so are their dead counterparts. It is not normal to encounter the remains of dead animal when moving over the land. Such encounters are not so rare as to be exciting or generate excessive curiosity, but they are not a normal part of walking the land. The guild of scavengers has fewer members than is the case farther south, but it is active. The remains encountered are virtually always reduced to bone, antler, and teeth. They are normally scattered and incomplete. Many show the gnaw marks of rodents.

If scavenging is to be considered as a possible human food source, it is necessary to consider the state of the carcasses likely to be available for scavenging. We have already indicated that intact carcasses are rare. At the other extreme, carcasses reduced to bone, antler, and teeth are more common but not terribly useful as human food. What remains are carcasses abandoned by predators and scavengers but that still retain enough flesh to be usable as human food. These also are rare. Most carcasses will be scavenged to the bone. Those that are not fully scavenged are most likely to be there because deaths occurred so late in the season that the carcasses froze before they could be fully consumed or, if a bear was the scavenger, because the carcass was abandoned because the animal had no further need of it before retreating to a winter den.

When an animal falls to a predator there is a pattern to its consumption. Assuming the prey animal was laying on its side as it began to be consumed, the abdomen would be opened and entered. The abdominal cavity is the easiest place to enter the carcass. It is also the location of the internal organs and fat that are favored for consumption. Predators or scavengers smaller than bears have difficulty rolling over the several hundred pounds of an adult large prey animal, and they lack hands for fine manipulation of the carcass. They eat and tear their way into the carcass through the abdomen. Secondarily, they tear their way through the exposed top and sides of the carcass wherever they can gain access and tear away flesh and bone. The effect is to consume the carcass from the top and sides downward (see Guthrie 1990 for an account of the examination of Blue Babe).

Carcasses left to be found by human scavenging would thus tend to have been consumed from the top down, with the remaining usable portions lying between the remnants of the abdominal cavity and the ground surface below. During the frozen months—the only time of the year scavenging is even probable—potentially usable portions of the carcass would not only be frozen and frozen together; the entire mass would also be frozen to the ground. We confess to never having tried to dislodge the remains of a large carcass frozen to the ground in weather that is often -20 to -40°F, and we are not sure how one would go about it. Thawing it would be a lengthy and energy-consuming process. Thawing it through the application of heat would also increase bacterial activity, which would spread through the meat, making much of it inedible. Once thawed, the carcass would have to be dismembered for transport. Presumably that would be the time to eliminate the least useful portions. The prospect of having to butcher a barely thawed carcass to remove contaminated or clearly inedible portions, reduce it in size to fit into whatever was being used to transport it, and then transport it to wherever it was to be consumed is daunting, particularly for a solitary hunter/scavenger rather than a group of individuals engaged in a collective scavenging expedition.

Marrow is a rich and nutritious food (as discussed in Text 2, Food Storage). Left inside the bone where it grew, as it would be in the absence of bone-crushing scavengers, it remains edible for considerable periods. It can last for several months under favorable circumstances. It should have been routinely available in whatever frozen carcasses were available for scavenging. The problem, as indicated earlier, is that there simply is not very much of it in an individual carcass. While individual hunters may well have recovered marrow from found kills for their own use, it is unlikely there was ever enough for it to be of much concern in seeking food for a group of hunters and those for whom they were hunting.

Streams, lake edges, muskegs, and ponds do not routinely collect usable caribou carcasses. Caribou do fall through the ice, but their remains tend to end up at the bottom of lakes, far from shore and away from human (or animal) detection

FIG. 1. Tundra at Damant Lake

FIG. 2. Rock Desert tundra

FIG. 3. Half a dozen caribou close by the location of Hunt 5

FIG. 4. Parts of two caribou being prepared for dry meat

FIG. 5. The leg meat of the two caribou cut into separate muscles

FIG. 6. The muscles being cut into sheaths

FIG. 7. Finished dry meat hanging on a dry meat rack before it is put into storage

FIG. 8. Eddy and Phil with caribou meat along the shore waiting for a float plane to arrive

FIG. 9. Wellington packing caribou meat up to the summer camp from the shore of Smalltree Lake

FIG. 10. The north-south bay, sand hill, narrows, and north shore of Foxholm Lake as seen from the highlands looking to the east

FIG. 11. Snow changes things

FIG. 12. The winter camp of 1975 on the small lake, showing the tree spacing in the forest

or recovery. There are circumstances that can produce mass kills of caribou and other large animals, but these are usually dependent upon types of events outside known experience here, such as floods or volcanic eruption. Normal events, such as river and lake crossings, can result in numbers of drowned animals; this has been reported for the Thelon River, but the Thelon is far away to the north. Drowning as an aspect of large numbers of caribou making water crossings might seem like a potential source of scavenged meat, but there is no Denésuliné interest in it. If caribou are abundant enough to suffer losses while crossing bodies of water, they are abundant enough for the Denésuliné to take what they need from among the living. Because of the mobility of the recent and ancestral Denésuliné, the dead caribou remaining in the water after a crossing (presumably more or less preserved by immersion in the near ice water) are of little value to them because the people would have moved away from the area long before they would have any possible need for the meat.

The issue of snow probes that has grown from Gamble's (1986: 387–88) work and his recognition that the identification of wooden shafts found in a particular archaeological context as snow probes provides a logical alternative to automatically assuming they are spear shafts needs to be addressed. The Denésuliné certainly know how to probe snow, but it is not something of particular significance to them. They make almost no use of snow as a construction material and have no need to probe it to determine its suitability for use in the construction of shelter. Their use of probes is essentially limited to probing ice surfaces, usually on small creeks, muskegs, or small lakes, to ensure a solid surface for walking. They do not make special tools to use as snow probes. If needed, these are made from whatever stems or branches are close at hand and discarded after use. They make no use of snow probes to search for material to scavenge, although they certainly know how to use probes and do use them if searching beneath the snow for a known object.

Human imagination being what it is, it is always possible to imagine some set of circumstances in which the search for a carcass is a plausible form of behavior. It is quite possible that in some circumstances under which scavenging could be a necessary activity, but the fact remains that organic remains consumable by humans are exceptionally rare, other than old bone that can be boiled for grease. Flesh usable by humans as food is both exceptionally rare and exceedingly hard to find. Scavenging as an organized activity would have to be restricted to those times of the year when it is cold enough to keep insects away from a carcass and allow the flesh to be preserved by the cold. These are the same times of the year when carcasses would be covered by snow and hidden from view. To search systematically for carrion in such a vast land would require more effort than to hunt systematically for living animals. Scavenging is simply not worth the time and effort that it would take.

In my (Karyn's) opinion the debate over snow probes as a method to obtain edible frozen carcasses is laughably improbable when one looks at a subarctic winter landscape. The time and effort needed to search a vast landscape systematically in hope of encountering a rare die-off would be a tremendous waste of effort and would likely result in the death of searchers before they were actually able to find something to eat. Alternative food resources such as ice fishing or pursuit of small game like squirrels and rabbits are much more effective food resources in which to invest your time and effort rather than randomly probing a snowy landscape. Among the Sayisi band of Dene in Manitoba, there are accounts of hunters placing carcasses along a riverbank for butchering, and in winter the snows would cover these carcasses (Petch 1998: 97). Descriptions of snow probes being used to find them for consumption during winter may be another source for the concept of probing snows for food. However, in this particular scenario the carcasses' location was known; the hunters knew the area of the riverbanks and the stretches of river used to store the carcasses. Probing such a limited spatial area to find them would not be a large investment of time. Whether meat could be removed in significant quantities is unknown; this is likely a practice that would have arisen with the arrival of steel axes and hatchets. As described earlier in this discussion, removing a frozen carcass covered in ice and frozen to the ground is difficult work, and it would not have been easily achieved with stone technologies.

The solution to the issues that the analytical interest in scavenging in northern climes imply is to be found in the methods of food processing and food storage used by the peoples of those climes.

Hunt 6

Wolf

By the end of the first week in May the move from the winter camp on the east side of Smalltree Lake (map 2) to the summer tent camp on the sand point on the west side of the lake had almost been completed. All the summer tents had been erected and occupied. There were still a few items that needed to be brought over from the winter camp, but the move was basically complete. The tents had been put up in a rough north-south line. Wellington's family's tent was the southernmost with Paul's a few yards north of it. Our tent was a few yards north of Paul's tent with George's bringing up the end of the line about ten yards to the north. The actual placement of the tents had turned out to depend upon the placement of large boulders left by the glaciers on the surface of the sand hill. These provided places to sit on or to shelter by if people sat on the ground. The various drying racks had been constructed, and the women of the camp had turned their attention to making dry meat. Most of the caribou meat was still stored on the ice of the lake in front of the camp, although with several of the dog teams now tethered along the shore, there was some urgency about getting the meat up to where it would be processed into dry meat.

George had constructed Joan's dry meat rack just behind their tent where she had wanted it. As he was carrying a load of caribou meat up the slope of the sand hill toward her drying rack, he saw a cow caribou trotting northward up the lake ice. The caribou was directly in front of the camp, about two thirds of the way between the west shore of the lake and the chain of islands in the middle. The islands were placed so that those directly in front of the camp (due east) formed a north-south chain. A series of small but long and narrow islands southeast of the sand point ran perpendicular to them from the middle of the lake toward its far western part. South of them, the lake opened into a large stretch of open water that continued to a large island that held a fly-in fish camp (Sharp 1988a).

George paused to watch the caribou move up the lake and realized it was being followed by a single wolf (map 2, H-6). The wolf was moving at about the same pace as the caribou, trailing a few hundred yards behind it and making no effort to catch up to it. When George recognized that a wolf was trailing the caribou, he hollered to his elder brother—who was in his tent—that there was a wolf on the lake. Wellington quickly got his rifle and put on his coat while George hurried to his tent to get his own rifle and coat.

The camp, which had been alerted by their calls, came out to watch what was going on. The two of them met by the Skidoo, which was parked near the front of my tent with a toboggan attached to it. They took off in pursuit of the wolf.

The wolf had become distracted from following the caribou when it noticed one of the gut piles on the lake ice. The gut pile, remains of a caribou that had been killed and butchered on the lake ice before we had moved to the summer camp, lay closer to the islands in the center of the lake near where the chain of long, narrow islands ran westward out into the lake. The wolf had gone over to the gut pile to investigate it. It then began to feed from the east side of the gut pile so that it was facing in the direction of the summer camp.

As soon as the caribou moving up the lake, a healthy pregnant cow, realized she was no longer being pursued by the wolf, she stopped. She turned back toward where the wolf was now feeding and stood to watch it eat. She then began to walk southward toward the wolf. As the Skidoo came off the sand hill and reached the lake ice, she turned to watch it as it began to move across the ice toward the wolf.

The wolf was quite engaged in feeding from the gut pile but soon heard the snowmobile. As it was facing the direction from which the Skidoo was coming, it quickly saw the source of the noise. The wolf abandoned the gut pile and trotted toward cover on the closest of the long, thin islands to the south of it. The islands had some tree cover and brush growth, but they were too small to support heavy growth and too narrow to provide the wolf with effective cover.

As the wolf, by now running, headed towards the island, Wellington and George stopped the snowmobile and took a shot at it but missed. They then approached the island where the wolf was hiding to drive it from cover. There began a twenty-minute pursuit. The wolf fled from island to island. The men chased it on the Skidoo from island to island, using the sound and approach of the snowmobile and the occasional shot to force it from cover. They were finally able to force the wolf onto the open lake ice. Once it was away from cover and on the open lake ice, they were able to kill it.

The cow caribou had apparently been fascinated by the entire spectacle. At the wolf's abandonment of its pursuit of her to feed at the gut pile, she had turned to watch. She then had started to walk back toward the wolf. She had continued to walk back toward where the wolf had first stopped at the gut pile to watch the snowmobile pursuit of the wolf. She stood there watching after the wolf was killed and put into the toboggan to be taken back to camp. She was still standing there watching when Wellington shot her.

The wolf, a gray yearling male, was brought back to the shore of the lake where Wellington, to the delight of the children of the camp, put it over his shoulders and walked back to his tent carrying it. In Denésuliné thought, killing an animal is not showing disrespect to the animal. Animal abuse is more about how the animal/spirit is killed and how its remains are treated. It involves an entirely different set of issues and categories far removed from the fact that the prey animal is killed. The price of wolf pelts had become so high that the Denésuliné, in a change of behavior within the lifespan of these men, had lost their reluctance to kill wolves and had become willing to do so whenever they could. Nevertheless, Wolf is a special being. After this one had been skinned, the rest of its remains had been taken into the woods several hundred yards from camp and hidden.

The caribou cow was later butchered, skinned, and brought back to camp. The fetus she was carrying, which Wellington gave to his mother, was cooked. As is the practice with infrequently obtained and somewhat exotic foods—like loons (*Gaver immer*), mergansers (*Mergus merganser, M. serrator*), or geese (*Branta canadensis,* occasionally *Chen hyperborea*)—May distributed it throughout the camp so that everyone had a taste.

Text 6

Camp Formation

The day following the killing of the yearling wolf, another wolf was seen out on the lake. Wellington and George again set off in pursuit in the Skidoo and were again able to kill the animal. This one was a large white adult male. Wellington estimated that its pelt would be worth two hundred dollars. By comparison, in 1972 the women of the village considered seven dollars and fifty cents a good price for a pair of handmade fur-trimmed, beaded, and smoked moosehide moccasins. Over the next ten days we heard other wolves intermittently howling close by the part of the lake where our camp was. May was convinced that it was the female of the pack calling for the missing members of her pack. She was most likely correct. After their calling ended, we never again heard or saw wolves that spring and summer.

Besides the two wolves killed after being spotted from the camp, several other caribou had been seen on the ice and killed. Twice before the ice melted, Paul saw what he thought were bear on the ice. One was too far away to investigate. When the other one was investigated, it was not possible to find sign of whatever he saw on the lake ice or tracks leaving the lake and going into the bush. Just after the camp had been set and we had moved in, Wellington and George put out a fence made of the tops of spruce trees or entire small trees cut to about three to four feet high. They were placed several hundred feet apart between the west end of the large island with the fly-in fish camp and led toward the tip of the sand point where our tents were. These were intended to act as a "fence" to direct toward our camp any caribou coming up the west side of the lake. If it worked, it did so only at night, as we saw no more caribou moving up that part of the lake.

One of the factors that had led to the choice of this particular location for the camp was the fact that it was possible to see long distances down the lake ice. For this purpose the site was effective. There was adequate clean water to be drawn from the lake and access to the lake from both sides of the point. There was a small pond—not used for drinking water—at the bottom of a gully on the south side of the sand point. It was possible to dig a few inches into the side of the sand hill leading down to this small pond and cause a flow of water sufficient to fill a container. This was melt water from the summer thawing off the permafrost, and was a good source of cold water on hot days. The camp was close to stands of timber large enough to provide adequate firewood for the camp and for the smoke fires of the dry meat racks. It was also high enough and sufficiently exposed to the wind to help blow away mosquitoes and black flies when they came out later in the season.

The Denésuliné knew all these things and were able to discuss them at considerable length. It is tempting to say that they gave the potential camp site a thorough evaluation—they did explore it to confirm Wellington's advocacy of the site—and came to a logical determination that it was the best place to set camp for the season to come. In practice, that is not the way it works. These people have chosen so many camps over so many years that there is no need for them to engage in this kind of conscious, logical evaluation of a campsite. It is much like driving a car. This kind of evaluation is much like how one approaches driving as a new and inexperienced driver. After sufficient practice and enough experience of different conditions and circumstances, the process of driving becomes almost automatic. It is clear, at least, that a lot of drivers are not engaging in any kind of conscious evaluation of what they are doing when they drive.

For the Denésuliné, all these processes of evaluation are carried on unthinkingly. They automatically adjust the process to conform to the different requirements that seasonality or the purpose of the camp introduces into the equation. In a summer camp, wind is a virtue because it blows the insects away; in a winter camp, shelter from the north wind is critical to the choice of a campsite. All these variations and factors— and a great many more—are dealt with when Denésuliné choose a campsite, but they speak of the choice of a campsite in terms of aesthetics rather than functionality. Their judgment about the suitability of a potential campsite will be expressed as a judgment about the aesthetics of the location rather than as a discussion about how close the wood supply is or how far they have to walk to get water.

Bush camps of this period were fairly simple. Most were home for fifteen to twenty people and comprised part of an extended family centered around two or more married pairs connected by ties of kinship or affinality. The Denésuliné preferred to spend the late spring through summer and into the fall dwelling in tents. Cabins would be used if they were already in place, but they were normally built only for winter camps. Camps are constructed in open areas rather than being shoe-horned into heavy timber. If the location is not open when the dwellings are constructed, the demand for timber quickly opens it up around the dwellings. The dwellings are clustered together, mostly facing south-southeast, but there is no real pattern to their placement on the ground. The closeness of the ties among the people who placed the tents or cabins is the major factor in how close together the dwellings are, but local topographical features, such as depressions in the ground or the rocks at this camp, are probably the most important factors in determining the exact placement of individual dwellings. People do like to have convenient places to sit or build a fire near the tents, and it is always convenient to have a large tree nearby on which to hang things.

Construction of larger settlements is a different issue. The contact literature (e.g., Hearne 1958) makes it clear that the Denésuliné did at times form large camps, sometimes of several hundred people. There was a now only seasonally occupied bush settlement to the south on Selwyn Lake, but there had been bush settlements or large temporary camps in that general vicinity for hundreds of years. The dynamics of these large camps are essentially unknown. Obviously the logistics of such a concentration of people are very different from those of a small camp. The land simply will not support such a concentration of people for very long without the use of resources drawn from the larger Canadian economy. Small game in the immediate vicinity of the camp is quickly exhausted. The fishing will decline from the heavy use that will be made of it. Firewood becomes scarce and too far away to bring back to the dwellings easily. Water supplies become contaminated. We have absolutely no idea how sanitation would be arranged. In summer bush camps the Denésuliné often prefer outside gender-segregated areas rather than outhouses as places to defecate or urinate. These have to be convenient to the tents yet provide adequate vegetation growth to ensure privacy. How all these things would have translated into the operation of a temporary bush settlement of several hundred people is unknown and will probably always remain unknown.

It is best to think of a camp as a focus or center for a series of activities that range widely over the landscape rather than as a separate entity that is closed in upon itself. This applies at a series of scales of distance. As the dwellings are occupied and put into use, activities begin to spread outward from them. People prefer outside fires to inside fires during the late spring through to the onset of colder temperatures in the fall (roughly from May to mid-September). There is an obvious reason for this when they are living in tents, but even when living in cabins the preference is to have the fire outside. This means choosing a location that is flat and sheltered from the wind. Cooking and making tea are tasks that cannot be delayed or be too far removed from where people sleep and rest. Firewood has to be brought in to fuel the cooking fire. Firewood is brought in from the bush in the form of logs. The logs have to be cut into usable lengths and then split. This means cutting it into near-uniform lengths if one of the locally made stoves constructed from half an oil drum is being used. Using either a saw or an ax to cut the wood generates waste in the form of sawdust and wood chips. A location will be developed for storing and cutting the wood that is close to the dwelling but that keeps debris from cutting and sawing away from the fire and the entrance to the dwelling.

As people begin to engage in other activities, they find locations for those activities that are suitable for them; ones that provide adequate light, or shelter from the wind, or whatever other specific requirements the task demands. The scale of distance moves from yards to tens of yards. The nature of the tasks partially determines where people choose to conduct them. Tasks that smell or that produce noxious debris are performed away from the dwelling. For example, cutting wood to make something or building a fire to heat an iron file so it can be pounded into a spearhead both generate debris—wood chips in one case, ashes and loud unpleasant noise in the other. These activities will be performed farther away from the dwellings than will other, less intrusive activities. Some activities cannot be mixed, so it is necessary to find a good working area for each one. Finding a series of acceptable work areas, each of which is appropriate to the specific task, becomes more and more difficult as the number of needed work areas increases. As the demand increases, it becomes necessary to range farther and farther from the dwelling in order to find suitable areas.

Beyond this, there are other demands that take up space. Each has its own requirements and may or may not overlap with any other activity. The dry meat racks have to be put up and a sufficient work area has to be left around them not only for the work itself but to keep the meat clean and the stored meat awaiting processing away from traffic.

Sled dogs have to have a separate place to be tethered. Dené-suliné sled dogs are not pets. They are working animals. Each dog identifies with its team. They will generally attack humans they do not recognize who stray within their reach. They will certainly attack individual dogs from other teams or take on an entire other team. This means that each dog team has to be tethered away from other teams at the camp. Even in the village it is necessary to keep the teams separated. It is possible to see the limits of where the dogs can reach as well as where they have been tethered by the wear they leave on the ground and the ring of dried feces that forms around their tethering post as each dog backs as far away from the post as is possible before defecating. The boundaries between teams and the amount of room left as separation between them can be read upon the ground—marked by the growth patterns of the vegetation. If only human social relationships and group affiliations were as easy to read upon the ground as are those of tethered dog teams. The dogs have to be fed. Once the snow vanishes from the ground they have to be watered. The closer the dogs are tethered to the water source, the less work it is for the humans charged to water them. This places a premium in keeping the dogs close to the lakeshore.

The dogs are vulnerable to mosquitoes and black flies once they come out. The mosquitoes appear as early as April—it is a bit of a mental adjustment to find oneself standing crotch deep in snow having to fight off ravenous mosquitoes—but not appearing in serious numbers until early June. The black flies normally do not appear in numbers until mid-June. The depredations of these insects are serious. They can weaken or ruin the health of a tied-up dog that has no shelter from them and may well be able to kill one under some circumstances. Denésuliné do not make houses for sled dogs at their summer camps. They rely upon the dogs digging holes into the ground to provide refuge from the insects. The area is too far north for fleas to live so the holes do not become flea infested. They do offer considerable refuge.

It is not a flawless solution, but it keeps the dogs alive and reasonably healthy. It also provides a view of natural selection at its most capricious for those few dogs that lack the instinct or judgment to dig themselves a hole. For the Denésuliné, it means that they have to find a location that allows the dogs to dig into the ground. The dogs have to be securely tethered; a factor in the choice of ground, as the stakes holding their tethers must be securely anchored. They have to be close to water and away from other dog teams; all this on ground that will allow them to dig a hole in the permafrost. In the absence of topsoil, this means the dogs must be tethered on sand.

Just as choosing a location to tether the dogs involves a whole series of competing requirements, so the choice of every work area involves a series of conflicting demands.

Beyond this, there has to be access to the lake—the drinking water source—that allows everyone to get down to the lakeshore to haul drinking water. The access has to accommodate not only healthy adults but infirm adults as well. Most especially, it has to accommodate the children of the camp, upon whom the task of getting water normally falls. The source of the drinking water has to be kept away from the dog beds or from work areas producing debris that will foul the water source. The lakeshore also has to provide a place to draw on shore any boats at the camp as well as a place for a float plane to approach the camp to load and unload. Since aircraft and boat motors deposit small amounts of petroleum-based products into the water as part of their normal operation, that also has to be factored into the equation, as does the decision to build or not build a temporary dock. (Docks do not do well in the ice of winter and the ice motion during spring break-up.) The scale of distance is now measured in hundreds of square yards rather than tens of square yards.

One point should be obvious. Any location the size of that needed for even a small camp cannot meet all the demands for space required by all the activities the people of the camp have to engage in in order to survive in this place. Since the activities have to be engaged in and since the topography of any small area is fixed, the only solution for the Denésuliné is to spread outward to find places in which they can do what they need to do in order to survive.

The construction and operation of gender is not a topic of this work but there are consequences of it that are at times relevant to topics considered here. One of those consequences is the way gender effects the movement of women about the camp. The bush is a dangerous place. It is not that every time you come around a large boulder you will find yourself face to face with something dangerous, but any time you come around a large boulder you might find yourself face to face with something dangerous. The bush is also the domain of things far more dangerous than ordinary animal/spirits (Sharp 1988a: 101–13; 2001: 48–58). The potentiality for risk is always an aspect of how Denésuliné deal with going into the bush. This far away from the village and free from government regulation that dictates what equipment they will carry when employment takes them into the bush, Denésuliné men do not go into the bush unarmed.

Denésuliné women do not normally handle rifles. Reasons for this, alluded to earlier, are tied to the sexual division of labor and Denésuliné perception of relations between post-pubescent females and animal/spirits. The effect is to keep women unarmed and largely within the camp or its immediate confines unless accompanied by an armed male.

Women do go into the bush. Toilet areas are outside the camp although very close by. Women wander off for short walks, often just to escape the activity in the camp and get a little peace and quiet. In colder weather some women will run short snare lines for snowshoe hares and a few will set out traps close to the camp. They sometimes have to go out to gather wood, particularly if the smoke fire for the drying rack has run low on acceptable wood. Depending upon the topography of area around the camp, they may get out berry picking or on a picnic. They go unarmed. This restricts the distance away from the camp that they are able to travel. If they wish to extend the distance they go, they need the presence of an armed male.

Even with these constraints on their movement, they move over an area of many hundreds of yards around the camp within which there is a potential human presence, an area within which any animal that enters may encounter a human and will encounter the smell and sound of humans as well as the debris humans have left behind. Children extend this area significantly. Free from the gender constraints that will affect their later lives, children up to nine or ten wander far beyond the confines of the area to which the adult women of the camp restrict themselves. As they age, the gender constraints begin to restrict the movement of female children of the camp, but they do not apply to the boys of the camp. By their early teens many of the boys of the camp carry .22s and sometimes heavier weapons. They are ambitious to display the skills of adulthood. One expression of this is the extension of the range over which they wander, often up to several miles away from the camp. They often hunt small game or whatever else presents itself to them. Because these camps are so small there are few playmates. Girls who in more densely settled situations would stay in camp and spend their time in all-girl groups wander along with their teenage brothers to distances far beyond those their mothers would choose to venture from the camp.

In all this activity, the children of the camp leave the sounds and smells—not to mention the trash—of a human presence. The area around the camp within which the human presence is a disrupting factor in the lives of the animals becomes not a thing of hundreds of square yards but a thing of square miles.

Over about the last sixty years the Denésuliné have made the transition from a bush-living people who visited the trading posts to a village-living people, some of whom choose to live part of the year in the bush. The reasons so many Denésuliné still choose to spend part of the year in the bush have become increasingly complex; perhaps even to themselves. What is clear is that economics—(as understood by the general populace of the more heavily settled parts of the United States and Canada as well as by corporate America and the extreme right)—play a decreasing role in those decisions. Economics may determine if Denésuliné have the resources necessary to live in the bush but not why they choose to go when they can afford it.

Unchanged is the fact that when in the bush they have to eat. That has remained a constant of this land for thousands of years. If you are to live from the land, you have to get out and hunt it. The men of the camp must range out from the camp in search of animals to hunt.

Using a circle on the ground is not an ideal way to represent the area a Denésuliné camp exploits and hunts. Individual areas used are too variable if only as a function of the variations in local topography. The presence of water is a constant, but the shape of water bodies varies enormously from place to place, and with that variation goes variation in how, where, and how far people can move by boat in their search for food. The presence of eskers can provide miles of easy traveling and the chance to range widely over the land, while rock hills and muskegs can restrict how far people can easily move. With freeze up and the switch to dog teams as the preferred means of travel, the distances a hunter can cover increase dramatically.

As local topography determines the distances people can travel, it also dictates the directions in which people will travel. The shore of a large lake can provide access to miles and miles of land and its animal life. A fertile stream course bordered by vegetation that supports an abundance of small life but that happens to be shallow and full of sharp rocks can be an absolute barrier to water travel. People have to follow the lead of the land and live upon resources they can reach.

Winter is better. When the water freezes on the lakes, and streams and muskegs turn solid, Denésuliné freedom of movement increases exponentially. Virtually the entire land surface becomes accessible to them. The shallow stream that would sink a boat becomes a sheltered pathway for the dogs. Muskegs impassible in summer become sheltered highways. There are tradeoffs, of course. Lakes that were highways become corridors for the blowing wind. The wind that blew down the middle of a lake in summer and posed a risk of high waves becomes an entirely different proposition when that wind is

-40° or -50°F. Travel still moves down the lakes, but in deep cold people move close to the shore and out of the wind.

Having said that it is impossible to represent the area a Denésuliné camp utilizes as a circle on the ground, there actually is something to be gained by doing exactly that. What is hopelessly inaccurate at a case-by-case scale has some offsetting merit at a greater level of abstraction.

Life on the ground is dictated by Denésuliné preferences about how they deal with that life. However they dealt with the circumstances of life in the bush in the past, by the time frame of this study the Denésuliné had come to prefer not spending nights away from their main camp when going out to hunt or trap. They will do it. They do do it. However, they prefer not to do it. This creates a pattern of land use in which how far they range is dictated by the preference that being out in the bush will be a single-day out-and-back excursion.

They can travel farther on large lakes if they have a boat with a large enough motor. Unfortunately, boats are hard to get into the bush—a boat on Smalltree Lake represents a 145-air-mile trip that has to be made over land by Skidoo or dog team hauling a bulky and relatively heavy boat or an extremely expensive float plane charter running to many thousands of dollars. Karyn's entry into the field in 2002, a one-way charter in a plane with two pilots and large enough to carry eight passengers and a canoe, was three thousand dollars. There is also the problem of gasoline. Even at the village, gas cost well over five dollars per gallon in 1975. Using charter aircraft to fly it to Smalltree Lake brought the cost of a gallon of gasoline to considerably more than fifteen U.S. dollars per gallon. Economics rarely determines but it does constrain how the Denésuliné go about their life in the bush. Using a boat and motor to extend the range that can be exploited from a bush camp is a rare and limited thing.

Come winter and the switch to travel by dog team, the range they can reach out from the camp is greatly extended. Travel back and forth to the village is by dog team; that same 145-airmile trip that is a much greater distance when traveling by land is a routine trip, especially among the Denésuliné camping farther south in the NWT. The problem is that when dog teams can be used, the days are very short, and conditions are harsh even on the best of days. It is a tiring and dangerous way to travel. The preference to go out and back in a single day comes in to play. With dog teams out of the camp, the Denésuliné restrict the length of their trap lines and their hunting trips to keep them within a distance allows that out-and-back on the same day pattern to hold.

The effect is curious: the area the Denésuliné can exploit using boats or dog teams is essentially the same as what they can exploit by walking. The effective area a Denésuliné camp can exploit is what lies within a 7.5-mile radius of the camp. This is the basic limit for an out-and-back trip within a single day. They do not, of course, walk out 7.5 miles to turn around and walk back. They move over the land as dictated by what they are seeking to do and by the lie of the land. They often walk far more than 15 miles per day. If they have to travel more than 7.5 miles away from camp, it tends to be a special thing for which they make special preparations and take extra precautions. The Denésuliné are fast walkers. An unhurried trip of 7.5 miles takes about three hours in reasonable walking conditions. The worse the conditions, the more slowly they will walk, the more often they will have to stop to hydrate (hot tea), and the longer the trip will take.

Their routine travel can well exceed 15 miles in a single day, but the range of their movements will almost always fall within that 7.5-mile radius. We suspect that 7.5 miles is about the maximum range at which an individual could make a caribou kill and still pack back enough meat to make a difference to a hungry family, but we have no way to test that assumption.

Obviously not every area within that 7.5-mile radius will be used equally. Much of any given plot of land will be useless for food production and will not hold prey animals. The amount of water in the vicinity of each camp that is usable by boat varies enormously. Some camp sites will be in areas where walking is easy and fast; others in areas where boulder fields, muskegs, creeks, wet ground, rocky hills, or bare unvegetated sand (to name only a few conditions) will affect how productive and how accessible the land is. We have not even mentioned the effects of variation in vegetation growth.

Even if we make no assumptions about the uniformity of the land around the individual camps, we can still go back to that idea of a circle around a Denésuliné camp. The area of the circle—a radius of 7.5 miles (squared) times 3.1416—is 176.715 square miles. This has a number of interesting implications.

The area exploited by the Denésuliné then living in Mission was roughly 45,000 square miles. Their area of exploitation was well over 50,000 square miles if allowance is made for the fact that they ranged out onto the tundra at least to the northern end of Merrie's Lake (named for one of May's sisters who drowned in the lake while emptying a fish net from her canoe; May pronounced it Merrie, but it is Mary on the maps). To use a conservative figure, 45,000 square miles seems reasonable, as some of the land was used by Denésuliné from other bands and some of the land to the south of the village had been unused for many years. During the period from 1950 to 1970 the population of the band centered at the village averaged about 500 people. As there were also non-treaty Denésuliné in the area, let us use a figure of 600 to be on the conservative side.

The average size of a Denésuliné bush camp has figured, at least indirectly, in theoretical debates about the nature and structure of bands among hunting peoples. It might be a contentious issue if anyone were left alive to care. It is no longer possible to sort out what things were like before the 1930s; perhaps there is no longer any way to sort it out at all.

Allowing for the fact that an unknown number of people—but substantial, often more than one hundred—spent their winter in the bush at the Selwyn Lake bush village (in its various transformations and locations) to offset the contribution of the non-treaty Denésuliné who lived in the area, the figure of 600 is reasonable. As both the total number and the number of individuals who did not live in the bush varied, the average size of the bush camps varied. The number of individuals in a winter bush camp ranged from two up to probably just over 30. To use a figure toward the upper end of the range, 20 persons should be reasonably accurate as the average size of a bush camp.

The Denésuliné population number we are using is 600. The average camp size we are using is 20. That means the average number of bush camps in the area we are considering is 30. At an average area of exploitation for each of 30 bush camps, the total land area in use at any given time (30 camps x 176.715 square miles per camp) was 5,301.45 square miles. In other words, to survive in the subarctic the Denésuliné need access to nine to ten times as much land as they can physically occupy at any given moment in time.

There are simply too many unknown variables for this figure to be taken too seriously. It does, however, give an indication of just how hard this land is and how difficult it is to support human life in this environment. Few areas in North America are as harsh as this. Most of the continent has far more topsoil than this part of the Canadian Shield and can support a far more luxuriant flora. Still, the ratio of the area of land needed to support a population of hunters this size might have some discussion value in examining the demography and ecology of other past and present hunting societies in North America.

If we return to the issue of the nature of Denésuliné camps, we face the issue that hunters have to get out onto the land to find enough food to feed the families of the camp. The 7.5-mile figure for their ranging out is probably greater than the distance they covered with any regularity. The 7.5-mile figure was rarely reached in the course of their hunts, although it was considerably exceeded in the course of a few hunting excursions made in the summer. On balance, the figure of 176.715 square miles is a reasonable estimate of their influence on the land and its wildlife. The issue of scale for this single camp has moved from square yards to square miles but square miles in the hundreds.

The footprint of humanity does not rest lightly upon the land. Even in this vast and almost vacant realm of northern forest, present and past signs of human presence scar the landscape and alter relations between the other animate beings that share that universe with humans. When snow cover comes, the Denésuliné develop a network of packed trails in snow to allow them to move over the land with a minimum of effort. These trails are encountered by other species that share the land. Some of these species use the trails. To other species, they are but a barrier to their use of the land. Human hunters leave gut piles miles and miles away from their camps. Each gut pile alters the feeding patterns and movement of animals both large and small that live close to it or pass by it. Hunters far from their camps have to stop and make fires to make tea and warm themselves. They use the bush as a place to defecate and urinate. Their dogs leave scat and urine as they travel. It may be difficult without firsthand experience of the north to realize just how far-reaching human influence can be in a situation like this. The sound and smell of humans spreads out from the camp and from the places people use to work and from where they hunt. Each disrupts the patterns of movement of the local animal populations.

At our 1975 summer camp on Smalltree Lake after the caribou had moved north when the migration ceased, the scars of a human presence remained. The expanding moose population remained at a considerable distance from the camp. George spent a few weeks of the summer in an intensive hunt for moose. It was clear from talking with him about where he searched for moose and where he sighted (and killed) them that the moose were avoiding an area of several miles around the camp. They were present at the lake in numbers never seen in living memory, but they avoided the camp and its environs. We have already noted that the wolf pack in the area, after its losses on the lake, vanished from our detection. It is likely that they abandoned the west shore of Smalltree Lake for other environs.

The small life of the forest and open spaces diminished around the camp. The only nesting birds or birds with young we saw after late May were water birds. What occurred here is even more pronounced on the tundra edges at Foxholm Lake. When the caribou come to Foxholm Lake it is easy to see how they react as they move along the game trails and encounter a human camp. They change the pace at which they move, hurrying past the camp in the woods behind it or turning back the way they came. We would often see bulls in late summer jump from the elevated shoreline over the boulders lining the shore into Foxholm Lake so that they could swim to the opposite side of the lake to escape our presence. Even the behavior of the ravens and sea gulls was modified as they gathered near our camps; never really finding food but always hopeful that something worth eating would come from the human presence on their lake.

This aspect, at least, of consideration of the nature of camps as the center of an expanding radius of human influence might be of value to those charged with interpreting and understanding the patterns of land use and the ecology of previous cultures. The sheer scale of the disruption that even a small human camp can bring to the behavior of other species that have to share the land with them is worth remembering. When we factor in the human use of fire to modify the environment, the consequences of long-term settlement in a single place or small area, or the increase in the effects of a human presence that come with the increased number of humans found in richer circumstances to the south, it might be possible to gain an even clearer picture of the disruption on local animal populations that come from even a small human presence.

Hunt 7

Moose

Hunting by Habitat

George had decided that he wanted to go moose hunting on the east shore of Smalltree Lake (map 2, H-7). Because Wellington was tied up with activities at the fishing camp, which only had one customer that summer before being closed down, and the two of them had come into conflict over ownership of a moose hide taken earlier in the year, George was spending much of his time moose hunting (Sharp 1988a: 124–26). My canoe had arrived by float plane a short while before, so the two of us were able to use it to get over to the opposite (eastern) shore of Smalltree Lake to check out a place George had in mind. The fourth of July was a bright, windless, and quite hot day. We departed the summer camp about midday, worked our way across the lake by heading through the small islands in the middle, and then headed south of the winter camp. It took us several hours to paddle across the lake. Keep in mind it was summer and the days were long, so the fact that it was late afternoon before we reached the other side was not an issue. Once we reached the eastern shore of Smalltree Lake we followed it southward until George saw the spot he wanted to check for moose.

We beached the boat on the shore and proceeded inland through the forest. George knew there was a good-sized pond a short way inland and that was the place he wanted to investigate. We worked through the woods as quietly as we could until we could see the pond a hundred or so yards inland. Sure enough, there was a calfless cow moose feeding along the east shore of it. We were able to sit within the forest cover and watch the moose for a few minutes before George began to work his way through the forest toward the west shore of the pond. I stayed behind him, intending only to act as backup in case his shot only wounded the moose and it attempted to escape. As there was no wind to carry his scent, George had little difficulty approaching close enough to have a clear shot at the moose. His first shot hit it in the neck and dropped it.

We then moved around the north end of the pond and approached the moose where it lay on the ground. As he came up to the animal, which had not moved from where it dropped, it made a noise in its throat and died. This set off a series of concerns as George feared it was a death rattle and a harbinger of ill fortune (Sharp 1988a: 131–32).

It is difficult to convey to anyone who has not experienced the insect infestations of the subarctic tundra and boreal forest just how heavy they actually are and how they impede human activities. Gangloff reports: "Researchers have found that as many as nine thousand mosquito bites per minute can be recorded during the summer in some parts of Alaska" (2012: 27). Even if the number of potential bites is off by a factor of more than 100 under more normal circumstances, it indicates the scale of the problem and the need to have effective protection. The blood loss that mosquitoes and black flies inflict on adult caribou can reach three and a half gallons—repeat, gallons—over the course of a summer. Local stories of humans or animals that are immobilized by injury dying from blood loss due to mosquito and black fly bites are not without a basis in fact.

The moose George had killed provided a quick measure of just how bad the insects can be. While the focus of attention is often black flies and the more than thirty mosquito species in Canada, they are not the only blood-sucking insects of the forest. The large deer fly, locally called a bulldog (*Tabanus affinis*) stands out because of its size. Deer flies are familiar in the eastern and southern woodlands, by sight if not through memory of their painful bite. Among these, the bulldog is excessive because of its size. Bulldogs often exceed an inch in length and reach the size of a man's thumb. Their biting mouth parts are so large that if one lands on your leg while you are seated, you can see it sawing through the layers of your jeans and long underwear to reach your skin.

Some things one just does not forget. All four legs of the downed moose were solidly covered by bulldogs attempting to feed on it. I have no expertise in entomology and made no effort at a scientific count of the bulldogs attempting to feed on the moose. I spent considerable time trying to estimate how many there were—without getting so close as to attract their attention! My best guess—as recorded in field notes—was at least two thousand large, hungry bulldogs on the four limbs of that dead moose. After forty years of reflection, I suspect five hundred hungry bulldogs trying to feed upon the recently dead moose is probably more accurate.

The moose died on the shore of the pond, so we did not have to drag it out of the water, but it was in such a wet and rocky place that it was not easy to skin or butcher. The normal weight of the barren ground caribou bulls of the tundra is about four hundred pounds. Moose generally run twice that weight, and bulls can exceed twelve hundred pounds. This difference in size makes butchering a moose a far different and more complicated process than butchering a caribou. Skinning, gutting, butchering, and dismembering even a big bull caribou is a simple one-person job. Skilled hunters can accomplish the task neatly and thoroughly in less than twenty minutes. Although a heavy blade is useful for separating bone on a caribou, a medium-sized sharp knife is all that is needed.

With a moose, the entire process is different. The massive head is difficult to remove from the spine and requires a large knife—or an exceptionally sharp one. The hide is so thick and heavy that it must be cut away from the flesh rather than being separated by a fist inserted between skin and flesh. Cutting the hide away, no matter how skillfully done, leaves far more tissue adhering to it and makes far more work for the person who has to prepare the hide. The bones of a moose are much larger and thicker than those of a caribou. It takes far more time and effort to separate them. Things like taking off the ribs require much more strength and effort as well as a much heavier knife; an extremely heavy knife or an ax is preferable. The same holds for dismembering the spine, separating the spinal column, or taking off the hips or neck. Many years later I sent Wellington two machetes I ran across in a hardware store; I had never seen them used in Canada. He was enamored of them and used them for many years, so often resharpening them that they were worn down to thin slivers before he finally discarded them.

Once the moose was field butchered, we went back to the main lake, portaged the canoe to the pond where the moose lay, and floated it the some seventy-five feet to the meat. We loaded the canoe with the hide and as much meat as we could get into the canoe. Once we paddled the canoe back to the other side of the pond, we unloaded it, portaged it and the meat to the shore of Smalltree Lake, and reloaded it. Because the day was windless and the lake was calm, we were able to load the canoe so that we had only a few inches of freeboard.

We were quite a few miles distant from the summer camp. The canoe was heavily laden and slow moving. It took us until 11:30 in the evening to reach camp. The distance was too great for a return trip to recover the rest of the meat. The weather was hot; the meat would spoil rapidly even if covered. Blowflies were at their height. Covering the meat would not keep them from gaining access to it. There were bear and fox in abundance in addition to the main scavengers of kills: seagulls and ravens. The probability of even well-covered meat surviving was considered so slight that it was felt it was not worth expending the effort and hours of travel to try and recover it. We did bring back several hundred pounds of meat and the hide. What was left behind was the less choice meat that had a higher bone content and would have been much harder to process and preserve.

Text 7
Summer Doldrums

Being high on a hill to look a long way down the lake ice, the function that had led to the original choice of this camp site, came into play but a couple of times over the summer. Small game, usually rafts of mergansers, would infrequently move down the lake past the camp. These would sometimes be pursued by hunters from the camp. We had moved north to Foxholm Lake before the blueberries became ripe, so the only berry picking expeditions by the women were short ones to look for muskeg berries. The only large game encountered over the rest of the summer, once George stopped moose hunting, was Wellington's unanticipated encounter with a grizzly bear farther south on the lake.

High summer in the bush is a curious time for the Denésuliné. For a physically active people for whom food production and food storage are such crucial issues, summer seems to work by different rules. The heat of summer makes it difficult to prepare food for storage and makes storage itself harder. Since Denésuliné meat drying depends upon air circulation for dehydration, the heat and occasional humidity make the process more difficult and less effective. Meat spoils more quickly in the heat, making it more difficult for what has been cut and hung to dehydrate quickly enough. Insect populations are at their highest levels during the warmer weather, so the numbers and kinds of flies are at their maximum. They make it harder to protect the hanging meat from becoming fly blown.

If meat does become fly blown it is not necessarily ruined. The smoking and dehydration of the meat cause many of the eggs laid on it to fail to hatch. The fly eggs, as well as the maggots themselves, can be scraped off without damage to the drying meat. The aesthetics may be disquieting, but the situation is far too routine to upset the Denésuliné. They long ago learned how to deal with it and simply clean the meat and continue to prepare it for storage.

Humidity poses its own problems. Increased moisture in the air of what is normally a very dry climate makes it take longer for drying meat to dehydrate properly. The longer it has to hang, the greater the risk of something else happening to damage it or render it unusable. The longer drying time increases the labor that has to be put into processing the meat. Higher humidity increases vulnerability not only to insect damage but to the growth of bacteria and mold as well. With both insects and bacteria, it is the places where the meat folds over upon itself to create crevices that are the primary locations where contamination can occur. These can be quite small and are far more vulnerable to infestation than is the actual surface of the meat exposed to the air and smoke.

Once the meat is dried, summer storage is far more troublesome than is storage at other times of the year. Throughout the fall and into late spring, dry meat generally freezes if kept away from the heated parts of the living area of the primary dwelling. Freezing does not harm it so long as it is protected from moisture when it thaws. Hanging the dry meat in a container that allows for air circulation usually suffices, but during the heat and humidity of summer, this becomes more difficult, and the risk of spoilage rises.

Joan used the tent George had built for her to dry the meat of the moose that was killed on July 4. It is an expression of basic Denésuliné values, particularly among those of these northern Denésuliné of the tundra fringe, that their focus is always upon caribou. Among them, moose dry meat is always a poor second choice to caribou dry meat. This expression of values translates into a lesser familiarity with making moose dry meat than with making caribou dry meat. Joan was far more practiced at making caribou dry meat than moose dry meat. She found moose meat harder to work with than caribou meat. The muscles of moose are larger and heavier than their caribou equivalents. She found it harder to cut it into sheaths to be hung and more difficult to get the sheaths cut to the uniform thickness so crucial to achieving a uniform state of dehydration. She did not get some of the meat fully dried and lost to spoilage some of what she had thought was finished dry meat. Maggots appeared on the stored dry meat by July 11. Once the maggots were removed from the contaminated areas, the meat was usable, but the entire process proved to be far more labor intensive and more of a nuisance than she had expected.

The same situation was experienced in Karyn's field season in 2003, when moose was our only game late that summer. The meat dried was thicker than would have been the case had it been caribou. Although the meat appeared dried, it soon became evident that it was not adequately dried. The smell of the rancid meat permeated the cabin as the meat was hung inside to try to continue the drying. When the time came to consume the meat, the rancid parts were cut off and fed to the local scavengers—the young puppy brought by one of my uncle's grandkids, birds, and various nocturnal animals we never observed—and we ate the rest.

Farther south in the boreal forest, moose provide a much greater part of the Denésuliné diet. The people who live there are more practiced at making moose dry meat and would likely have had little difficulty making dry meat from the moose meat that George brought in. In 1975 he killed four moose that summer, but making the moose meat into dry meat and then storing it proved to be such a pain that this was the only one from which dry meat was made. (For moose hunting in the boreal forest see Jarvenpa and Brumbach 2008: 54–78, and Tanner 1979.)

In 2003, before we were lucky enough to get our moose, we relied on the fish caught in a net. It was checked once a day and the catch was brought in and distributed among the camp members, with the male checking the net getting first dibs on fish selection. For almost two weeks we had nothing but fish for our fresh food, the rest being canned and boxed products flown north with us. When the first moose was killed the net was abandoned. In fact it stayed in the water unchecked for two days after the first moose kill before the net was retrieved and the fish caught in it were returned to the lake and shores for scavengers. Our fish being dried, unsuccessfully, and the fish stored in the muskeg pit were discarded and forgotten with the arrival of fresh red meat in camp.

Subsistence shifts during the summer. Smalltree Lake is too far south of the tundra to have access to caribou during the summer. Small environmental changes and variations in micro-environments matter a great deal in this country. It is but thirty-two miles (on a map) from the camp on Smalltree Lake to the winter camp just off Foxholm Lake, but that distance is sufficient to place the former well within the transitional zone of the boreal forest, while Foxholm Lake lies at the edge of the tundra. During the years when we wintered at Foxholm Lake and Wellington wintered at Smalltree Lake, that distance was sufficient to make the difference between mosquitoes staying active (and abundant) at Smalltree Lake until October although they vanished from Foxholm Lake no later than mid-August. Caribou usually arrived at Foxholm Lake by mid-July but often did not arrive at Smalltree Lake until mid- to late October.

During the summer, fish become the primary source of food for both humans and dogs. Other lakes in the region were far more productive than Smalltree Lake was, both in terms of the quantity and the variety of their yield. Even though it was not a terribly productive lake, a single net in the water generated a sufficient daily catch to feed the four families and three dog teams in the camp.

Many other food resources are more abundant in summer than they are at any other time of the year. Small game animals have maturing young to boost their numbers. Waterfowl are also raising young. Early in the season this means a readily available supply of eggs; arctic tern (*Sterna paradisaea*) eggs are a particular favorite. One of the changes that has accompanied contact with the larger Canadian economy, especially as the relative cost of travel by float plane has come down over the last half century, is the greater usage of supplies brought into the bush from the points of trade in Saskatchewan. This has reduced the need to rely upon local small game and bird populations for primary subsistence. Things like waterfowl, arctic hares, eggs, grouse, cranes, and swans have ceased to attract systematic harvesting effort. Fish have remained a primary subsistence item, and berries, which come in later in the summer, are still harvested in some quantity.

With the switch in sources of food comes a change in the way it is obtained. The fish net has to be checked daily but only once a day. The net belonged to Wellington, and the aluminum boat was the only boat in camp really suited for checking the net. He would go out in it once a day, usually in the early evening, and remove the fish from the net. When he returned to shore, he would take what he needed for himself and his dog team and leave the rest in the boat. Paul and George would later come to the boat to take what they needed for their own families and dog teams.

Wellington and Paul ceased going into the bush to hunt for large game. George spent several weeks on his moose hunting, but once he had enough moose hides he ceased to hunt for them. Once the tourist fishing season was over, the men of the camp had to struggle to keep themselves busy. Paul rebuilt an old canoe. George and Wellington were mostly involved in carpentry, making furniture and other things for their tents. The men still felt the need to get out and explore around the lake but did not do so by going hunting. Instead, they went fishing. These fishing excursions were made in the aluminum boat. What could be caught by rod and reel served as a supplement to what came from the fish net, but the primary reason to go fishing was to get out of camp. If they encountered waterfowl or small game, it would be taken, but there was no systematic effort to seek it out.

The lack of things that needed to be done was one of the banes of male summer bush life. Prior to the late nineteenth century the men would have had little difficulty keeping busy making tools and other implements for the upcoming fall and winter seasons. The adoption of metal tools and manufactured implements greatly reduced their need to manufacture the basic implements of daily life. The boredom of summer bush life was one of the major factors that drew the Denésuliné into Saskatchewan and life around the trading posts. With the increased importance of life at the settlements in Saskatchewan—and the increasing periods of time spent there—placing a camp in the bush became an aspect of a yearly seasonal movement into the bush rather than the simple relocation of a camp that was already there.

The choices of the Denésuliné who lived in Saskatchewan were complicated by the presence of registered trap lines within that province. This meant that where people chose to live was regulated by the provincial government through the Department of Natural Resources. Those Denésuliné who trapped and lived in the Northwest Territories were not subject to that kind of regulation. They could choose where they wanted to go.

The issue is not without theoretical significance. Where a hunter chooses to place himself—and the camp of people dependent upon him—on the ground is a decision that may well determine the economic success of the upcoming trapping season as well as determining the food supply available to support that camp. It is the kind of decision through which should be expressed, and in which should be visible, the calculations and considerations expected in a veritable plethora of theoretical models. If in fact the theoretical approaches that academics use in trying to understand human hunting behavior do have some validity, this is the kind of issue in which those concerns should be reflected in the behavior, thoughts, and choices people make on the ground. There should be some mechanism at the systemic level that governs where people go and how they pick a local environment to exploit. Calculation, analysis, prediction, and rational choice should all be to the fore in a self-maximizing species.

It is interesting that all these things are on display when the Denésuliné have to justify themselves to whites and white authorities. The Denésuliné are not particularly fond of being called upon to explain themselves, but by now they have a lengthy history of having to deal with whites and their institutions in situations where there is an asymmetric balance of power and wealth. If called upon to explain why they have chosen to go to one place rather than another, they are perfectly capable of offering an explanation that will satisfy outside inquisitors and get them to go away without the speaker having to give away very much. It is instructive that those answers generally are vaguely couched in economic terms: terms that play to the officials' values and expectations. This usually means a vague reference to the potential for economic gain to be found within the area under discussion: for example, "Lots of caribou" there, or "lots of fox" there, or "lots of marten" there.

In practice the Denésuliné generally go to an area where they have a personal or family history of having gone before. They choose to go where they are familiar with the locality. To places where the land itself has acquired meaning through its history of shared use by people who are important to their own individual lives. They choose to go to places their own experience has taught them are attractive and pleasant. This does not mean that they do not explore places where they have never before spent a season or do not respond to the draw (and urging) of kin or friends to camp with them. It does not mean, in this vast land, that they do not rotate their camps throughout particular areas so that they can camp in places where they have not been for some time.

The systemic mechanism analysts seek does exist, but it is located within that part of the cultural system that determines how people structure their relationships to each other through kinship, affinality, and friendship. It works through how particular individuals internalize their understanding of their land through their ideas about the beauty of particular places. It works through the trust they have in the animal/spirits to provide them with the opportunity to survive everywhere within their land.

The lifetime of a camp is generally quite short. If simply moving a camp from one place to another place close by, pure aesthetics are as likely to determine where the new campsite will be as is simple convenience.

Conspicuous physical remains of human occupation are curiously absent from Denésuliné land in this part of the Northwest Territories. The processes of decay are extremely slow in this part of the world. If abandoned and left standing against a tree, a simple wooden object like a shoulder yoke for packing goods over a portage can take several lifetimes to fall to the ground and begin to rot away. Even simple packaging, like a paper box for holding rifle shells, can last for years. When we moved from the temporary tent camp made in June 1970 and used for less than two weeks, I left an empty cartridge box on the ground inside where our tent had been placed. By 1975 signs of where the walls of the tent had been placed and the packing down of the reindeer moss ground cover where the inside of the tent had been were distinguishable from the surrounding ground only by the presence of a few of the poles that had supported the tent, the bits of cord adhering to them, and the remnants of the spruce branches that had been laid on the ground to line the floor of the tent. The shell box was still there, but it had been worn away to the single outside wall of the shell box that had been in contact with the ground. By the summer of 1977 the ground where the tent had been set was unmarked. A few of the poles were still scattered around the area where the tent had stood. The rifle shell box still remained. When I picked it up to examine it, the printing and the color on the side of the box that had faced the ground was intact. It still looked new. By the summer of 1982, the next time I was in the area, only a few of the poles remained in the area.

The walls of abandoned cabins collapse in time, but their collapsed remains last for several generations if not recycled for firewood or lumber. The land around the cabins returns to a pristine state considerably more quickly than the cut logs that made up the cabin decay away. After a campsite is abandoned, the land around it undergoes a regular process of succession. Within a few decades the reindeer moss has returned and looks undisturbed. The stumps of trees that have been cut down may remain for centuries, but they become darkened and aged and fit into their space without drawing attention. The fading of a campsite with log buildings occurs at just about the pace that humans live their lives and fade from the memory of those who once knew the people who made it.

In time the scars of a human presence become inconspicuous, and the landscape again seems clean and empty to those who are not looking for such signs. About one hundred feet behind the tents we pitched at Smalltree Lake was a well-drained, gently sloping incline. It ran west for several hundred feet before merging into rougher ground that was wetter and covered with timber. That open incline was covered by hundreds of tipi rings: scars from where ancestral Denésuliné had pitched their tents. Among the many hundreds of partial tipi ring scars, it was possible to find dozens that were so recent (or so well preserved) that the circular outline of the edge of the tipi was clearly marked by the faint scar formed in the ground cover as it grew back. Buried beneath the ground cover at many of these scars could be found the rocks that occupants had carried to their tipi to hold down its outer walls to keep out the wind. To illustrate his point that the ancestral Denésuliné protected the bones of caribou from consumption by dogs, Paul one day took me out to the tipi rings. With a few moments' searching he identified a clear tipi ring scar and moved to the center of it, where he said the fire would have been. It took but a few moments for him to squat down and dig with a hatchet into the ground where the fire had been (it still supported a few dried strands of the prior year's grass, something that served to mark the hearths, as grass grew nowhere else on the incline), and he recovered the degrading remains of small pieces of bone that the tipi's occupants had protected by throwing them into the fire to keep them from the dogs.

Humans are not the only creatures to use and scar the land. When we came up on the hill top to examine it for possible past human use, the most conspicuous mark upon the land was the scar of an old wolf den site by the path at the very front of the sand hill, where the path led from the hill top down to the shore of the lake.

Hunt 8

Caribou

Long-Distance Hunting

The social situation at the Smalltree Lake camp had become complicated (Sharp 1988a: 142–59), culminating during the third week of July with George packing his family, possessions, and dogs into the canoe that Paul had rebuilt and moving north to the small lake just across the portage from Foxholm Lake. The direct line distance of his trip was thirty-two miles on the map, although local bush pilots referred to it as a fifteen-mile flight. The trip was hazardous, especially in an overloaded canoe with several small children along. Within the week, Wellington and I made a long circular reconnaissance by canoe that intersected George's course of travel to ensure that he had safely passed. A garbled short-wave radio message about George's departure—including tales of murder—led to a surge of aircraft visiting our camp. This strange influx of float planes allowed us to confirm that George and his family had arrived safely.

On July 24 Eddy and his wife Virginia (one of Paul's and May's daughters) arrived at our camp. They had come to spend several weeks visiting. Eddy hoped to find caribou so that Virginia could make dry meat. He especially wanted to take fresh meat back to Discha to keep in their home freezer.

Caribou were not present at Smalltree Lake that summer. The influx of transient aircraft had brought word from George that caribou were present on Foxholm Lake, although they were not there in great numbers. As the situation with George's move sorted itself out and it became clear that caribou would not come to Smalltree Lake during the time Eddy had allowed for their visit, he and Wellington decided to make a canoe trip to Foxholm Lake. Their primary purpose was to hunt for caribou there, but the visit would also allow them to confirm that George and his family were safe and would relieve his parents' concerns.

Thirty-two miles on a map is a rather different kind of thing than is making the actual trip. In early August Eddy and Wellington departed in my canoe. There was not room in it for a third person if they were going to be able to bring back any caribou meat. They chose not to use the canoe's small motor. They departed from the camp and paddled west. Their plan was to follow the shoreline near to the west end of the lake and then make a series of portages to reach a lake that had a small creek running from it that intersected the river chain (Sanderson Lake) that flowed close to the southwest corner of Foxholm Lake. They would be able to follow that river northward to its source in the small lake that was just across the portage from Foxholm Lake. This was where George had settled into the winter camp (map 1) left from 1970–71.

Sanderson Lake and the river proved to be no difficulty for them. There was only one narrows section where they had to use a rope to haul the canoe through rapids, and one other spot where three creeks met that the water was fast enough and rock filled enough to be dangerous (see Interlude 1 and map 1). The journey between Smalltree Lake and the river proved a different matter. The route they had chosen required a considerable number of portages, and some of the ground they had to cover proved difficult to negotiate, especially while packing the canoe. The year had been dry, and there had been a great many forest fires fifty to a hundred miles to the south. (This was most likely the reason there were so many moose around Smalltree Lake that summer.) With the lack of rain, the small creek they had intended to follow proved to be in a low water condition. Instead of being able to paddle down the creek as they had expected to do, they found the creek's water level so low that it had become a rock-filled obstacle course they often had to negotiate by walking the canoe down the creek and around the rocks.

The trip took them a day longer than they had anticipated. They did not arrive at George's camp until the third day after their departure. Their time at Foxholm Lake was further complicated by the fact that a survey team of archaeologists from the Canadian Archaeological Service had just passed across Foxholm Lake (1988a: 156–57). George had injured his shoulder during his trip and was in a state of general distress, not least because of the RCMP sending up an aircraft to see if he had been murdered or not. He did not know the survey party was in the area, and the sign of their passage had greatly disturbed him. Dealing with this took time away from Eddy's and Wellington's time to hunt.

Caribou were far more common on Foxholm Lake than they were across the portage in the areas to the south of it. Eddy and Wellington had to focus their hunting there and portage the meat they took three-quarters of a mile back to the small lake. It took a few days to reassure George that there were no more unknown persons on Foxholm Lake and to take enough caribou to begin the journey back to Smalltree Lake. Eddy and Wellington returned by a different route, which kept them on the river longer and made use of a different series of small lakes and ponds to cover the distance from it to Smalltree Lake. They entered Smalltree Lake near the river at its north end and returned to camp on August 8, 1975.

Text 8

Transporting Meat

As a hunting expedition, the trip Eddy and Wellington made was a mixed success. They did get to their destination and they were able to kill caribou at a time when caribou were not available at Smalltree lake. Long distance hunting trips like this are rare, particularly when the land is not frozen and snow covered, for fairly obvious reasons. A summer hunting trip is slow and demanding unless it is along an unrestricted water course. The energy and effort they require tend to inhibit the Denésuliné desire to make such trips. They are rarely all that productive.

This lack of productivity comes not from the success or lack of it in the hunting itself but from the wastage that comes from having to transport the meat once it has been taken. The warm weather of summer decreases the time it takes for meat to spoil. It took at least one day from the time the meat was killed until it could be transported back to the winter camp on the small lake and prepared for transport in the canoe. The trip itself took two days, and the meat arrived at the camp on Smalltree Lake late in the evening. Processing of the meat that was transported back to Smalltree Lake could not begin until daylight the day after it had arrived in camp. Even though the meat was covered in the canoe, it was exposed to a minimum of three days of daytime temperatures before it could be worked on.

Since it was now too late in their trip for Virginia to make dry meat, the meat still had to endure several more days' exposure to warmer summer temperatures before it could be gotten to Discha and into a freezer. The only practical source of cooling for the volume of meat they had brought back in the canoe was immersion in the lake water. Storing meat in the summer waters of one of the large lakes of this country helps, but doing this near the shores, where it is possible to get the meat into the water and have access to it, is not as effective as refrigeration. The temperatures of shallow water are just not as cold as the interior of a refrigerator. There are ways to increase the effectiveness of lakes as summer meat storage devices, but they all require preparation and special effort or equipment.

The basic principle is getting the meat deeply enough into the lake to reach colder water. There are relatively few places where deep water is easily accessible from shore. Having to take the meat out onto the lake far enough to reach deep water poses its own set of problems. It requires a boat to get the meat out there. Once the meat is taken over cold, deep water, the question becomes what to do with it? Simply dumping it into the water will work, but how is the meat to be recovered once it has been dumped into the lake? Aside from the fact that few Denésuliné can swim, these lakes are far too cold, and the water is often too deep, to jump into the lake and swim down to locate and recover anything. The Denésuliné have no technology suitable for searching lake bottoms to locate and recover meat dumped into deep water.

The situation is different in winter, when the ice covering the lake provides a platform capable of supporting meat immersed in the water, but during most of the time the lakes are frozen over, meat will freeze on land so underwater storage is unnecessary. It would be possible to build a platform to float on a lake's surface to support meat immersed in its colder and deeper waters, but making a platform large enough to support the meat and strong enough to resist the wind and wave action of the lake would be a significant undertaking. Such a device would be so totally a special-purpose creation that it is hard to imagine circumstances in which it would be a practical solution to anything.

The simple fact is that water storage of meat is a short-term fix, a two- or three-day measure to address to a temporary problem rather than a long-term solution. This is the case even without consideration of how meat texture and taste quickly begin to deteriorate from immersion in water. Eddy is quite particular about the freshness and quality of the meat he and his family consume. The morning after he returned to camp, he took all the meat out and arranged it on the rocks by the shore. He inspected and smelled each piece carefully to determine if it was fresh enough to store for transport back to Discha when the plane came for them. What he did not regard as fresh enough he discarded by throwing it out beyond reach in the lake. What was fresh enough to keep he carefully placed into the lake water where he could get to it. As it turned out, slightly more than half of what had been transported back from Foxholm Lake had deteriorated to the point that it was discarded rather than being taken south.

The process of transport itself is destructive to the meat that is being transported. Portaging a canoe sounds simple enough, but it means the contents of the craft—in this case the raw meat—must be taken out of the canoe and placed on the ground until they can be picked up and carried over the portage and placed back into the canoe. Even if the meat is well wrapped for travel, each portage means exposure to risk of physical damage, contamination, contact with the ground, and exposure to outside air temperatures. Wrapping the meat for transport is itself an issue, as the meat cannot be wrapped in plastic or sealed away from the air. An airtight container increases the rate at which spoilage occurs.

When transport is a determining issue, the weight and quality of the meat to be taken becomes a crucial issue in the selection of what is to be brought back. Ease of transport becomes the key to deciding what is taken from each kill that is made. The premium is on meaty cuts suitable for making into dry meat or for cooking. Bone becomes dead weight during transport, so every effort has to be made to eliminate it. Parts of the caribou that would be used were the camp close by have to be discarded because they are not suitable for long distance transport. In turn, this means that the number of caribou that have to be killed to make up the load increases to compensate for what has to be discarded because it cannot be transported.

Unless the trip can be made entirely by water, long distance summer hunting is unnecessarily wasteful. It is not popular among the Denésuliné and seems to occur only under special circumstances. Long distance hunting once snowfall has come and dog teams can be used is a different matter. Dog teams pulling toboggans are faster and can more readily make return trips between camp and kill. They are far more effective at transporting meat than are boats that have to be portaged. Long distance hunts are far more common in winter than are summer boat hunts that involve portaging.

The loss of meat resulting from Eddy and Wellington having to transport it back to camp illustrates a recurring conundrum of aboriginal and fur trade Denésuliné life: the choice between moving meat to the camp or moving the camp to the meat. Prior to the advent of the fur trade and the Denésuliné adoption of dog teams and Algonquin-style canoes, it seems clear that the balance was shifted heavily toward moving the camp to the meat. After their adoption of the technology derived from the fur trade, their ability to transport heavy loads increased greatly, and the choice became more complicated.

We have frequently pointed out the sheer scale of the Denésuliné homeland and the paucity of large animals within it. Movement across the land was always the basis of aboriginal Denésuliné survival. Their primary adaptation to the scarceness and erratic distribution of the animals was their ability and willingness to move from place to place within their homeland. The dominant image of the lives of their ancestors that was to be gained from talking to the elders in the last third of the twentieth century was of a life lived on the move. This image holds more than a grain of truth.

The Denésuliné walked through their land to an extent not obvious to urban peoples dependent upon motorized transport and for whom a three-mile walk can mean an excursion into strange, dangerous, and alien worlds. The current image of the life of ancestral Denésuliné is of a people in constant motion, leading a life of continuous camp movement in which men wandered out hunting while women loaded the camp on toboggans they hauled from kill to kill.

The accuracy of this image is not at issue. What matters is its encapsulation of the need for movement and willingness to live in almost constant movement.

The reality of the lives of the ancestral Denésuliné was probably less demanding than this image suggests, but it contains in quite abstract form the essential elements of aboriginal life in the subarctic. When food was scarce or when people could not transport what they had killed to their camps, the Denésuliné moved their camps to where they had made a kill. In times of crisis or when they could not supply their own food, they moved to those points of contact where there was food—to their kin and affines—until they were again able to supply themselves. This translated into a culture in which long distance movement across the land was routine. Seasonal trips of 100 to 150 miles on foot, by entire camps consisting of women, children, and the elderly, ill, and infirm were not only routine—they could occur several times within a year. It is not that everyone made trips this long every year, but walking trips of these lengths were a routine part of life.

Parties of males, removed from the responsibility to feed anyone other than themselves, made trips that were hundreds of miles long and that sometimes lasted for months.

With the fur trade, Denésuliné travel began to change. The adoption of southern-style birch bark canoes and dog teams greatly increased the weight and volume of material they could carry with them. With this increase in carrying capacity came an increase in what the Denésuliné chose to carry with them. As the fur trade settled in and seasonal travel transitioned from foot to boat and dog team, the number of trips and the distances traveled began to decline, and the routes of travel changed. Travel by foot simply takes people over different routes than does travel by boat or by dog team.

A large freight canoe can carry an entire family and far more goods than they can pack, but canoe travel is slow. Canoes are vulnerable to being upset by wind-caused waves on the lakes. The September canoe trip from the village to the Smalltree Lake area often took an entire month, as people had to lay up and wait out rough water conditions caused by the winds of September. Even though the canoes could carry large amounts of freight, people often had to consume so much of their supplies while waiting out the wind and storms that they arrived at their destination inadequately provisioned.

With the full fur trade, the Denésuliné were not immune to the changes induced by the presence of points of trade in Saskatchewan. The Caribou Eaters, the northern Denésuliné of this work, formed "All-Native Communities" (Helm and Damas 1963). These were mostly around Selwyn Lake. These communities became the center of their lives, and it was not uncommon for boys who grew up during the World War I era not to go into the points of trade in Saskatchewan until they were in their midteens. Young women of the same birth cohorts often did not see the points of trade until they were adults. Well into the 1920s it was common for northern Denésuliné never to have seen a white person before reaching adulthood, other than possibly a priest.

As the localization of Denésuliné life began to break down after World War I and their lives began to center more and more around the Saskatchewan trading points, ground travel began to decline. Winter land trips between bush areas and the stores—where the village at Mission came into being after 1953—persisted into the 1970s even as air travel by float or ski plane began to replace land travel.

All mammals large enough to live upon the surface of the ground live within a web defined by their contact with others of their own kind. It matters not if they are social or solitary, territorial or migratory. The defining feature of their lives is the presence of others of their own kind and the boundaries imposed by their contact with those others. What humans add to that web is the alteration of those points of contact into points of assistance and support. Within the web of human contact defined by other Denésuliné—that part of the world within which individual Denésuliné could move without fear of attack by other humans—they used the presence of other Denésuliné to construct a world of security through the simple transformation of those contacts into sources of food and assistance during times of need (Sharp 1978: 61–64).

Interlude 1

Land Use and the Terrain at Foxholm Lake

Foxholm Lake seems to embody the distinction between forest and tundra. Patches of trees are found hundreds of miles north of this lake and patches of tundra are found dozens if not hundreds of miles south of it, but when you stand on the shores of this lake, it seems as if the two zones meet here (C on map 1; see Sharp 2001: 34–41). If you stand on the north shore and look south, you see solid forest extending as far as the eye can see; forest broken only by splotches of muskeg and patches of tundra or bare lichen on the high ground of the hills. If you are on the south shore of the lake and face north, as far as the eye can see there is nothing but tundra north of the opposite shoreline, save the tops of trees breaking from depressions surrounding sheltered lakes and patches of timber along the odd stream course snaking off into to the distance. The impression is almost pure: to the south is forest, to the north is tundra.

Foxholm Lake is a large lake. Throughout the summer and into the fall its north shore was the primary hunting area for the Denésuliné portrayed in this book. Except for the relatively shallow narrows at the lake's far northwest end, it is wide enough to restrict caribou movement across it. They are able to swim across the lake, but most of it is so wide that they are not likely to do so. This has consequences for how the Denésuliné use the land on the south shore of the lake and south-ward from it—the focus of this interlude. The lake has many bays, several large arms, small offshoots, connecting lakes, and entering and departing streams. Foxholm Lake is so large that its northern half either borders the tundra or is in the widely scattered mature forest that is so common close to the tundra edge. Its southern end is in the transition zone of the boreal forest. Where this distinction is most crucial is in the appearance of caribou. They are far more likely to appear over the summer at the edge of the tundra and for a few miles into the beginning of the forest. Even a few miles south of this tundra border, caribou may not appear until they begin their fall migration toward their wintering areas. In practical terms, this can mean the difference between having caribou in late June or early July compared with not having access to them until October or even early November.

Prior to 1960 the lake was the fall and winter home for several camps of Denésuliné who were dispersed around it. According to Paul and May's memory, the lake once supported eight separate camps through a fall and winter season. This seems to have been about the maximum number of camps that were viable, as both of them commented on how crowded it had seemed and that this number of camps was never reached again. By the 1970s with the withdrawal of the Denésuliné from bush life, Foxholm Lake was no longer in use every year. It was now a favored locus for Paul and May, but it was only one of several areas in which they spent the fall season. They maintained a larger camp with more elaborate cabins, including a two-story one, on the north end of Wholdia Lake, which they used in 1972. They occasionally spent the trapping season at the Selwyn Lake community and had begun to winter sometimes at Small-tree Lake in the company of Wellington and his growing family.

Denésuliné usage of Foxholm Lake is mostly geared toward gaining early access to caribou. When the Denésuliné come here for the fall and winter seasons, they tend to come earlier in the summer than they choose to go into the bush if they are wintering farther south.

George had adopted Foxholm Lake as his favored base for his own trapping and hunting. He would continue to base himself there after Paul's ill health forced him to abandon spending the fall in the bush. George would eventually construct a multi-building complex on the north shore of the lake (see Hunt 15). As George himself aged and ceased to spend time in the bush, his sons would take over his camp and continue to base their own trapping and hunting operations from it. They continue to use that camp as a base for their hunting and trapping as this is written.

The activities of this group of Denésuliné were centered upon the northwest corner of the lake because this was the part of the lake that Paul preferred. The summer tent camps were located on the north shore of the lake. Winter camps throughout the 1970s were on the small lake just over the portage at the far west end of the lake. Over their married lives Paul and May had camped all around Foxholm Lake. Wellington, who was born in a camp on the south shore of the lake in the 1940s, was one of two of their sons to be born at Foxholm Lake. Their preference was for the northern half of the lake. This part of the lake was closer to the tundra and more likely to have caribou present in the summer. During the earlier part of their married life, it was common to make the trip from Mission to Foxholm Lake by canoe. As soon as it became practical—a combination of the appearance in the north of float- and ski-equipped Norseman aircraft in the 1930s and the lowering of the cost of charter flights to a point within the reach, though still expensive—they began to make the trip north by float plane. If coming this far north by canoe, it was customary to leave Mission in August. If making the trip by float plane, it was customary to depart in September.

At the west end of the main lake is a shallow narrows some hundred feet wide (D on map 1; the location of the loon hunt portrayed in Sharp 2001). The narrows connect into a north-south-running bay perhaps three and one half miles in length (E on map 1). From the narrows Foxholm Lake extends to the east and south. About six miles to the east a very large arm extends northward. After several miles this arm of the lake ends at the entrance of a stream that drains the country between Foxholm Lake and the next series of large lakes to the north. The land north of this large arm of the lake was little used by this group of Denésuliné. Fred Riddle's poisoning operations extended into the lakes north of this part of Foxholm Lake and were part of the reason the Denésuliné avoided the area (Sharp 1988a). On the east side of that arm was another inflowing stream or river that drained a series of lakes and their connecting stream. It was out along this stream course leading northeastward that Joe's Camp was located (Hunt 1). Other than passage during the occasional trip to Joe's Camp, the area to the northeast and east of the large north-projecting arm of Foxholm Lake was little used. It was simply too far from the base camps for it to be easily exploited either by boat or by dog team in winter.

The south shore of Foxholm lake opposite the northward-projecting arm was the termination point of the large sand esker (see following discussion) cut by the shallows on the stream that drained out of the small lake.

Foxholm Lake continues southward for miles, widening out to become ten to fifteen miles wide in places. At the southeast corner of the widened lake is an outflowing river that drains the lake southward. This drainage, after passing through a number of lakes, ultimately feeds into the northern end of Anaunethad Lake. These parts of Foxholm Lake were far too far from the camps at the northwest end of the lake to be of use to hunt or fish. Getting there by boat required so much gasoline that going down to that part of the lake was no more than a twice a decade occurrence. It was close enough for exploitation by dog team in situations where food was in very short supply and the taking of one or two caribou could make a difference.

At the western side of this widened southern end of Foxholm Lake, Sanderson lake/river enters it. This river, which drains several hundred square miles, extends northwestward for more than a dozen miles. It is fed by a number of creeks, lakes, and small rivers. This was the river that Wellington and Eddy used in their trip up and back from Smalltree Lake (Hunt 8). One of the sources of this river, at this point a large stream, was a nearly circular lake roughly a mile in diameter (A on map 1), which lay on the east side of a sand ridge. This sand ridge (F on map 1), about three quarters of a mile in width at this point, runs between the north-south bay of Foxholm Lake and the small circular lake. The sand ridge is all that prevents Foxholm Lake from forming a massive circle. As the closest point between the small lake and the bay on Foxholm Lake, it had for many hundreds of years been used by the Denésuliné as a portage between the two lakes.

The nearly circular form of Foxholm Lake has consequences for the land within the circle; the land that, if Foxholm Lake were a doughnut, would be the doughnut hole. Because at all but its far northwestern parts the width of Foxholm Lake inhibited caribou from swimming across it, it was difficult for them to reach the land of the doughnut hole from the north shore of Foxholm Lake. As caribou movement near Foxholm Lake during the summer was almost always in a northeast-southwest direction, this large area was always relatively devoid of caribou. Other game resources seemed to be normal for the area, but the caribou resources were decidedly less than those of the areas to the north and west of Foxholm Lake. The effect was to make the Denésuliné avoid the area of the doughnut hole at times of the year when there was no snow and the lakes were unfrozen. Trapping occurred along the western fringes of the doughnut hole and the parts of it along the south shore of Foxholm Lake after the lakes froze. Paul ran his trap line along the stream course, but otherwise the area was ignored.

In the course of a long walk for a picnic in 1970 Paul was taken by a place along the shore of the small lake. He so liked the spot that he built his winter camp there (B on map 1). Before 1975 George had built a small cabin for himself at the same location. After getting married he expanded that cabin by extending it to the rear. In 1975 George's father-in-law decided to spend the fall to winter trapping season here with his family. This was the first time in his life that he had wintered near the edge of the tundra. Early in the fall of 1975 George and his father built a far larger cabin for George's father-in-law and his family than they used for themselves. This was the third—and last—time this location would be used for a winter camp. By 2012 the camp had been razed, mostly for firewood, by one of George's sons.

The camp was set on the west shore of the small lake (which did not seem to be named) on a patch of slightly sloping sand. It was no more than 150 feet from the lake shore to the base of the sand hill behind the camp. To the immediate north of the camp was a small inlet (fifty feet by fifteen feet) connected to the small lake. North of this the land was scrub timber with thick scrub growth along the shoreline of the small lake. Along the south side of the small inlet, rising steeply from its rear, was a sand and gravel ridge that rose upward to the main sand hill of the portage. That ridge served as the pathway between the camp and the main body of the sand hill. It was the southern terminus of the portage route to Foxholm Lake. When humans were not around, it was a game pathway used by large animals moving between the two lakes.

The south shore of the small lake was lined by a series of beautiful white sand beaches ten feet to fifteen feet deep. At the back of each beach was an abrupt rise of two to four feet; a vertical cut formed by the collapsing edge of the spruce-covered sand hill. A stream flowed eastward out of the southeast corner of the lake (G on Map 1), the connection between this lake and the stream and lake system that flowed into the southwestern end of Foxholm Lake. This stream, which turned into a river as it flowed southward and was fed by other inflowing streams, was the main route of water travel to gain access to the areas south of the winter camp. (In winter, when the ground froze, the muskegs and low-lying land to the west provided quicker access to these areas.) When people were based in the winter camp and there was no ice on the water, there was boat traffic fairly regularly—once or twice a week. Most of this traffic was to reach the lake and low-lying areas west of the sand hill (see following description), but attention was always paid to the tracks of large game passing through.

As the stream exited from the small lake, it took a southward turn within thirty feet of leaving the small lake. On the east side of this turn was a narrow boulder-filled connection to another lake (about the small lake's size) bordered by muskeg to the north and connecting sand flats to the east. These formed the shores of a series of other lakes near the south shore of Foxholm lake. This area, part of the land of the doughnut hole, was essentially ignored by the Denésuliné of the camp. There might have been some traffic into the area in deep winter (the Denésuliné did tend to get out and explore by dog team until the snow became so deep that travel off their trail network became too laborious), but we never saw any traffic into the area once the ice had melted.

A few hundred yards south of this connection between the eastern lake and the stream exiting the small lake, the stream, now some thirty feet wide, became only three or four inches deep (H on map 1) as it cut through a long esker. From this shallow narrows, the northeast-southwest-running esker—which rose 100–150 feet above water level on the left side of the stream when going south—ran for some miles until it reached the south shore of Foxholm Lake at the base of its northward-projecting arm.

These shallows were the only spot along the entire stream course of twelve plus miles where it was possible for a large animal to cross the stream without having to swim. For animals to move into or out of the northern part of the land of the doughnut hole, this was the easiest crossing. From the top of the northeast-southwest-running esker down to where the stream cut through it was a game trail used by animals moving along the esker between the south shore of Foxholm Lake and the higher, dry ground of the flats farther to the west. The shallows provided a perfect ambush point for caribou moving across the stream. It was one of the places where we found moose tracks in 1975, before the caribou arrived, but even though we checked it every time we passed, there was relatively little animal traffic over it.

To the west of the shallow narrows was a north-south-running sand hill paralleling the course of the stream. That sand hill rose some fifty to seventy-five feet above the water level, continuing for several miles to the south until it ended in an abrupt vertical face on its southern and western sides. As one moved southward along the sand hill, its sides became progressively steeper until they were sheer vertical drops. Access to the top of the hill from everywhere except the shallows or the trail leading from the winter camp was so difficult that little game was ever encountered there. People used the sand hill largely as a route of foot travel to get to the southern end of the hill, where it was possible to overlook several miles of small lakes and lower-lying terrain to the west and south.

The sheer southern face of the sand hill fell away to a series of muskegs and a pond one or two acres in size. A deep, meandering creek of dark water (darkened with tannin from the muskeg) ran through these muskegs. This creek flowed from the west into the larger stream from its origin in a lake. It was a place where we often saw otter and beaver sign. Barely a hundred feet before this dark tannin-laced creek joined the stream, a considerably larger stream flowed into it from the east. That stream drained a series of lakes lying in the land of the doughnut hole south of the large northeast-southwest-running esker bisected by the shallows (I on map 1). This created several hundred feet of fast and slightly turbulent rock-filled water that was dangerous to negotiate in a canoe or small boat. It was also a dangerous place in winter as the water currents were liable to weaken the ice that formed on it.

The tannin-laden creek was only several hundred yards long, but it provided water access to the land westward of the sand hill with the steep sides. That land was largely flat and considerably more waterlogged than most of the land in the area. It held several black water muskegs, some of which were exceedingly dangerous for the passage of any large animal with foot pressure exceeding that of a caribou. This low-lying area was difficult to access until the ground and muskegs froze solid. The wetness and muskegs did not bother caribou. Until the ground froze and snow started to cover the land, this was a preferential feeding area for them. Access to them in this area was so difficult that the Denésuliné ignored their presence. After the ground froze, travel into and through the area was easy, but it was no longer as attractive to the caribou as a feeding area and they rarely concentrated there.

The tannin-laced creek connected to a medium-sized lake (roughly one mile in diameter) that lay along the west side of the sand hill that ended in a vertical face. This lake had an inflowing shallow creek and rapids system on its west side as well as a creek entering on its northeast side that drained the low land west of the highland. The creek and rapids system led westward toward territory sometimes used by Denésuliné from Fond du Lac and the denser, more fully boreal forest country individuals from that band seemed to favor. As usage of this country by the Denésuliné from Mission declined, there was some pressure from Denésuliné from Fond du Lac pushing into the area. Occasional irritations developed over trap lines and the treatment of animals found in the traps of other trappers. It was along this creek line that George's father-in-law, on Paul's advice, chose to run his trap line later in the fall, and it was along the north side of this creek that the bear destroyed one of his caribou caches (Hunt 14).

To return to the shallow spot on the creek flowing out of the small lake, the land behind that shallow spot rose to the sandy ridge of the north-south esker. The ground dropped westward of the sand ridge then rose into a "highland," perhaps a hundred feet above the level of Foxholm Lake and extending for several miles to the north and northwest (J on map 1). The northern edge of this highland paralleled the west shore of the north-south bay of Foxholm Lake and extended northwestward for several miles. The highland was fairly dry and relatively well drained, with small ponds scattered over it but not too many muskegs. It was largely covered with reindeer moss. As the fall advanced and the summer vegetation was gone, it became a good feeding ground for caribou. Once the ground became snow covered and dog teams and toboggans could be used, it became a primary hunting area (although with the onset of winter conditions the lower-lying and wetter areas to the west of the highland became even better areas for trapping and hunting), and use of the north shore of Foxholm Lake was largely abandoned.

In the fall and winter of 1975 Phil began to run his own trap line. As he did not have his own dog team, he had to run a line that he could walk when he could not borrow his father's team. His trap line went over the portage trail to the north-south arm of Foxholm Lake. From there it went to the far northern end of the creek that fed into the north-south arm. At the end of the lake and creek, it turned west over the highland. It crossed the highland and then turned southward, along the border between the highland and the low-lying (but now frozen) wetlands just beyond, before looping back to the winter camp. George's trap line followed a similar course but was longer. His trap line went over the portage, up the north-south bay, and up the creek. Out of deference to his younger brother's efforts, he did not place any traps along this first part of his trap line. At the end of the creek, his trap line continued northward to the shore of Spider Lake and then turned westward along its southern shore. After a number of miles it turned southward through the now frozen wetlands. Like Phil's trap line, George's continued southward before looping around and returning to the winter camp from the south.

These two trap lines meant that two hunters went out into the frozen low-lying wetlands (or along their eastern edge) on a regular basis. As the lowlands were a regular feeding ground for whatever caribou were in the area after the fall migration had passed to the south, it meant that the lowlands became the camp's primary source of fresh caribou meat once the serious cold began to set in.

It was several miles from the north shore of the small lake to the south shore of Foxholm Lake. The land along the east shore of Foxholm Lake's north-south bay ran in a nearly straight north-south line. That shore was the typical jumble of rocks and boulders until a small conical island (elevated some thirty feet above the lake's surface) marked the presence of several small sand flats and the narrows that connected the north-south bay to the main body of Foxholm Lake. Inland from the boulder-lined shores on this north-south stretch, the land was covered by fairly thick mixed spruce forest (*Picea mariana, P. glauca*) that extended eastward for several dozen yards. Inland from the forest strip, the elevation dropped a few feet and the land was largely wet and covered with muskeg (Hunt 14). In places were boulder piles that had become moss covered and were more damp than wet. These were difficult to move through but provided habitat for some of the odder small animals living at the extreme northern end of their range: quite a dense population of red squirrel (*Tamiasciurus hudsonicus*) and a small creature that looked like a cross between a northern flying squirrel (*Glaucomys sabrinus*) and an arctic ground squirrel (*Urocitellus parryii*).

At the junction of this patch of land and the south shore of Foxholm Lake, the muskeg wetness gave way to a wet mixed forest in which were the only large white birch trees on this part of Foxholm Lake. The Denésuliné cherished the location for memories of the past, when the bark of this white birch stand provided the last chance to patch canoes before moving out onto the tundra for the summer. The next few miles farther east along the south shore of Foxholm Lake were largely mature forest broken by patches of muskeg and the odd patch of tundra on the sides of the higher sand hills.

Reaching eastward or inland one to two miles from the wet muskeg-covered shore of the north-south bay, the land stayed low, but there were patches of sand that were covered by lichen and reindeer moss. This area was dominated by a tall conical hill (Hunt 9). It was broken up by small lakes and muskeg ponds. By two miles inland there was a series of substantial lakes, but we could not discern a drainage system connecting them. It looked much like anywhere else in this vast and amazing land.

The south shore of the north-south bay of Foxholm Lake formed a beach about one hundred yards wide upon the sand hill. The beach was divided into three nearly equally sized sections. Facing south, the left side of the beach terminated in an outcrop of bedrock granite some seven to ten feet high and roughly fifteen feet wide (east-west). Some eighty feet of the outcrop, running north-south, showed above ground before becoming buried in the sand that formed the portage. It created a barrier between the beach and the eastern shore of the north-south running bay. Climbing over this outcrop was difficult and I never saw it attempted. People rarely moved from the beach to the east shore, and when they did, they did so by moving up the sand hill portage route and turning east once the granite deposit was buried by the sand hill. It was up this sand hill from the beach that the portage route had run, and moving up off this beach onto the sand hill and through the forest to the small lake was the favored route of the people now living here.

The first and second beaches were separated by another granite outcrop, a small one some fifteen feet wide but low and easily climbed. The granite of this outcrop was largely covered by sand supporting lichen and moss ground cover and a small stand of trees. This beach was off the portage trail, as a muskeg lay just inland of it. Another small granite outcrop separated the second and third beaches. The terminal outcrop of granite that ended the beaches at the west (their right side, facing south) had substantial tree cover and was most noteworthy for the fact that the lichen and moss ground cover and trees covered more than thirty birch bark canoes that had been abandoned there.

Beyond this last beach, the land was wet and covered with a heavy growth of scrub hardwood timber. This scrub-timber-covered rising ground was a favored area for black bear to den for the winter. The land rose steeply from the beach to the top of the highland; it was from the highland just above this area that George first spotted the caribou in Hunt 14.

Hunt 9

Bear

Failed Hunt

George and I went out into the low, flat land north of the small lake to climb to the top of a conical hill that projected from the mixed muskeg and sand patches between the north-south bay of Foxholm Lake and the first of the inland lakes south of Foxholm Lake. The hill (H-9 on map 1), projecting more than two hundred feet above the water level of Foxholm Lake, looked like a perfect dwarf volcanic cinder cone. It could be seen from miles away and was the most visible landmark in the area. We carried rifles and were watching for caribou, but our primary reason for the walk was curiosity. George had not been to the top for years, and I had never been there. There were stories about strange constructions on the hilltop and I wanted to see what was there.

We took an easy course to the hill top, which was several miles away, by moving inland from the west shore of the small lake then heading northeast to the hill. At the very top of the hill were indeed the remnants of a structure. All that remained on the surface was an elliptical ring of stones. These were all dark rocks—I remember them as almost black—stacked three high. The rocks must have been carried to the top of the hill as they were unlike anything on its ground surface. Whatever had been there was long gone; George thought it was an old sweat lodge, and Paul felt it had been a place for drumming. The ground surface inside the ellipse was identical to the ground cover outside it, but the ring of rocks supported a heavy growth of dwarf shrubs amplifying the shape of the base cobbles by outlining it in living vegetation. Several years later Phil—at the time in his mid teens—would become an accomplished artist and something of a visionary. He would create upon the ground within the circle artistic-spiritual devices focused upon the moon and part of his own communion with the spirit world of the Denésuliné.

After we had been on the hilltop for a short while and had finished inspecting the remnants of the construction, George saw a black bear on the flat land near the inland lakes. The bear was several miles from our location and was just south of the south shore of Foxholm Lake. It was moving rapidly in a southeasterly direction, paralleling the west shore of the first of the large inland lakes, already out of the muskegs and moving over the dry moss- and lichen-covered sand outcrops. George pointed it out to me. We watched the bear briefly and he explained what he thought the bear would do. I thought it was far too far away to do anything but watch it, but George gathered his things together to go after it. We set off in rapid pursuit, taking a course down toward the inland lake's shore to try to intercept the path the bear was taking. We moved rapidly; a combination of very fast walking alternating with spells of sprinting or trotting, headed toward where George thought we could intercept the bear.

His course headed directly down the east side of the hill, slightly north of east. The bear's pace was a lope that was nearly a run. When I first saw the bear I thought it was running from something. It was moving so quickly that George assumed it would slow its pace or stop to search for food. His assessment of the bear's probable behavior was off. The bear must have kept up its near running pace. By the time we had covered the distance to get close to the shore of the inland lake, the bear was long past and out of sight.

Text 9

Looking for Game

This is the first failed hunt we have examined, but failed hunts are an all too common experience for the Denésuliné. My assessment of the situation when we were on the hilltop was the correct one in terms of the outcome of the hunt. The bear was too far away and moving too fast for us to get close enough to kill it. The problem is that this judgment on my part was also wrong. George's judgment was correct: the bear might well have slowed down or stopped to feed. Something entirely different might have caused the bear to slow its pace or alter its course so that we might have been able to close with it. However correct my assessment of the situation was, acting on it would necessarily have precluded any chance of killing the bear. George's assessment was the correct one to act upon even though the outcome was a failed hunt. My assessment was intended to spare us the expenditure of a good deal of effort and reflects exactly the wrong approach to subsistence hunting.

One of the most basic things the Denésuliné have to shift the balance of predation in their favor is their willingness to expend effort and energy in attempts that a reasoned judgment indicates will end in failure. With my approach a 100 percent failure rate was guaranteed. With George's approach, failure was likely but not guaranteed. Wellington's oft repeated "I'll try it" clearly reflects this difference in approach and is a far better way to approach hunting. The harsher the conditions, the scarcer the game, and the more dangerous the situation, the more this difference holds true. Sometimes the only chance of survival in this land comes from willingness to expend time and energy doing things that seem to have no chance of success.

The fact is that the bear moved far too fast for us to have any chance to close with it. This reflects a basic fact of life in the subarctic: virtually all the land animal life moves far faster than humans can move.

The failure of this hunt was particularly interesting as it involved hunting from a high place. The image of early hunters seeking out high ground from which they can see game in the distance and move to intercept it is a widely featured aspect of the interpretation of hunting and land use by our ancestors and other human species. It is also the source of a great deal of stuff and nonsense written about those hunters. We have seen it used for everything from explaining Neanderthal extinction (noble human ancestors took the hilltops of Europe away from the inferior Neanderthals, who then died out because they were unable to hunt effectively) to perpetuating romantic images of our ancestors as noble savages (images of early European hunters gazing from the high hilltops in search of game are remarkably like and clearly a continuation of politically charged nineteenth-century contrasting reconstructions of Neanderthal vs. Cro-Magnon). This image is particularly pervasive in popular literature, but it shows up everywhere from paleoanthropological and archaeological literature to science shows on television.

On this point we do not intend to throw the baby out with the bathwater. . Homo sapiens and presumably our ancestral and related species are visual creatures. The effectiveness and clarity of our distance vision has been a crucial factor in our survival. Humans, including the Denésuliné, do use visual searches from high places to gain an understanding of what else is in the environment and use that understanding to improve hunting success. Looking for game from high places where it can be seen far away—from distances of five or ten miles or more—could provide useful knowledge. Not knowledge that would be of immediate use for the people on the high ground to go and hunt but knowledge that would be useful in planning future hunts or the movement of the social groups to which the hunters were attached. In a few circumstances, the ability to use high ground to observe the surrounding area could be quite effective as a means of hunting. Obvious examples are situations where animals migrate in large, closely packed herds: caribou on the open tundra, wildebeest on the African plains, and perhaps buffalo on the American and Canadian Great Plains.

However, these are special cases. All involve open country where it is possible to see for long distances inhabited by migratory animals that move in large, tightly packed herds, a situation that is not terribly common. Standing on a high hilltop gazing off into the distance to spot the approach of a herd of ten, twenty, or thirty thousand animals is one thing. Gazing out over that same landscape to spot a group of three, five, or ten animals is something quite different. Animals come in groups of three, five, or ten a great deal more often than they come in groups of tens of thousands.

There are problems even with these cases. It is not clear how plausible the case of buffalo actually is given the considerable variation in local topography found on the Great Plains and other parts of buffalo range. Just how many of these high hills are out there and how conveniently located are they? The tundra has some of these problems with the variability of the land surface as well. There is also the fact that almost no one has ever lived on the high tundra—certainly not in any great numbers—and we have almost no idea how they went about hunting caribou there. The problem with using high places to locate migrating wildebeest may have more to do with the scarcity or absence of "high places" from which to observe their movement than anything else. In any case, it is far more likely in the case of wildebeest that human hunters would have watched for the dust clouds the animals raised while migrating rather than for the animals themselves; not a big deal, but it does detract from that image of the noble and clever humans standing on the hilltop gazing off into the distance looking for game to go and intercept.

The problem is interpretive overuse of the idea in trying to understand hunting behavior. Long distance spotting occurs, but it occurs rarely and is a far less significant factor in hunting for a living than our popular and non-popular literature indicates. As noted earlier, all hunting is local. That means that while hunting does make use of the human ability to see long distances and to make careful use of terrain while hunting, hunting occurs at a scale of distance that is well below that assumed in the interpretation of human hunting as seeking the high ground to spot game at long distances.

There is the problem of distance and movement. The higher the ground, the taller the hill from which game is spotted, the greater the distance hunters must travel to intercept the game. Aside from the fact that the prey animals can, and generally will, move far faster than the humans trying to reach them, there is the fact that increasing the distance at which the hunter sees them also increases the number of directions in which the animals can travel and the number of routes the animals can take in the time required for the hunter to close with them.

Barring exceptional topographic circumstances that channel the movement of the animals through particular routes, in essence through choke points, increasing the distance at which the potential prey is seen is, beyond a reasonable scale of distance that can quickly be covered by a hunter on foot, of little immediate value.

Hunt 10

Caribou

Calves

AUGUST 1970

FOXHOLM LAKE, NORTHWEST TERRITORIES

H unting caribou is not just about meat. Aboriginal Denésuliné life depended upon the caribou as their primary animal resource. Hides, sinew, bones, antlers, and fat were all critical necessities for Denésuliné survival. A fact reflected in the deep emotional and symbolic involvement they have with their prey. This simple fact, that animals are used for far more than their flesh, is something that is difficult for people to understand if they have not experienced life in this manner. The emotional and symbolic involvement of the Denésuliné with their prey is even harder to grasp and factor into the attempt to understand the Denésuliné and other hunting peoples. Even if our intellectual understanding of the point is sound, most people lack any experience of the natural world comparable to the depth of the involvement hunting peoples have with the prey upon which they depend. The absence of that experience complicates the effort to grasp the deep emotional aspect of bringing down animals that is so critical to the Denésuliné relationship with the caribou. In situations where Westerners try to reconstruct or interpret the actions and behavior of hunting peoples, their lack of practical experience and emotional and symbolic involvement lead them to take too narrow a focus. They often forget or overlook the fact that the use hunting peoples make of their prey is but one part of a complex of practices, symbols, and values.

Caribou had come early to Foxholm Lake in the summer of 1970. They were present from our arrival at the lake in mid-June. From mid-June through to late July they were taken sparingly for fresh meat. The hides, with their seasonal short hair, were saved in quantity. Some dry meat was made, but it was not until the sheaths of fat began to build on the backs of the bulls in late July that the women began serious dry meat production. Two weeks into August the camp was well into laying up an abundant supply of dry meat. Caribou were available in sufficient supply for the women to be able to devote time and effort to drying necks, ribs, and other bony parts as well to boiling bones for grease. The women were busy, but their work was that which came from abundance rather than from shortage, and they were able to engage in a range of subsistence activities often absent in years when caribou were scarcer.

Among the things they were concerned with was the presence of infants and toddlers in the camp. Since they planned to remain in the bush until the Christmas season, they had determined that the toddlers would need caribou hide clothing for the coming winter. A special dress set of clothing would have to be made for the day of their return to the village. Because of the toddlers' small size and their lack of strength, these sets of clothing would have to be made from the thin hides of calf caribou.

Because cow caribou and many of the yearlings are far to the east at the calving grounds in June, it is normally the bulls that first arrive at Foxholm Lake. In early August the cows and calves began to arrive. The women, who had long known that they would need calf hides, had said little about it because there were no cows and calves at the lake. They immediately made known their need for the calf hides upon the arrival of the cows and calves. It was not a high priority for the men, but it was a need that could be met.

Once again, hunting is not a sport. Indeed, the concept of hunting as a sport would be essentially incomprehensible to most Denésuliné, if not an actually sickening concept. Hunting for calf hides—shooting calves off their mothers—is not a pleasant task. The calves were still nursing, had never seen humans before, and had no idea that humans were a threat. Like the very young of virtually all large animals, they are cute, playful, and essentially defenseless. Where and how sentimentality is applicable is a cultural variable, and the men never talked about this among themselves, but it was clear that no one was particularly thrilled at the prospect. It fell to Wellington, George, and me to complete the task.

At the time we were camping in tents on the north shore of Foxholm Lake (L on map 1). We had moved from the hillside on the bay close to a mile to the east of where the float plane that brought us had dropped us off. The new camp was on the east side of the bay on a triangular shelf of granite projecting into the lake. It was partially covered with sand so that parts of it had what passes for soil in this country. There was a partial ground cover of reindeer moss and lichen. At the back of the camp the ground sloped gently upward for some two hundred yards until it reached the higher rocky ground inland of the north shore of Foxholm Lake. The campsite was bounded on the west by a patch of timber along a stream that flowed into the lake. On the east, the shore curved out into the lake and rose to higher ground (perhaps twenty to thirty feet). Late in the day the three of us walked about 75 yards north of the tents then turned northeast for 150 yards or so, where we entered a relatively flat, dry, reindeer moss–covered meadow of perhaps three quarters of an acre. The meadow was scattered with erratic boulders up to half the size of a small car (H-10 on map 1).

The cows and calves had entered this meadow from the east and were wandering around feeding. The calves were at most two months old. They were small and still nursing. The weapon of choice for taking them was the .22 rifle. This small caliber weapon has sufficient stopping power to kill a calf with a well-placed shot and has the virtue of not making so damaging a wound as to ruin the hide by punching large holes in it, as the shell of a large caliber rifle would. A .22 shot would take the calf down but it did not make enough noise to frighten away the calves' mothers. Ignoring their own potential peril as we began to take the calves, the cows ran around their fallen young, bleating and calling to them. At times we had to shoo them away from their dead calves by walking toward them and shouting or making other kinds of noise.

The half dozen calves that were taken (along with one cow) were quickly skinned and butchered. Unusually, the cow was gutted and carried back to camp otherwise intact. The calf carcasses were carefully skinned and then gutted. The heads were removed, but the carcasses were not cut into sections as adult caribou taken for meat normally were. Instead they were placed over one of the glacial erratics with the open intestinal cavity fitted onto the top of the rock. When we ran out of suitable erratics, the remaining carcasses were cut in half at the mid-back and placed upon one of the flatter erratic boulders. The flesh of the calves was never destined for human consumption as we had an ample supply of meat in the camp. However, this group of Denésuliné was reluctant to waste meat. With the cool nights and coming colder weather of fall, they felt this mode of storing the calf carcasses, even though the outer surface would be fouled by birds, would preserve them long enough to provide food for the sled dogs later in the season.

The calf skins were taken to the camp and turned over to the women. Because it was so late in the day, the calf hides were folded over and stored for the night. The following morning the women placed them out in the sun to dry, fur side down. The hides were staked into position so that they would not shrink as they dried. The hides were out all that day and were again brought in for the night. It took two days outside for the hides to dry sufficiently to be placed inside, where they were kept until the women had a chance to work them and prepare them for sewing.

Text 10

Hides

Use of animal hides by historic and prehistoric hunting peoples is one of the aspects of their lives most overlooked in interpreting how they lived and how they interacted with their environment.

Contemporary Denésuliné are no longer as dependent upon caribou hides as they were in even the near past (early twentieth century), but in the first half of this study they still made considerable use of them. They used caribou hides for winter clothing as well as for ground cloths, blankets, and sleeping bags. Besides keeping people warm, hides served almost as general-purpose cold weather tarpaulins used for everything from liners of toboggans to protective wrappers for things (including people) that had to be exposed to the cold.

Caribou hide has a number of characteristics that are reflected in the use Denésuliné make of it. Considering that a barren ground caribou bull runs about four hundred pounds, compared to twelve hundred pounds or more for a large moose or two hundred pounds for a large white-tailed deer, caribou hide is a relatively thin hide. It is thicker and apparently stronger than deer hide but thinner and less strong than moose hide. The females of these species are substantially smaller than the males, and the thickness of their hides reflects the difference in their size. Hides of bull caribou and bull moose vary a great deal in thickness over the animal, as the hide thickens to provide protection during intraspecific conflict. The hides of females are not as strong as the thicker hides of the males, but they are more uniform in thickness and far easier to scrape and work. Cow hides are favored over bull hides for all but a few special purposes. As the hides have to be hand scraped and hand worked, it is far easier to work a cow hide into a finer, more uniform, and more flexible finished product.

We call it a finished product rather than leather for a reason. The Denésuliné use two different processes to produce what can loosely be called leather. The closest analogy to the leather found in modern societies is produced by a process known as brain tanning (originally using the animal's brain to provide softening chemical action). This is a long and complex process—sometimes taking weeks—that is used to produce a prepared hide suitable for use as clothing, footwear, and gloves or mittens. Making this kind of leather from moose hide requires mounting the hide on a frame strong enough to support one or two women sitting on the hide. They must scrape it to a uniform thickness, carefully removing all the non-skin material from the inside surface of the hide. The hide then needs to be soaked for several days before all the hair can be removed from it. It then has to be treated chemically to remove all the fat from the skin. By the 1970s the Denésuliné had learned to make use of modern household chemicals to improve their traditional processes. When fabric softener became available at the store in the 1980s, they began to experiment with it as a means of removing the fat from the tissue. Once the hide had been stretched, dried, and soaked, and had had the hair and fat removed, it had to be worked until it was soft and flexible. Only at that point could the now snow white hide be smoked to add the desired brown color and an increased resistance to water.

This is a complex, lengthy, skilled, and labor-intensive process. The quality of the smoked moose hide that results can vary enormously. After all the work that is required to prepare a moose hide for the final step, smoking, failure can still result. Even a few moments of inattention while smoking the hide can cause it to come out too dark to be usable. A slightly incorrect choice of wood for the smoking fire or allowing the smoke to grow too thick can blotch its finish and result in a nearly unusable finished hide. The Denésuliné—particularly female Denésuliné—evaluate one another on the quality of their products. Reputations can rise or fall depending on how a moose hide turns out. When the process works, the result is a leather that is strong and flexible and that will breathe. It has tremendous insulating properties. The Denésuliné make moccasins, gloves, and mitts both as decorative items to wear around the village and as work wear. The difference between them is in the decorative beadwork placed upon them and the amount and type fur used as decorative trim. Work gear wears most quickly on the soles, palms, and fingers. Gloves in particularl are subject to being cut by axes and knives. If at all possible, damaged or worn items are repaired and kept in use. At least into the early 1990s, moose hide was irreplaceable for use in making mitts, gloves, and moccasins.

Denésuliné in this part of Canada rarely use moose hide for coats or decorative clothing (other than mitts and moccasins) and only occasionally make decorative clothing from it for sale, as do the Cree to the south. The primary drawback of tanned moose hide is that as a leather that is not oiled, it is vulnerable to surface moisture. Use in wet conditions or rain stiffens the leather once it has dried and greatly reduces its insulating properties. To protect their moccasins around town, where they were in and out of heated buildings, the Denésuliné favored wearing thin, light rubbers over them.

Going to all this effort was largely reserved for moose hide. The products that were commercially available through the store and by catalog were far too expensive and nowhere nearly as effective as the locally made hand- and footgear. The Denésuliné kill far fewer moose each year than they do caribou. Raw moose hide is always in short supply. Often it is promised to female relatives by male hunters months, sometimes even years, before the moose is actually killed. Through the mid-1980s, when demand began to drop because of changes in Denésuliné life style and the improvement of commercially available substitutes, the skin of a killed moose was valued more than its meat and it would be recovered before the meat was.

The alternative to tanning and smoking a hide is to "sun dry" it and then scrape it into a flexible state. Caribou hide is normally prepared this way. Because it is a much thinner hide, it dries quickly and rarely has to be scraped to remove bits of flesh or other material from the inside of the hide. Processing the hide involves inspecting the inside surface to ensure that it is in the correct state for processing. Any bits of dried tissue are pulled off or if necessary scraped away. This is usually done with the fingers or a large spoon if scraping is needed rather than the heavy, specially made moose leg bone scrapers used for moose hide. Once the hide is deemed ready, it is laid flat, hair side down, and a handful of water is put on the hide. This is smeared over the inside surface, and the hide is then folded over and allowed to sit for a short while. When the hide has absorbed enough water to be flexible and ready to work, it turns a conspicuous blue color. Care has to be exercised not to soak the hide too much, as that greatly increases the amount of scraping necessary to prepare the hide for use. Fortunately, the wetter the hide, the darker blue it turns, so the color of the hide provides a guide to its wetness.

The preferred way to scrape the now damp and soft hide is to sit down before a heavy, smooth, woven steel cable (3/8 or 1/4 of an inch, whatever can be scavenged from village life or construction trash) that has been tied to tree trunk, the logs of a cabin wall, or a post set into the ground for this purpose. The cable is tied at its top and bottom so that it makes a bow away from the post and is flexible yet securely attached. (We do not know if this method, using a substitute for the cable, was a traditional method or if it is a replacement for a traditional method.) The person working the hide then sits in front of the cable and begins to draw the damp blue side of the hide back and forth across the cable. The hide has to be stretched as it is pulled back and forth.

This is a task that takes considerable strength and is hard on the hands and back. As the hide dries from the repeated motion back and forth across the cable, it tends to bunch up and shrink. The person working the hide repeatedly has to take the hide off the cable and stretch it, both as a whole hide and in smaller sections throughout the entire area of the hide. It takes several hours of work to finish a cow caribou hide in this manner. When the hide is finished, it has become snow white as well as soft on the inside where it was worked. The previously flat inner surface of the hide has become uneven and puffed up, almost fluffy in texture.

What should be noted about this worked but untanned leather is that it is prepared with the hair still on the hide. Caribou hide prepared with the hair on is extremely warm and extremely light. There seems to be an urge for every specialist who deals with arctic and subarctic animals and peoples to insist that the hide of their favored animal provides the warmest clothing in the world. We doubt that anyone has actually measured this, except perhaps the U.S. Army. In any case, caribou hide clothing prepared with the hair on is certainly near the top of such a list. Most of the men in this camp had spent many nights sleeping outside in temperatures below -20°F with just a caribou hide ground cloth and a caribou hide sleeping bag.

Caribou hide worked in this manner was the basis of pre-contact Denésuliné winter dress. It can be used for winter moccasins by making the moccasin with a double layer of hide: one side hair out, the other hair in. These are appreciated for their extreme warmth, but they are fragile and are made only when tanned moose hide is not available.

For all its virtues, caribou hide—both worked and as a raw, dried, hide—has its flaws. Caribou hair grows throughout the year. Come midspring, the new year's hair is just starting to grow in and the old hair is starting to be shed. Shedding is not a smooth or quick process. Patches of old hair can remain on the animal until well into the fall and sometimes into the following winter. From late spring through late summer, caribou often look ragged and blotchy from the patches of old hair adhering to them. If hides are taken during these times, they have to be cleaned of the excess old hair to be usable. The continued growth of their hair has other consequences. By mid- to late September, their hair has grown so long that Denésuliné women do not like to use it for clothing because it sheds too badly. This means that there is only a narrow window during the late summer and early fall when it is possible to take caribou hides in prime condition for making clothing. By October, Denésuliné will use the hides only for ground cloths, tarps, or prepared leather if they have any choice in the matter. Concomitant to the continuous growth of the caribou's hair is the tendency for it to shed. Unless hides are kept frozen—an easy thing to do in a subarctic winter—even worked hides will lose so much hair that they cannot be used for a second season. This means that making clothing from caribou hide that has its hair on for insulation has to be an annual process. Finished clothing cannot be stored for use in a second year.

Seasonality is a major factor in the use the Denésuliné make of caribou hide. Caribou are a heavily parasitized species. Parasites affect the suitability of their hides for Denésuliné use. As the fall progresses into winter the warble fly (*Hypoderma tarandi*) larvae that have been laid on the caribou begin to grow under the skin of the animals. These larvae, which can reach the size of a human thumb, are reported sometimes to parasitize individual caribou by the hundreds. They live between the skin and the muscle tissue, burrowing under the skin and feeding until they mature enough to leave the animal in the warmer weather of spring. They keep a hole through the skin open in order to breathe. To leave the animal, they burrow through the skin to reach the outside world. Both their feeding and their burrowing leave scars on the caribou's hide or holes through it. These holes are points of weakness where the hide can easily tear as it is being worked into leather. The damage they cause reduces the value of the hide for leather. By winter, unless there is no choice, caribou hides are not made into leather because of the damage from the larvae. They are not made into clothing both because of damage from larvae and because of the length of the hair. Winter hides or hides that are not in particularly good condition can still be made into small pieces of leather, but they are normally used for ground cloths and serve a tarp-like function. Their condition partly explains the willingness of Denésuliné to leave the hide on winter-killed animals to protect the meat from the dryness and cold.

The Denésuliné did make leather from caribou hide. The leather produced from caribou hide has much the same characteristics as hide worked with the hair on. It is lighter than moose hide, but it is also thinner and not as strong. It does not insulate nearly as well as moose hide does. Its primary contemporary use is for the flaps at the top of moccasins. These fold over to cover the pants leg and are tied together to make a seal around the pants and over the bottom of the moccasin. Making and using tanned caribou hide has been rapidly fading since the 1930s, but it was a critical resource for the Denésuliné before that time.

The use of caribou hide for clothing diminished with access to commercially made cloth clothing. Normal dress no longer involves hide clothing, but there are certain kinds of winter gear for which it remains preferred even if it is no longer irreplaceable.

The now infrequently made caribou hide parka and pants are the items most valued and the most difficult to replace with commercial gear. Making a complete outfit—a parka and pair of pants that fit over the bottom of the parka—requires the hides of several caribou. Cow hides with the very short hair of mid- to late August are preferred. There is no superior winter gear for the dry cold of the Canadian subarctic.

The demand for caribou hides in traditional Denésuliné life was far greater that it has been for the last century. White traders used log buildings from their first appearance in the country. The Denésuliné would have been exposed to them as soon as they entered direct contact with the Hudson's Bay Company traders after 1715. The ancestors of Denésuliné now trading into the area around the village would have been familiar with small log cabins from that point onward. Trading posts were not established in areas close to these Denésuliné until the nineteenth century. As some Denésuliné began to winter at the trading posts, they would have begun to build log cabins for their own use. These should have appeared around the trading posts by the middle of the nineteenth century.

It is not clear when the Denésuliné began to build log cabins for their own winter residences out in the bush. Until they did, they continued to use tipis (Osgood 1933: 97) as their year-round residences. Even after they began to use log cabins, they continued to use tipis as their primary residence during late spring, summer, and into the serious cold of the fall. Many continued to use them year-round until well into the twentieth century. Smaller versions of the tipi form were used for shelter while traveling and for all-male winter hunting and trapping trips. The same form was used to make "tents" for smoking meat as well as for menstrual seclusion huts or for giving birth.

Some of these tipis were constructed from spruce. Spruce tipis are still made, often serving as outhouses in bush camps. The use of spruce branches as the covering for special purpose tipis reduced the demand for the caribou hides from which tipis were normally made. A tipi requires many hides. The accepted figure given by elders in 1969–70 was twenty-seven hides per tipi, although a few thought it was possible to get away with twenty-two for a smaller tipi. Caribou hide used as part of a tipi covering did not have a long life. It is not clear from the elders' memories if a new tipi had to be made every year or if it was possible to get longer service out of one. The opportunity to store the tipi when it was not in use as well as variations in weather, local conditions, and the care given the tipi during transport or storage when not in use were factors affecting how long it lasted. There is a bit of an image among those elders of the time of going out onto the tundra as a time of having to make a new tipi.

As mentioned earlier, caribou hide provided their winter clothing. Outer clothing for winter use would have been made from caribou hides prepared with the hair still on the pelt. Leather made from caribou hide would have been used for clothing year-round. It would have served for winter clothing that was worn mostly inside or under the outerwear. It is not clear just how many sets of clothing an individual would have. A complete winter outfit was a major undertaking: parka, pants, footgear, clothes to be worn under the outer wear, gloves and/or mitts, and a weapons case. It is unlikely that a hunter would have had more than one set of outerwear. Still, it took a considerable number of hides—again, cow hides were the preference—to outfit a hunter. There was less agreement on this number in the memory of the elders, but seven hides per hunter is a safe minimum number.

Besides the hunters, everyone else in the camp would have had to have been clothed. There was no stated memory by the elders of just how many hides this would have taken or of just how much clothing any single person would have had to have. Clothing in the subarctic is a serious matter. Not only is there the problem of extreme cold—there is the near constant risk of hypothermia from exposure to water. When the problems of the cold vanish, insects are out in force. When they are out in force, being covered in the bush is not a question of convenience or comfort. It is far more serious than that. The blood loss and skin damage they can cause are serious threats to human health and the ability to function. People have to be covered year-round (Hearne 1958: 198).

The issue here is simple. Clothing and housing people in the subarctic using caribou hide means there is a tremendous demand for caribou hides. The demand for hides is cumulative, and there were many more uses to which caribou hide was put.

Caribou hide was the source of the cordage used to make nets and snares. Denésuliné winter hunting as well as summer hunting out on the barren grounds made heavy use of nets and snares to capture caribou. When people set up drives, with or without fences, or when they established fences to lead caribou to a central point, those central points were in effect corrals. Wood is scarce on the tundra. Where wood would be used as fencing in the forest, on the tundra they had to use brush and netting. The nets made from strips of caribou hide had to be strong enough to hold a caribou until someone could approach it to dispatch it.

Nets were also used in the forest during winter. How many and how much we simply do not know, but we can be certain that they were used (Hearne 1958: 49–51). Some of the usage on the patches of tundra found on high places within the forest would have been much as during summer on the tundra. Nets were also set along the trails caribou made when they came off the lakes to feed. Again, how many, how much, and how often are ethnographic unknowns. However, they were used and were another source of demand for caribou hide. The Denésuliné also set snares for caribou. They used snares in conjunction with pounds both on the tundra and in the forest. They also set them along the winter trails caribou made through the snow. With a caribou snare, the intent is not to kill the animal but to immobilize it until a hunter can come to dispatch it. This requires a cord of sufficient strength to hold a desperate, struggling animal that weighs several hundred pounds.

The Denésuliné also made fish nets. They made their fish nets from caribou hide. By all accounts they were difficult to make, did not work very well, and were abandoned as soon as cord nets became available through the trading posts. Still, nets were once another source of demand for caribou hide. By the same token, other Denésuliné fishing gear was also made of cord from caribou hide. Not a great source of demand for caribou hides but one more thing among many demands. Jigging for fish through the ice in winter was a major source of food during travel or moving camps from place to place. They would have been careful to make their gear and keep it in shape.

The list is probably endless. Aboriginally, Denésuliné used dogs as pack animals. Toboggans were used, but they were pulled by women rather than dogs. The dogs needed pack sacks and other gear; all were made of caribou hide. Storage containers were needed for holding meat and other goods. If moose hide was not available for footgear, caribou hide had to do. Everything the Denésuliné had that was to move from camp to camp had to be packed or dragged on a toboggan. There was demand for caribou hide to provide cord, sacks, harness, and countless other things.

This demand for caribou hide has to alter the way we look at Denésuliné hunting. So far, as in most of the literature on humans and related species, hunting has been viewed in terms of food production. We think it should be clear by now that this is not an adequate perspective. Hunting to meet the demand for hide is not more important than hunting for food, but it is clear that it is nearly as important as hunting for food. The issue would not be so significant if the hides taken as a byproduct of hunting for food were sufficient to meet Denésuliné needs. This is not the case. There are several points at which the demands for food and the demands for hides are in conflict.

The most conspicuous point of conflict occurs in the fall hunting when the Denésuliné are trying to lay up meat, dry meat, and fat reserves for the winter. By the time fall arrives, the cows are beginning to recover from the stresses of birthing and nursing their calves. Although they are starting to recover, they have not yet recovered and are not in prime condition. The quality of their meat is improving and suitable for human use, including for making dry meat, but they have not built up fat the way the bull caribou have in preparation for the rut and the coming winter. However, at this time the cows' hides are in prime condition for working with the hair on for making winter clothing. The holes made by the season's warble flies have healed as well as they will ever heal, and the hide itself is as intact and unholed as it will ever be. The window of time in which this is true is, at most, but several weeks. This is not only the best time to take hides for winter clothing (and for quality leather); it is an irreplaceable time. If it is missed, the Denésuliné have to make do with inferior quality hide, which will result in inferior quality winter clothing. Something that might haunt them throughout the entire winter and into midspring.

In late July to early August the caribou start to build fat for the winter season. By late August into mid-September, the fat buildup on the backs and rumps of the bulls can exceed an inch and a half in thickness. This fat is the critical resource for humans having to cope with the caloric demands of a physically active and demanding outdoor life in the intensely cold weather that normally comes with the late fall and early winter before they retreat to the village for the Christmas season. The meat of the bulls is also at its best at this time of the year. Winter meat storage, both as dry meat and as frozen meat, as well as fat production have to focus upon the bull caribou.

At the same time that the cows are starting to recover and their hides are in prime condition, the bulls are at their peak condition of the year. They have built up substantial fat reserves to carry them through the rut and into the winter. Their hides are in prime condition, but bull hides do not really work for clothing. They are useful for tipi covers and other heavier duty usage but not for being tanned with the hair on. When it comes to making dry meat or putting up meat for winter use, this is the time of the year when bulls are most desired. The fat buildup on the caribou is the crucial issue. Bear, which are generally scarce—Paul's best year in his life was the one in which he killed five black bears at Foxholm Lake—are the only alternative source of animal fat. They cannot be counted on to provide an alternative to caribou fat.

By October the bulls enter the rut. The onset of the rut seems to vary from late September (rarely) into November, with October the accepted time. It has a dramatic effect upon the bull caribou. Aside from the weight loss that comes from the bull's frenetic activity and fighting, the hormones that prepare it for the breeding season change the internal chemistry of the animal. Its meat takes on a pinkish red color and it develops an unpleasant taste and smell. Coupled with the weight loss from increased activity, the fat layer rapidly begins to be used up (as well as turning red). In effect, the animals soon smell and taste bad and grow skinny. The Denésuliné saying is that eating the meat of bull caribou just after the rut is like eating ice.

Drying meat is about the condition of the muscle tissue of the caribou. The taking of fat is about the nutritional status of the caribou as it prepares for winter. Making clothing is about the condition of the animal's hide and the length of its hair. Making leather is about the condition of the hide itself and the absence of damage caused by the maturing of the winter infestation of warble fly larvae. Taken together, these factors pose a set of somewhat contradictory demands.

Setting aside meat for the winter, making dry meat, and building up stores of caribou fat all indicate that taking bull caribou should be the hunter's priority. During our time frame, this was where their energy was directed. As the demand for caribou hides has steadily declined since the Denésuliné stopped making their own clothing out of caribou hide and switched to building winter cabins, what happened during the first half of this study probably mirrors the situation that prevailed for the eighty or so years before that. However, when the Denésuliné lived in tipis and made their own clothing year-round, the balance of energy expended in taking cows for hides and bulls for food must have been different. The conflict in demands was definitely there. Exactly how it differed from what we saw and how the Denésuliné resolved those conflicting demands we shall never know.

A partial way out of this conundrum is provided by yearling animals and cows that fail to become pregnant. Yearlings of either sex do not face the demands of pregnancy and lactation. Their hides are in good condition. The only drawbacks to focusing upon them—aside from issues of prey selection that we take up later—are their relative scarcity and lack of the fat buildup found on the bulls.

We think this discussion of hides has significance for understanding the behavior of other hunters elsewhere in time and space. For those who inhabited cold climates, it should be clear that the need for animal hide was a significant factor in their lives. It could well have exerted as much influence on how they went about hunting as it did upon the Denésuliné. The Denésuliné need for caribou hides is not something particular to them. The prey species differ from place to place and over time, but the basic situation does not change: humans need clothing. It is unlikely that the flesh of Neanderthals or *Homo erectus* froze at substantially different temperatures than does the flesh of modern humans. Temperatures in the subarctic routinely drop into the -40°F to -50°F range. If you live in the cold, you need clothing to protect you from it. Protection from the cold means complete protection from the cold. In subzero temperatures humans have to be covered from head to foot. If human ancestors lived in subarctic conditions, they must have had the technology and the knowledge to make functional clothing that covered them from head to toe and kept them from freezing.

As noted, it was not just the cold. Humans also need clothing to protect them from the insect infestations that characterize the boreal forest and the tundra. You cannot survive there in your birthday suit. If you try it, the insects will kill you. The insects seem to go with the country and the climate. They were certainly there in the past. That means, simply, that if humans lived there, they had the technology and the knowledge to make clothing to protect themselves from the insect populations.

Certain points about how humans hunted and lived follow the proposition that animal hide was the basic material for human clothing in the deep past until cloth became widely available. Hunting was not solely a matter of procuring food. It would also—perhaps equally—have been about procuring animal hides and other animal materials for use in clothing and for other purposes.

This has its own consequences. Humans are specialists in hunting and killing medium-sized game, game that ranges from under a hundred pounds up to game that weighs a ton. Humans could and did kill megafauna, but they never specialized in hunting and killing the megafauna. Remember what we said earlier, that killing is the easy part. All it takes is a cutting blade into the abdomen, something that will cut the intestines as the animal moves. Once this blow is delivered, the animal is dead. All people have to do is commit the time and travel to wait for it to die of the wound and ensuing infection. Bringing down the megafauna has never been the issue. The issue is what the megafauna could and could not provide.

This is partly an exercise in scale. Humans are not terribly large animals. There is a size range that humans can handle and make use of, and humans have always tended to hunt and depend upon animals falling within that size range.

People certainly killed megafauna when they could. They may have hunted these animals for ritual purposes. What they did not do was hunt them for daily subsistence or to meet their other needs. A dead mammoth might provide an awful lot of meat until it went bad. However, how do you make children's clothes or the clothes for an entire camp from the hide of a mammoth? How do you work the hide to the point that it is thin enough and soft and flexible enough to be put to the myriad of human purposes? If nothing else, trying to use such thick hides for these purposes would have so increased the demands on the labor of the women of the group—who have to scrape the hide and reduce it to a uniform and usable thickness—as to risk their ability to perform their other tasks.

The need for hides directed human hunting toward smaller and more usable animals, Ones with hides that could be worked and put to use. People needed animals with body parts that could be used for tools, sewing, or a thousand other purposes; animals with flesh in quantities that could be worked, prepared, transported, and stored. Even if humans routinely made use of the megafauna for food, they would still have had to pursue mid-sized game actively in order to meet the myriad of needs for the material required for them to live.

Recognizing this issue of scale and human need has another consequence that should affect how we look at other hunters, past and present. The subarctic is a severely restricted environment in terms of the resources it offers humans attempting to survive in it. Humans were never purely hunters if they had any choice in the matter. They have always sought out and exploited a diversity of resources to develop a subsistence system making use of the diversity of resources available. Wherever they had access to a richer, more diverse environment, any human population or ancestral species would begin to exploit those resources.

Hunt 11
Jackfish

MAY 22, 1975

SMALLTREE LAKE, NORTHWEST TERRITORIES

By late May caribou were long gone from Smalltree Lake. The lake ice had melted away from the shoreline. The snow pack was almost gone, but we had one more six-inch snowfall to come the following week. In places, open water was as much as ten feet from the shore. It was possible, slowly and with considerable difficulty, to use the aluminum boat from the fish camp to get out and move up and down the lakeshore near camp. In camp the dry meat making was near its end. All that was left on the dry meat racks were a few of the thick, heavy pieces that required longer to dry than did the smaller, thinner pieces of cut meat. The latter had long been placed into storage.

This was a period of enforced inactivity for the men of the camp. The lake ice was usable only by pulling the boat over it, a tiring and dangerous thing to do. There was not enough open water anywhere on the lake to justify the effort and risk involved in getting to it. Fish taken by rod and reel would have provided a change in diet, but the open water along the lakeshore was not wide enough to bother with trying it.

As an escape from inactivity and to check the country for sign of game, George began to make walking trips out into the bush. On May 22 he was out on one of these trips. He had taken along the teenage son of a widowed elder brother who was spending the spring with us. As always when Dené-suliné men are in the bush, he was watching for game. They were moving along the shore of the lake when they encountered jackfish (northern pike, *Esox lucius*) in one of the inlets with heavy reed growth along its shore. He shot several with a .22 and brought them back to camp.

This led to several days of our taking the boat out along the shore searching for more, but there were few suitable bays and we were unable to find any more.

When the ice first melts away from the shore of the larger lakes in the spring, it melts most rapidly at river mouths, stream inlets, in the shallow water of bays, and around the shores of islands. As the small lakes and bays lose the ice along their edges, female jackfish come up to the shores as part of their breeding behavior. Apparently territorial, they occupy preferred locations in reed beds in shallow water. The most dominant females tend to be the larger ones, and they prefer quite shallow water close to shore. They come into such shallow water that although their heads remain underwater, their backs are often out of the water and their fins project several inches into the air. Jackfish can grow quite large. The females in the reed beds often exceed thirty pounds.

Large fish in a few inches of water less than three feet from shore are quite visible. They are accessible if reasonable caution is taken in approaching them. Shooting them is done from shore. It is necessary to identify the fish you are after and approach it until it is possible to get a clear shot. They are generally approached from an angle. Care has to be taken not to startle other jackfish in the reed bed lest one is scared into fleeing. If one goes, the others will follow suit and all will vanish in a flash. In shooting the fish, the idea is to kill or cripple it so that it cannot escape to deeper water. The ideal first shot is one that breaks the spine to immobilize the fish. All that then remains is to wade into the water to retrieve the fish.

Obviously, this would have been a good time to take them by spear. The fish are so aggressive about taking and holding their place at this time of the year that the Denésuliné regard them as a routine source of food for the local wolves.

Our search for jackfish continued for several days, but as the water on the lake opened up, attention shifted to fishing by rod and reel from the boat and to taking the occasional waterfowl out on the lake.

Text 11

Women's Labor

To understand Denésuliné hunting and subsistence, it is necessary to talk about women's labor. The Denésuliné are a small-scale society. Over the long past their population was small and was scattered over a vast area. Even in modern times this has consequences for those trying to live in the bush. As one drifts backward in time, modern technology and the resources that came with involvement in the fur trade vanish from Denésuliné life. Their absence intensifies the effects that come from being a small-scale society scattered over a vast area. Subsistence had to come from locally available resources. There was no escape to a village or trading post when things went wrong in the bush. Large settlements or gatherings were rare and could not be sustained for long. The bush was all there was. Normal life for the Denésuliné was that of small camps. These had to be highly mobile as life was a constant search for resources.

Because so much of Denésuliné life was lived in small camps, each with a small number of individuals within each category of life—adult male, adult female, youth, elder, etc.—there had to be a certain flexibility within the division of labor. When illness or accident strike a small camp, the necessary chores of human life do not go away. The fire has to be kept going regardless of whether or not people are sick. Firewood for that fire has to be gathered. Children in diapers still have to be changed. Moss for the diapers still has to be gathered. Water still has to be hauled in from the lake. Most times in a camp of twenty people or so, there are still functioning individuals able to perform these tasks when illness or accident strikes. Most times, it will be possible to maintain the sexual division of labor in the completion of necessary tasks even in the face of illness or accident. Most times, illness or accident strikes individuals within a camp rather than the entire camp. In a camp of twenty people there may be three adult men or three adult women. The numbers provide a buffer; others can fill in for the sick or injured.

The smaller the camp, the fewer individuals there are to occupy the various roles and perform the designated tasks within a sexual division of labor, the less this holds true. The buffer that comes from numbers diminishes. It is in circumstances like these that women are most likely to have to act as hunters for the camp. If the scale moves to that of a married pair living alone in the bush in order to establish their independence, that buffer is gone. Spending time in bush camps of fewer than twenty people was a normal part of the life cycle of Denésuliné prior to World War II.

Because of the risk of illness or injury in a small to very small camp, and because men have to get out to hunt and trap, it is sometimes necessary for women in bush camps to spend time alone or only in the company of other women. Because men do go off on hunting or trapping trips, they have to spend time in the bush when they are alone or only in the company of other men. This has consequences for the division of labor: individuals of each gender have to be competent in the basic work skills of the other gender. If men are to live alone in the bush or only with other men, they have to know how to cook, how to make bannock, how to sew their torn clothes, how to clean the camp site. If they want dry meat, they have to know how to make it. If they need a freshly worked caribou hide with the hair still on it in order to repair or make a winter garment, they have to know how to prepare the hide and how to sew it. If women are to live in a small camp where they might find themselves alone or only in the company of other women, they have to know how to get out and get firewood. If there is a fish net in the water, they have to know how to go out in a boat to check it and recover the fish within it. They have to know how to care for the tethered sled dogs. They have to know how to set snares and obtain food. They have to know how the rifle works and be proficient enough in its use to take large game.

The sexual division of labor is exactly that: a sexual division of labor. It is not an individual division of labor and it does not mean the skills of individuals of either sex are limited to the tasks they preferentially perform within the sexual division of labor. The tasks allocated to each gender within the sexual division of labor are reserved to those occasions when individuals of both sexes are present in sufficient numbers to allow them to follow the conventions of the division of labor without destroying the necessary functional operation of the group.

Although we presented the section on making dry meat in as gender neutral a manner as we could, it should be apparent that making dry meat is women's work. Making hides is women's work. Sewing is women's work. The nature of the work taken on by women in Denésuliné society is such that they do not have periods of enforced idleness. No longer needing to make stone tools and weapons, among so many other things that used to have to be made, has left a void in men's activities that can lead to periods of boredom and idleness. Women have not had this problem. Women's work is relatively constant. It has its peaks and valleys but it never so diminishes as to force women into long periods of inactivity. Boredom is an intermittent condition in Denésuliné bush life, but it is a disruptive one. Traditional Denésuliné are active individuals who use work as a means of staving off boredom. Even today, the individuals who thrive in bush life are physically active. We have seen periods of inactivity sufficient to lead women to seek out tasks that they do not have to perform in order to cope with those periods of inactivity, but those periods do not reach the intensity or duration of those affecting men when they cannot get out of camp and into the bush.

We do not want to give the impression that we are saying that it is just that women are saddled with "busy work" or the routine tasks of child rearing and camp maintenance. Women's labor and the products of women's labor are the crucial factors in determining the economic and social success of the camp. It is their ability and willingness to perform the productive tasks they engage in that determine not only how comfortable life within the camp will be but how successful the camp will appear in the eyes of other Denésuliné.

Before the fur trade introduced a source of income to the Denésuliné, along with a supply of goods to be obtained with that income, the measure of a camp's social reputation rested on the products that could be obtained by hunting. Then, as now, this was a male task. It was the skill at which a man had to display a sufficient degree of competence if he were ever to be able to marry. There obviously were differences in the skill and competence of individual men. Borderline competence at procuring basic food and materials from the bush might well have restricted a man and those attached to him to a life of political dependency or at least to a lack of independence and a life lived in a subordinate position within a larger group.

However, the differences between men were measured less by the quantity of meat or other resources they could produce than by the products that the labor of the women attached to them could create from the raw materials they supplied. Appearance mattered among the Denésuliné. Success and prosperity were judged in part by how the tipis looked as well as by the look of the clothing people wore. All of these were the result of women's labor. Sewing, like preparing hides or drying meat, was seen to reflect variation in the skill, character, and creativity of individual women. Other Denésuliné noticed the quality of the hides women prepared. They would see the hides on the tipi; they would sit on hides when they visited. Guests would share food and would notice if the dry meat was well prepared. They would notice the clothing worn by the individuals within a camp. Denésuliné women, in particular, paid attention to the quality of the sewing done by other women. Sewing was a task all women performed; a task that interested them. They would examine sewn items, noticing the quality of the stitching and decoration as well as the execution and choice of designs upon the clothing.

The quality of a woman's work reflected not just upon her own reputation and the social assessment of what she had accomplished; it also reflected upon the reputation and status of her husband and that of the entire camp in which she lived.

The amount of work that fell to women was staggering. Hides had to be prepared, both as leather and worked with the hair on. Cooking, childcare, pregnancy and childbirth, housekeeping, sewing, dry meat making—the list seems endless. Traditional Denésuliné did not use dog teams. Dogs were pack animals. The Denésuliné used toboggans, but as mentioned earlier they were pulled by women rather than by dogs. When camps moved, the men ranged out searching for game while the women moved the camp. It was women's year-round responsibility to pack, load, and then pull or pack the entire camp and everyone in it to the location of the next camp.

Denésuliné women's work tends to make different kinds of demands upon the human body than does men's work. Women's tasks now rarely involve heavy lifting or pulling. Few require sprinting or running. Tasks that require raw strength are shifted onto males. The tasks women have to undertake are nevertheless tiring and demanding. Their successful completion takes perseverance and endurance. Women's tasks are varied in their nature, but many of them are sedentary. These require the ability to stay put and engage the task with constancy, often for hours at a time. Much of this time is spent sitting upon cold ground. Constant sitting while engaging the upper body, as in preparing hides, places considerable strain upon the back. Hand strength is at a premium. Pulling and stretching hides, holding and swinging a bone scraper to smooth a moose hide, or twisting and pulling a caribou hide that is being worked with the hair on all place very different kinds of demands on the body than do tasks like cooking, cleaning, or getting firewood, which allow the individual to be up and to move about.

Sewing and beadwork, which even during the time frame of this work could demand hours upon hours, have their own demands. It is close and fine work that demands careful attention to detail. Sewing is indoor work often conducted under conditions of poor lighting. The close vision that sewing requires, particularly in the absence of eyeglasses and modern vision care, generates eyestrain and headaches and, over the long term, is deleterious to vision. Sewing is indicative of a whole category of tasks women perform that require dexterity rather than raw strength.

The tasks women have to perform under the Denésuliné sexual division of labor are not just demanding and tiring—they are endless. Male tasks, which demand different kinds of persistence and endurance, are based more on raw strength and exposure to risk. The difference between them is almost, to make a bad analogy, like the difference between aerobic and anaerobic activity.

There are consequences to the difference in the nature of male and female tasks. Many female tasks can be conducted within a small area and are ones that can be done in the company of others engaged in the same task. They allow a degree of socialness generally lacking in male tasks. This applies especially in small camps where so much male activity involves solitary travel in the bush. Much of women's work is so labor intensive that it generates a particular kind of disparity between men's and women's work. Men are essentially generators of raw materials. Women are generators of finished products. When the raw materials are from animals' bodies, the quantity that can be procured reflects variations in the abundance of the local animal populations. It helps if we think in terms of a single pair of people: one man producing raw materials for one woman to process. In bad times the issue is producing enough raw material (meat) to prevent starvation. The rest of the time raw material can be generated in a far greater quantity than it can be processed into a finished state.

Under normal circumstances a reasonably competent and reasonably hardworking man is able to generate more raw material than a single woman is able to process into finished material. This creates a productive advantage to social arrangements that allow women to work in the company of other women engaged in the same tasks.

Since so much of the reputation and status of a social group as well as the reputation and status of the male(s) attached to it depends upon the work of the women of the group, the division of labor creates an avenue for the expression of will by the women. Skill varies from woman to woman, as do other variables in the production process, such as strength and motivation. Motivation has many components. We are not going to push the implicit analogy between labor, capital, and a production process too far. Any analogy with a work stoppage or strike would be going beyond what our data can support. Nevertheless, we can also note that slowing down or working less hard or less skillfully are viable ways for women, either individually or collectively, to express dissatisfaction with the circumstances of their lives or relationships with others in the group to which they are attached.

Even though the work women have to perform is quite consistent from woman to woman throughout their life cycle, the same cannot be said for their temperament. Denésuliné women vary from person to person as much as do women anywhere in the world. The same is true for Denésuliné men. Some are more physical or more athletic. Some are more reflective or aggressive than others. Some enjoy physical activity more than others do. Some individuals enjoy isolation; others do not. The work may be the same for all Denésuliné, but the interests and temperaments with which they approach that work are not.

From the standpoint of the camp as a social group engaged in a set of tasks necessary for its survival, there is a value in having a balance of temperaments within the camp. The tasks camp members have to engage in to survive are so varied, and the physical and climatic conditions in which they live are so demanding, that different temperamental characteristics within the group can add to the camp's chances of survival. Hyperactivity can be a burden in an urban setting or a classroom—both for the individuals and for those around them. That same hyperactivity can become a survival advantage when the impulse toward physical activity drives a hunter to get out and hunt while other hunters think hunting is not worthwhile and choose to stay in camp. The shyness that drives an individual to avoid the company of others and seek solitary activities can become an asset to the group's survival when translated into sewing, or making arrow shafts, or engaging in other productive activities when no one else has the time or inclination to engage in them.

This is more than just a question of individuals seeking out that which suits them. There is a decided advantage to the camp's operation and survival if among its members there is always someone who is driven to more physical activity—and if there is always someone driven to seek solace in solitary work, or someone who will question or wonder about and go out to check on what the animals are doing and where they are. The issue is not the specific temperaments but the balance of temperaments. Maintenance within the camp of a sufficient variety of temperaments makes the group more effective at exploiting the resources and opportunities the environment presents.

Hunt 12

Bear

Stalking Prey

At Foxholm Lake the summer of 1977 did not follow the expected pattern. It was a warm summer and the lake levels were low throughout the country. Many river and stream mouths that were normally passable by boat and were key junction points between water routes were blocked. Boulders normally far enough below the water surface to allow the safe passage of our boats projected to near or above the surface. What had been water passages became portages, something annoying when traveling by canoe but far more serious when traveling by aluminum boat. Many entire streams were now so filled with projecting boulders or sharp rocks that they were unusable for water travel.

The insects—both black flies and mosquitoes—remained in force nearly to the middle of August instead of vanishing to a minor nuisance by the end of July. It was late in the season when caribou finally arrived at the lake. We were camped in tents on the sand hill at the point by the narrows between the north and south shores of Foxholm Lake. Until the caribou came it had been a summer of frustration, of eating fish and wishing for caribou. When the herds did come, they did not remain on the lake. They would be present for a few days, only to vanish overnight, not to return for several days or a week, sometimes remaining away for nearly two weeks.

During one of these periods when the caribou had vanished in mid-August and the camp was low on fresh meat, George decided the two of us should take an afternoon off from the other things we were pursuing to search for caribou. We took the boat and headed east along the north shore of the lake, following the route we would have taken to go to Joe's Camp. We had gone but three and a half to four miles east of the camp when we saw a black bear feeding in a wet (but not muskeg) area a few yards from the shore.

The wind was from the north, and we were west of the bear's location, so scent was not a factor. George killed the motor on the boat and we paddled carefully toward shore about a hundred yards west of the bear. The shore consisted of cobbles and rocks punctuated with a few boulders, but unlike most rocky places along the shore, the tops of the rocks barely extended above water level. There was water between the rocks all the way to the shore. A low ridge, no more than twenty feet high, extended from a hundred yards inland down almost to the shore. Where George chose to take the boat to shore, this ridge was between us and the bear; it could not see us from where it was feeding.

We tied the boat and carefully headed inland, George in the lead. We stayed along the base of the west side of the ridge, moving at a quick walking pace, making sure to minimize the noise we made. George followed the ridge to where its northern base emerged from the higher ground inland before he moved up onto higher ground. He turned east toward the bear. On the higher ground we were inland among scattered timber, but after we topped the ridge we came out onto open ground. We were now perhaps two hundred yards inland and about thirty yards west of where the bear was still feeding. The bear, which proved to be a thin old animal with many missing or broken teeth, was concentrating so intently on feeding that it did not see us. Once we got into the open and saw it, we watched it closely as we moved east. The bear seemed oblivious to anything other than the food it was searching out in the wet area—apparently sedges and roots.

As we moved away from the ridge along the higher ground inland, wind direction and scent became an issue of concern. The farther east we moved, the more the wind would blow from us toward the bear. George quickly headed to a spot directly in line with the bear but between it and the higher ground inland that was its logical escape route. He closed to within a hundred yards of the bear before sitting down to shoot. The distance between us and the bear was a result of the wind and topography rather than a function of the distance itself.

Experienced Denésuliné hunters sometimes kill denning black bears with axes by constricting the den exit so that the bear can be struck in the head with the flat of the ax as it attempts to leave the den once disturbed. Still, bears are formidable creatures. He wanted to stay on the dry ground higher than the wet flats where the bear was feeding and be far enough away from it to have time to react if things went south.

Once we sat down, we were able to watch the bear and talk softly for a moment or two as we prepared to shoot. George wanted both of us to shoot at the same time. We fired together and the bear dropped to the ground. As a safety measure, George, Wellington, and Paul all carried their rifles without a shell in the chamber and often transported them unloaded. Like many Denésuliné men, George had more than one rifle, but he had only a single ammunition pouch, one made and decorated by his wife. To fit whatever rifle he was using at the time, he often carried shells of different calibers in his ammunition pouch. George's rifle had been unloaded for the boat trip. As we approached the bear from the boat, he had not taken time to load the magazine of his rife. As we sat watching the bear, he decided to fire his rifle in single shot mode rather than taking the time or risking the noise that might come from loading the magazine.

After his first shot he was in a hurry to reload his rifle for a second shot in case the bear was not dead. Watching the bear instead of his hands, he loaded his rifle with the wrong caliber shell. The shell jammed in the chamber and could not be quickly extracted, so he was unable to fire his rifle again. As it turned out, the bear had been knocked down but not killed. It bounded to its feet and had to be shot again.

Once we were sure the bear was down for good, we went down to inspect it. George prepared to skin and butcher it. Bears are large animals, and their hides are thick. Skinning a bear, particularly a fat one, is not a quick or easy process. Most of the hide has to be removed by cutting it away from the carcass rather than separating it from the carcass by hand, as is done with caribou. With a fat grizzly bear there is so much fat adhering to the hide that once the hide is removed from the animal and laid out on the ground, it will very visibly twitch and move around as the fat cools.

The Denésuliné kill far fewer bears than they do caribou or moose. George had had little practice at skinning bears and this was only the second one he had ever butchered. This one was not a fat animal, but it still took him quite some time to skin it. While he worked on the bear, I went back to get the boat and move it closer to where the bear was down so that we could load it into the boat more easily. The shoreline rocks near where the bear was being butchered proved worse than where we had first beached the boat. Rocks just below the water surface extended at least ten yards out into the lake. It was difficult to find water deep enough to get the boat close to shore or to move anything (including ourselves) over the rocks to the closest place it could be left without damaging its bottom. The situation was worsened by the fact that it was rapidly getting dark.

George took the hide, prepared the head symbolically to protect his relations with Bear, and took some of the meat. Because the bear was old and not in good physical condition, he sharply restricted the amount of meat from it that he was willing to take back to camp. Not until well after dark were we able to get the boat loaded and out into deeper water to head back to camp.

Text 12
Prey Choice

The Denésuliné almost always pursue certain animals whenever they are encountered. For wolf and bear this makes a certain kind of sense because of their size and the value or utility of their hides; the same applies for moose because of the value of moose hide in leather making. Many of the fur-bearing species are pursued regardless of the season. Even if the fur is unsalable, it has value as trim for clothing. It would be convenient to advance an economic rationale for the Denésuliné willingness to pursue these animals, but an economic explanation will not work. If Denésuliné hunting is not just about food, neither is it just about the commercial value of the animals they hunt. Among the species the Denésuliné try to kill almost every time they encounter an individual are beings such as the loon or the merganser. These are not creatures with any commercial value. The amount of food they provide does not justify the time or cost that the Denésuliné are willing to put into trying to kill them.

Geese provide another curious case. They are large birds, and the Denésuliné are quite fond of eating them. When they fly over a camp someone is almost certain to run out with a rifle and try to shoot them out of the air. Yet at least along tree line, the Denésuliné make almost no effort to hunt them systematically. Rifle shells are expensive, and the quantity the

Denésuliné can afford to take into the bush is rarely close to what they would like to have to last them a season. Yet they will often expend four or five valuable rifle shells trying to shoot geese out of the air. It may be possible to shoot them out of the air, but we have never seen anyone succeed when they attempted it. Waterfowl in general and ducks in particular are another resource rarely hunted systematically away from the vicinity of the village. Close to tree line, hunters take these birds if they are encountered while hunters are out in a boat and if they have a .22 along. They do not shoot them with larger calibers—(unless hit in the neck or head, not much of a duck is left if they do)—and make no systematic effort to search the ponds for them or go out hunting them.

Denésuliné hunting and prey choices are not reducible either to economic analysis or to other analysis that is based upon some kind of rational choice assumption. It does not matter if the analysis refers to calorie yield, work expenditure, or time usage. Economic theory or theories based upon the assumptions that underlie economic theory just do not work (Gould 2002: 121–25). There may be great value in attempting to model in economic terms the hunting behavior and the choices hunters make in allocating their effort and resources, but that value is limited by the fact that the resulting model is no more than a model of what people do—not of why they do it. Causality—the reasons why Denésuliné do what they do and make the choices they do—rests within the realm of culture and the field of meaning it generates. In the case of the Denésuliné, the causality for what, why, and how they hunt rests within their conceptualization of animals as simultaneously natural and spiritual beings and the relationships that exist between the Denésuliné and those animal/spirits. In other words, the causality of Denésuliné hunting behavior rests in the Denésuliné conceptualization of the moral order of the universe and their place within it.

The topic of this section has been a matter of much discussion between us. While trained in behavioral ecology I (Karyn) admit that there are many aspects I still have to comprehend fully. However, in my perspective the advantage of an economics-based assessment is that it provides a measure. Every archaeologist or behavioral ecologist would acknowledge that there are day-to-day influences and cultural factors that affect human behavior but are not evident or retrievable. Trying to assess human behavior based on nothing more than "what may be possible" results in a myriad of plausible outcomes. The human imagination is capable of conceiving almost any scenario to which a person must respond or that one might encounter. Trying to assess human behavior based on cultural preferences or human desire cannot truly provide any way to understand past human behavior effectively, or as a whole, in the same kinds of ways that are evident archaeologically or evolutionarily. I try not to hypothesize about the symbolic conceptualizations or systems of meaning of our ancestors; we can barely understand our contemporaries' symbology and meaning, even though we can communicate with them directly.

The Denésuliné approach is culturally specific. Although elements of their culture are shared by other Northern Athapaskan peoples, their culture is theirs alone. It is not something that can be used as a template to explain the hunting behavior of other hunting cultures elsewhere in time or space.

Recognizing that the causality of Denésuliné hunting behavior rests in the specificity of their culture poses a serious issue for the interpretation of hunting behavior in cultures elsewhere in time, where ethnographic work is not possible. It means recognizing that the causality determining the hunting behavior of those societies rested in realms that have no presently knowable physical expression, as we are currently able to read physical remains. There is at present little we can do about this other than to recognize that knowledge of this causal layer is absent and to be sensitive to its absence in our choice of the kinds of explanations we offer and in deciding what can be inferred from physical remains.

This hunt and the moose hunts (Hunts 2 and 7) serve as illustrations of how hunting tactics and techniques must vary as a function of the kind of prey being hunted. A far greater degree of specificity is involved in hunting animals that are found individually than in hunting animals that are customarily found in groups. With those found singly, the hunt is focused upon a specific animal in a specific place and under specific conditions in a manner that does not apply to caribou, which are usually found in groups spread out over a considerable area of ground. The most obvious variation comes in the way stealth is used in the approach. With single animals it is much more necessary for hunters to conceal their presence completely from the prey. Hunters must much more completely hide their scent as well as hide their movement and the sound they make. Animals that normally live singly are far more likely to flee at the first indication of a human presence than are herd-living caribou.

Hunt 13
Missing Hunts

There are a series of kinds of hunts that have yet to be considered in this account. These are contemporary ones that are solitary in nature or ones using techniques that have now passed from Denésuliné practice. What they share is that we have not witnessed them. Because we have not seen or participated in them, the kind of information we can present about them is different than it is for hunts we have witnessed or in which we participated. An adequate understanding of Denésuliné hunting requires us to speak about them, but in the absence of direct observation and participation, our accounts need to be considered in a different manner than is what we say about hunts we have actually observed or in which we participated.

Solitary Hunts

The vast majority of Denésuliné hunts are best characterized as the actions of a single hunter who encounters game while out and about in the bush. Contemporary solitary hunting is normally an adjunct to other activities, such as running a trap line. It is of note, however, that Denésuliné men are capable of moving through the bush by themselves even in this harsh and dangerous environment. This is not something that can automatically be presumed of other human hunters or those of other species. There may have been many times and circumstances in which a single hunter was simply too vulnerable for hunting to be a solitary activity.

Denésuliné men always go armed into the bush. They are always hunting. Hunting is what they do; hunters are what they are. It is their identity as well as their occupation. They are always prepared for an encounter with game and prepared to make a kill if they have any need for the animal they encounter. Denésuliné men make their living in the bush; it is their workplace. They spend much of their waking time in the bush and go there for an enormous variety of reasons.

Deliberate pursuits, when the hunter enters the bush seeking sign to follow up as in Hunt 2, are quite rare among the contemporary Denésuliné but happen more with moose than with other animals. Moose hunting has characteristics different from caribou hunting. Moose are not migratory in the same sense that caribou are migratory. They are far more likely to remain within a defined area for an entire season than are caribou. The Denésuliné of the boreal forest know the areas where habitat is favorable for moose and are well aware of the local history of successful moose hunting. Hunting moose is likely to be a planned activity that involves making a trip of several days to an area known to have a high probability of having resident moose.

For caribou, situations like those at Smalltree Lake in 1975 are more common. The difference lies in the way these hunts were organized. The need for caribou was understood. It was the reason the group was in the bush at all as well as the reason they were camping where they were. Nearly every day George, Wellington, and Paul went out looking for caribou. Caribou are migratory and they were in the process of migrating at that time. Their direction of movement was known. The country and circumstances were different from those in Hunt 2. The caribou were moving up lake ice. It was possible to see them from long distances away, unlike moose, which prefer the much denser cover of the forest. The actual process of hunting was organized on a different basis than moose hunting would have been. Instead of picking an area of good habitat and searching it for a resident animal, as in Hunt 7, the hunters could let the caribou come to them. They would each day choose an area or a direction they wished to venture into, a side of the lake or a direction of travel. Within this designation—intended as much as anything to keep them from interfering with each other and out of range of each other's weapons—they could conduct long distance visual searches. The idea was to create a situation that placed them so as to increase the chances for that accidental or opportunistic contact to happen.

Times when the need for caribou is so forefront in Denésuliné bush life are relatively infrequent and generally seasonal. Midwinter, early to midspring, and late summer to early fall are the times of the year when large numbers of caribou are most needed by the Denésuliné. They are the times of the year when this deliberate search aspect of hunting is most common among the contemporary Denésuliné. Over most of the year meat is needed in lesser quantities. Hunting can become an adjunct to other activities. The previous statement needs to be thought about carefully. Among those Denésuliné who still choose to live part of their lives in the bush, hunting is still the basis of male identity. Hunting is a continuous state of being in the bush, but the Denésuliné do have to do things other than hunt.

Away from the times of demand for large quantities of meat, most Denésuliné hunting comes as a result of accidental contact with a prey animal when hunters are out and about for reasons other than hunting. If caribou are seen—and needed—while the hunter is out checking his trap line, pursuing the caribou will take precedence over running the trap line. If game is spotted while on a journey, and is needed, pursuing it will take precedence over the trip. If game is encountered when it is not needed or if the contact is too far away from camp to transport back any game that is killed, then the game will be watched. The Denésuliné enjoy the presence of the animal/spirits with which they share the land. They are perfectly willing to stop and enjoy the presence of animal/spirits without pursuing them.

Over the course of a season—in earlier times over the entire year—most of the fresh meat a camp consumes derives from these accidental encounters with prey rather than from deliberate hunts. The bulk of the meat a camp consumes will come from the processed and stored yield of deliberate hunts, but these accidental contacts with prey are the basis of the continuing supply of fresh meat that is so crucial to Denésuliné nutrition and health.

Winter Hunting

Winter hunting in a bush camp falls within the pattern of hunting by accidental contact while out and about in the bush. It mostly occurs when the hunter is moving over his trap line and encounters game. There are odd occasions when there is an inadequate supply of meat in the camp, and the hunters will make a deliberate trip out in search of game. This usually happens when caribou move into an area the camp normally exploits after the animals have been out of the area for some time. At least since the start of the twentieth century—we do not know when the Denésuliné in this area adopted the routine use of dog teams—winter caribou hunting has been based upon movement by dog team.

Winter hunting out of the village is a different kind of activity than is winter hunting out of a bush camp. By the Christmas season almost the entire population has retreated to the village for the seasonal activities and the sale of any fur that has been trapped. After the Christmas season ends, few individuals and fewer families return to the bush. The concentration of people within the village creates a great demand for meat. Even families from bush camps that had plentiful supplies of meat rarely have the financial resources to hire a large enough ski plane to transport back to the village both themselves and enough meat to supply them through the balance of the winter. Traditional methods of transport—a dog team pulling a toboggan—are not able to pull a large enough load of meat to be a useful means of bringing in meat from the far outlying bush camps, because they also have to carry supplies and gear for the trip. Many of the bush camps are more than ninety miles away from the village. It takes too long and is too hard on the dogs to make multiple trips between camp and village just to haul meat. Snowmobiles can make the same trip much more quickly than a dog team can, but the distances involved are often beyond their safe operating range.

The demand for meat is aggravated by the state of the caribou herds. The herds the Denésuliné of this village use went into a "crash" situation during the 1940s. It is the nature of caribou herd dynamics that caribou have to maintain their numbers within a narrow range. If the herd size gets too large or if it gets too small, the population will crash. Caribou population dynamics are a contentious issue that we will happily leave to biologists but crashes in caribou numbers are a regular feature of Denésuliné life and have been recorded many times in the past since Europeans arrived to keep written records. On the ground, the consequences of a crash are dramatic. The size of the herds can drop by 90 percent within a year or two. The caribou herds had not returned to their earlier size by 1970. Their numbers improved but remained erratic through the latter part of the twentieth century. Since the serious onset of climate change—in the north it is warming—with the onset of the twenty-first century, caribou have become a borderline threatened species for which the future is uncertain.

The consequences of the World War II crash in the caribou herds showed up in changes in their winter range. The herds ceased coming as far south as they had come in the recent past. At the height of their numbers in the earlier part of the twentieth century, caribou ranged far down into Saskatchewan and even crossed the Churchill River during their winter movements (Jarvenpa, personal communication). After 1950 caribou wintering as far south as the village became an unusual occurrence, and during winters when they did come that far south, they did not come in numbers approaching those of the past. Wintering caribou sometimes did not come within seventy air miles of the village, and their presence was erratic even there.

This created a particular kind of midwinter caribou hunting dynamic out of the village. If word came that caribou had been sighted within range of the village, about a ninety-air-mile maximum, individual hunters would load a dog team and depart the village almost as soon as they got the word. During the winter of 1969–70, when hunters learned that caribou were on Selwyn Lake ninety air miles away in the Northwest Territories, it was possible to sit all morning by the window of a cabin in the village and see a dog team and hunter depart the village every three or four minutes to start on the trail north after caribou.

These hunts were of a particular nature. The initial caribou sightings were often by pilots rather than from within the Denésuliné population and usually indicated that large bunches of caribou had been seen from the air on particular lakes. This information did not indicate how widespread the caribou were or how far they ranged from east to west. The Denésuliné would all head toward where caribou had been seen. They departed individually but often joined other hunters as they traveled north, because they all used the same trail. If they encountered anyone traveling south on the trail, they would be able to get updated information about the situation farther north.

The key to finding the caribou once they arrived in the general area where the caribou were thought to be was information from other hunters and the trail network the caribou created as they departed the lakes—which can be more than forty miles long—and moved inland to feed. Even in midwinter and deep snow, caribou are mobile animals that move around a lot; the trails departing the lakes tell the hunters where the animals have been and if they are still using the routes. Although the hunters departed individually, they camped in groups. Joint camps provided security, company, places to get the latest information, and a safe place to leave the sled dogs.

The actual hunting was conducted individually or in small parties on land and by foot. The key was locating the caribou while they were dispersed to feed. On the lake ice the caribou could see the hunters from too far away and were liable to flee en mass. If disturbed enough, they could easily move to an entirely different lake. There was also the problem of the sled dogs when hunting on the lakes. Sled dog teams will pursue caribou on sight, and it is almost impossible to stop them once they have taken a mind to chase caribou. Being chased by a dog team does nothing to settle a bunch of caribou or make it easy to approach closely enough to get a good shot.

An area where caribou were present in numbers could quickly end up with a number of small camps and quite a few hunters. If hunting pressure became too great or if they were disturbed too much, the caribou would move off to a quieter area. With so many hunters moving into an area, the caribou would often remain only a day or so before moving on.

Each hunter was able to transport a maximum of two to three caribou back to the village. The animals that were killed were gutted but usually not skinned and only sometimes dismembered before their transport back to the village.

As time passed into the latter part of the twentieth century snowmobiles and later all terrain vehicles replaced dog teams for use close to the village. ATVs came after our fieldwork in the village, so we do not know their effective range out from it. The usable range of snowmobiles was still in flux into the early 1990s. The machines could quickly cover distances of ninety or a hundred miles. The trip north that was an overnight two-day journey with dogs was but a half-day run for a snowmobile. The drawbacks of snowmobiles involved mechanical reliability and gasoline usage. It was a long walk back if the snowmobile broke down. By the mid-1970s some individuals had already had to make midwinter journeys of forty miles or more on foot after a snowmobile broke down. Gasoline was expensive, and the space committed to carrying fuel cans was hauling capacity that could not be committed to bringing back meat. Contamination was also an issue when transporting fresh meat in close proximity to oil and gasoline.

Snowmobile hunting has other problems. The speed of the machines makes it possible to run right up on a caribou herd on a lake, which has damaging effects upon the energy expenditures of the caribou. They live on a knife's edge in terms of energy expenditure, and being chased around by snowmobiles does not aid their survival. The machines are also noisy, another disturbing factor for the caribou. Perhaps the biggest problem deriving from snowmobile hunting had to do with who used the machines. The older, more experienced hunters had the least access to them. The people who could afford to buy them were the most westernized youth of the village, the very people who were least experienced in hunting and dealing with animals. The speed of snowmobiles made it possible for the youngest, least knowledgeable, and least responsible parties to make quick excursions from the village without guidance from those older and wiser, a situation that led to unnecessary stress upon the herds as well as excess kills and wastage of what was killed.

Endurance Hunts

One of the first things to have vanished from Denésuliné hunting with the arrival of modern repeating rifles was endurance hunting. Endurance hunting is a category unified by a common feature: pursuing game until it is exhausted beyond the ability to flee. It does not mean pursuit until the prey dies of exhaustion. It may not even mean pursuit until the prey lies down from exhaustion. All that is required is pursuit until the prey reaches the point that it stops and turns, allowing the hunter to close with the animal. Turning and facing pursuit is sometimes an effective strategy for dealing with wolves—the only other predator that attempts endurance hunting of caribou or moose—but it is not effective against the weapons humans use and have used.

Endurance hunting requires deep snow to be useful against a healthy prey animal. It can sometimes be used for a wounded prey animal when there is no snow, but in the absence of deep snow, even a wounded animal is liable to move too far and too fast to make the practice worthwhile.

In either case, the issue is endurance and the behavior of the animal. Wounded deer have a tendency to flee only until they feel they are no longer threatened. At that point they lie down to recover. Their adrenaline levels drop, their body temperature drops, and their muscles stiffen. They continue to hemorrhage and often enter shock. It becomes more difficult for them to regain their feet and resume their flight. When in pursuit of wounded prey, it pays the hunter to allow a certain amount of time for the animal to feel secure enough to lie down and stiffen up. If the animal is healthy enough to regain its feet and move off before the hunter can reach it, the hunter needs to increase the pressure by forcing the animal to keep moving until it can no longer sustain its escape. It becomes a judgment call as to whether a wounded animal that flees the place where it was wounded is worth the effort of continued pursuit.

It is necessary to remember that it is not just a question of being able to catch up with the animal and kill it. Consideration must involve how far the animal can move. Killing it is pointless if it has moved so far that its flesh cannot be transported back to where use can be made of it. The remains of any other animals killed at the time another was wounded may also be an issue: it does little good to pursue a wounded animal only to have scavengers destroy the remains of others that might have been killed at the same time.

When the prey is a healthy animal, the technique seems to have been used on moose more often than it was on caribou. As a moose hunting technique, it was probably only a technique of desperation for times when there was no other food available. As on a contemporary moose hunting expedition, pursuit seems to have been more of a planned search rather than the result of a casual encounter. Running down a healthy moose could be an affair of several days. Moose are semi-territorial, more like white-tailed deer than caribou. At the least they have some sense of a preferred area. When they are pursued they are more likely than caribou to use circling movements to stay within a familiar area. Caribou, although reluctant to leave the frozen lakes in winter, are far more likely than moose simply to take off and keep moving away rather than circling. This tendency does not make them any easier to run down, but it at least keeps the kill within a closer distance from the start of the pursuit than is the case with caribou.

With both animals, the key issue is the use of snowshoes. These greatly increase the speed at which humans can move through deep snow and allow hunters to move through snow conditions that would otherwise immobilize them. Humans are not nearly as fast as either moose or caribou. Although both species are faster than humans and can run for considerable distances, they are not endurance runners. Their escape from predators is based upon sprinting away such that predators decide it is not worth the effort to continue the pursuit. Other than wolves, most predators, at least among the cats, are not endurance runners. When a human launches in pursuit of a healthy prey animal in deep snow, he is forcing the animal into a form of energy expenditure for which it is not designed. Snowshoes allow the human hunter to sustain a steady, rapid pace that is fast enough to allow the animal no chance to rest and recuperate before exhaustion sets in and the hunter can close with it.

It should be noted that in this type of hunting, the Denésuliné often delayed the actual killing of the animal once they were able to close with it. An animal in a state of exhaustion has its blood supply largely dispersed throughout its muscle tissue. This gives the meat an unpleasant taste. Particularly if the animal is on the ground, allowing it to recover enough to begin to stir improves its taste, so there is a preference to wait until the animal begins to stir and show signs of trying to rise before killing it.

Given the limits of human physical ability, endurance hunting is obviously not a first choice. It requires a hunter in exceptional physical condition and was most likely limited to hunters in their mid-thirties or younger. Using the technique as a way to maximize the take from an encounter of several hunters with a group of animals by pursuing those that were wounded and escaped is plausible as a routine practice. While some hunters went in pursuit of the wounded game, those not up to the pursuit could butcher and prepare the game already killed.

Running down animals may never have been common practice, but memory of it is a significant feature of contemporary Denésuliné understanding of their past. It is likely that the ability to run down a healthy animal in winter was highly valued and that it afforded considerable status to those able to do it. Memory of this having been done likely serves as a marker of just how difficult life was in the past as well as a prideful indicator of just how rugged and capable their ancestors were.

There may certain conditions of snow cover that would decrease the time of pursuit involved in running down a healthy moose or caribou, as there are for wolves pursuing the same animals, but determining exactly what those conditions were or how often they occurred reaches beyond our data.

Snares and Nets

Snares are a staple of Denésuliné food production although they are currently used only for small game. Snowshoe hares are the favored prey. The Denésuliné have become partial to snares made of brass wire, which is light, flexible, and strong. It is also easy to use. Wire snares are most commonly used after snow has covered the ground and the trails the animals use have become visible to the person placing the snare. With small animals, the snare is placed so that the animals become caught in its loop as they move along the trail. As the animal fights the snare, it closes and tightens around the neck. It can cause suffocation. With small animals, if the snare does not kill by suffocation, the animal is immobilized and unable to reach shelter and may die from the cold. Before wire was available the Denésuliné had to make snares from locally made cord. Caribou hide was likely the most frequently used material, but within the boreal forest it was possible to use other kinds of materials as substitutes.

The Denésuliné used a variety of deadfalls as a substitute for snares in taking small animals. They were also used for trapping fur-bearing animals once the fur trade began. They do not seem to have played a major role in food production.

In the past snaring was not restricted to use on small animals; animals as large as caribou were snared. These much heavier and stronger snares were made from caribou hide and were designed to catch the animal by its antlers rather than by closing around the neck. They were regularly used in conjunction with pounds erected on open ground. With large animals the snare was not designed to kill the animal but to prevent it from escaping until a hunter could approach it and dispatch it. On open ground, posts—if available—could be sunk into the ground to hold the snare. If strong trees or saplings were present, the snare would be attached to the trunk. If they were lacking, the snare would be attached to a pole that was left on the ground. Once the animal was caught in the snare and attempted to flee, the pole dragging after the animal would become entangled and prevent its escape.

It is not possible to determine how often snares were used by themselves as a means for capturing large game. Hearne's account (1958: 49–52) from the 1770s indicates that pounds and snares were used all winter long. Snares were one of the regular means of capturing caribou driven into the pounds constructed on the barrens or in open areas within the forest. Details about placing snares along caribou trails where the animals entered or left the frozen lakes are less clear. Some descriptions of how snares were attached to an anchor indicate that they were regularly used in areas that were either wooded or had substantial undergrowth. Some of the elders' statements indicate that snaring was a regular means of obtaining caribou even within the forest, but it was not possible to obtain any clear idea of where or how frequently.

The Denésuliné still occasionally used nets to capture game during the period of this work. Old fish nets would be set along lake shores for spruce grouse (*Canachites canadensis*) during the fall. These birds, which are very tolerant of a human presence, form large flocks in the fall. They fly quite close to the ground and can be netted effectively in places where a barrier—

such as a lake shore and its ringing vegetation—breaks up their flight over open spaces. At the height of the spruce grouse fall movement, nets were set along the shoreline even within the village. We were told of the use of fish nets to capture ptarmigan (*Lagopus lagopus, L. mutus*) in winter but did not observe it.

The nets used for large game were made from caribou rawhide. They were a primary means of confining caribou within the pounds that were the focal point of fences built upon open ground on the tundra. How nets were used for large game away from these pounds is less clear. Elders' statements indicate that they were sometimes used along caribou trails by frozen lakes throughout the winter, often in conjunction with snares, but it was not possible to get clear indications of how often they were used or the precise circumstances involved. There was no indication of any attempt to use nets for moose.

Water Crossings

Caribou are excellent swimmers. They swim strongly and quickly. They are comfortable in the water and enter it readily. Both healthy and injured caribou will run into lakes if under threat from predators. Wolves will sometimes follow caribou into the water and occasionally kill them there even when the water is deep enough for all of the animals to be swimming. Getting into the water is not a perfect escape for caribou, but it is often far safer for them to be there than on land. Most of the shorelines of the larger lakes are rocky and boulder filled. The land surface is elevated several feet above these rocks. Essentially, the edge of the land is worn down by the action of the lake ice as it moves around during break-up. This creates a shoreline consisting of a narrow rim several feet lower than the ground surface. By preference, caribou enter the water from places where they can walk into it. If they are under threat, they will jump completely over the shoreline and into the water from ground surfaces set well behind the rocky shoreline and above the water line.

Caribou are capable of—and comfortable with—long distance swimming, often choosing to swim across small lakes (a half mile or less in diameter) rather than following the shore. By swimming from island to island, caribou rarely have to swim more than a few miles to cross all but the widest parts of the lakes within the areas considered here. Still, caribou generally prefer to be on solid ground rather than in the water. This means that the local topography channels their movements.

Caribou do not feed in lakes as moose sometimes do. Their feeding areas lie on the land between the lakes. They remain in constant movement wherever they are, moving from feeding area to feeding area in a constant attempt to escape the insects that plague them until cold weather arrives. If they are moving in a direction that is intersected by one of the larger lakes, they tend to move parallel to its shoreline until they reach a place where entry into the water is easy and exit on the other side is readily accessible.

The predominant ground cover of reindeer moss is slow growing and easily disturbed. It can take decades to return to ground that has been disturbed. Even if caribou are only in an area for a few weeks every year, their passage damages the reindeer moss along their favored routes. Those parts of the land that are sand slowly become packed down where caribou pass over it. This causes their trails to sink slowly into the ground from repeated use. The land in this area is dynamic, but those places most comfortable for travel remain relatively constant from year to year. In most places in North America, game trails still mark the land. Here the trails are clearly visible; indeed, they are the most visible thing to be seen while walking the land. They form a conspicuous network used by species of all sizes for moving about the landscape.

The Denésuliné use these trail networks as much as any species. As predators, they read the network for its generations-deep history of the movements of any caribou that have used an area. Trails tell not only where caribou have been but where they are likely to be or at least the most likely routes by which the caribou will get to where they are going. This information becomes most useful where the trails intersect the lakes as it indicates to the Denésuliné the places on the ground where caribou are most likely to cross the lakes. Any information that makes caribou movements determinate—such as where they will walk or where they will enter or leave the water—is of immense value to a hunter trying to figure out where he should position himself to hunt. Because the caribou trails that lead to and from the lakes often pass through territory constricted by topographical features or vegetation, it might often have been more productive to ambush them along those trails than to hunt the water crossing itself.

Hunting caribou when they are swimming or when they enter or leave the water was a staple of Denésuliné subsistence for hundreds of years. By carefully choosing the water crossings they hunt, the Denésuliné are able to create certain useful advantages for themselves. Choosing a water crossing to hunt requires careful analysis on the part of the hunters. If they have boats—canoes—they are able to approach the swimming animals. The hunter needed to be at a sufficient height above the animal to be able to strike downward from inside the canoe with a spear, the favored weapon. Stabbing them in the kidneys was the favorite thrust. The chosen location needs water deep enough to allow them to approach the animals while they are still swimming, as if the canoe is below the level of the animal's back, the hunter will not be able to use the spear as intended. Caribou swim quickly, so the location chosen has to have water wide enough to allow the hunters in the canoe time to close with them before they reach land. A favored technique in verbal recollections of spearing caribou was to drive the canoe up over the back of a bull caribou until the prow rested between his antlers. This allowed the hunter to kill other caribou as the bull swam among the rest of the bunch. It freed the hunter from having to paddle the canoe, but it was a rather risky approach as a twist of the bull's antlers could upset the canoe. We have no evidence on how frequently this method was used.

Killing caribou in the water had certain advantages. Through practice, Denésuliné became skilled at reading the wind and water currents and were able to estimate where the caribou would wash ashore. This allowed them to establish a butchering and processing operation at that point, saving the labor of having to transport the carcasses to a central point.

It was not necessary to kill caribou in the water to take advantage of a water crossing point. Again, it is a question of choosing the right location. There has to be adequate cover to hide the hunters and their gear when the animals are approaching the crossing. It has been a long time since caribou in this area have been subject to predation by large cats or other ambush hunters. This has allowed their human predators to use the tactics of ambush hunting on them effectively. If there is a camp, it has to be far enough away from the crossing for the sight, smell, and noise of it not to deflect approaching caribou away from the crossing. This also holds for concealing canoes from the approaching caribou if the intent is to use canoes to approach the animals and spear them in the water. During the time from late June until the snow starts to fall in September, caribou are not the most cautious of animals. How difficult it would have been to avoid scaring them away is difficult to tell. Surface examination of known crossings indicated that there had been a considerable human presence around them; it may not have been too difficult to conceal hunters and their families and equipment adequately.

Entering or leaving the water is a time when caribou are particularly vulnerable. They are following a fixed route heading toward a fixed location. As their movements are always difficult to predict at a local scale, in choosing a crossing point to exploit there is always a risk that the caribou will not cross there or will show up in the middle of the night when no one is ready for them. Yet a careful choice of crossing point can lead to large payoffs. A hunt in a fixed location like a crossing allows the hunters to seek out those that have the best cover, which makes it easier to approach the caribou—an important consideration when spears or bows are the weapons in use. Under circumstances like this it was much easier to close with the animals so that a spear could be used than would be the case on open ground.

Killing caribou at a crossing is a dramatic image. There are particularly choice locations, still in use elsewhere in the NWT, that regularly produce kills of caribou. How common these places are and how frequent this practice still is are another question. Nothing we gathered from contemporary Denésuliné recollections of their past indicated much use of caribou water crossings to produce mass kills or even very large kills. The dramatic idea of mass kills at water crossings probably plays to images within our own culture that have given it a greater place than it deserves in our understanding of earlier hunters and hunting cultures. As with most things Denésuliné, what we see as activities involving many hunters and leading to mass kills were far more likely to be things conducted by a few hunters to produce kills of fewer than ten animals.

Drives and Pounds

Past Denésuliné use of drives and pounds reflects that their range was once centered upon the tundra (Hearne 1958; Gordon 1996). We do not understand the dynamics of their use of the tundra. Neither do we entirely understand their abandonment of their use of the high tundra. We do understand some of the factors behind the shift. Foremost was increasing involvement in the fur trade coupled with the nineteenth-century peace between the Denésuliné and the Cree that was brokered by the Hudson's Bay Company. The arrival of modern repeating rifles was certainly a major factor as they allowed a more effective exploitation of caribou at the tundra edges and in their wintering grounds as well as an improvement in the Denésuliné ability to take moose within the forest.

Several aspects of caribou behavior underlay the Denésuliné ability to live upon the tundra. The key to understanding this is recognizing that caribou center the birthing of their calves within a small area. Their reproductive strategy involves the cows gathering in a common area to give birth. Nearly all give birth within a three-week period. Coming together in a single location far out on the tundra reduces the number of predators that can be present for the birthing. Travel to and from the calving areas is difficult for large numbers of predators. Even though the period around the births would provide abundant prey, the predators have to eat before that period as well as after it, and the land simply cannot support them. The second factor is that the birth of so many young at a single time overloads any predators present. So many calves suddenly appear that the resident predators are not able to make a dent in their numbers.

Once the calves are born, the cow caribou disperse from the calving grounds but remain upon the tundra for the balance of the summer. Being out on the tundra in summer allows them to draw upon the summer growth of vegetation. It also keeps them far away from most of their predators—then dispersed to raise their own young—as well as keeping them in open country where the wind can provide some relief from the mosquitoes and black flies. Many yearling animals remain with the herds of cows for the summer. Many of the bulls do not go near the calving grounds, instead spending the summer on other parts of the barren grounds. On occasion some bulls spend the summer close to tree line, as happened in this area in 1970, when they were present on Foxholm Lake, hundreds of miles from the calving grounds, at least as early as mid-June.

From a Denésuliné standpoint, the crucial factor is that caribou are present on the tundra all summer long. It is simply a case of having to find them. When herd numbers are high, there are likely to be caribou nearly everywhere. When numbers are down, finding them becomes an issue. Aboriginal relations between the Denésuliné and the Inuit populations were hostile, making parts of the tundra dangerous for the Denésuliné to occupy. The ancestors of this group of Denésuliné roamed widely over the tundra south of the Thelon River across to Dubawnt Lake. Through the generations they developed a deep knowledge of the animals and the dynamics of their movement. Even though caribou movements are variable and unpredictable, the people had a pretty good idea about where to find them at each season of the year.

The first part of the survival equation came from the fact that the caribou are on the tundra all summer and that the Denésuliné had a good idea where to find them. The second part of the equation came from a quirk of caribou behavior.

When caribou are moving across open places—either on land or on lake ice—they display a behavioral oddity. Faced with a linear obstacle, they tend to turn and parallel the obstacle rather than crossing it. This is a most peculiar behavioral characteristic. Caribou spend at least half the year living in forest or scrub forest. The presence of trees does not bother them. Approaching a tree line or a forest edge does not deflect their motion or alter their course of travel. Although studies were conducted on caribou movement with the construction of the Alaska pipeline, we are not aware of studies determining what constitutes an obstacle in the mind of a caribou in natural surroundings out on the tundra. From Denésuliné statements as well as observation, it seems that linearity is one of the critical variables causing caribou to turn and parallel the obstacle. We do not know how caribou perceive linearity or if linearity is simply a human perception projected onto the caribou. Linearity is how Denésuliné perceive the situation and is the factor they use to exploit this behavioral characteristic of caribou.

The Denésuliné exploited this tendency to turn and parallel a linear obstacle by constructing fences on the tundra and on open spaces within the forest. Use of these fences was the basis of aboriginal Denésuliné subsistence upon the tundra. Bush pilots who fly over the tundra in this area confirm the stories of the Denésuliné: caribou fences are found on the tundra by the dozens. They are seen from the air in open areas along the bush pilots' routes of flight all the way south to Saskatchewan and are common from Wholdia Lake northward.

Fence may be the best word for what the Denésuliné erected to alter the movement of caribou, but in this case it is a somewhat deceptive term. Timber, by definition, is lacking upon the tundra. The Denésuliné had to make their constructions out of stone. This is not as intimidating as it may sound. The fences did not have to be continuous walls to be effective. They were made from stone piles that could be as far apart as fifty yards or more. What mattered was that they were sufficiently intrusive in the environment for caribou to recognize them as alien and that they were built in a line, causing approaching caribou to turn and parallel them rather than crossing between them. The fences were built in a simple V shape. The arms of the V could extend outward for more than a mile.

At the base of the V the Denésuliné built a corral. It was fenced with brush, stone, timber, nets, or whatever else the Denésuliné could find to create a barrier. Within the corral the Denésuliné placed snares and nets to entangle caribou that entered the corral until they could be dispatched. It was an elegant system that was made to work by the actions of the Denésuliné manning the corral. Individuals would be hidden along the arms of the V. As the caribou passed, they would come into the open behind the caribou to drive them forward into the corral. The opening of the corral could be quite narrow. There would be more Denésuliné hidden nearby to frighten the caribou through the opening into the constricted place within. Other Denésuliné could patrol the outer wall of the corral to keep the caribou from jumping over it or breaking through it. All these tasks could be done by women and children as well as by the elderly. The hunters themselves would be inside the corral engaged in killing both the free animals and those that had become caught within the snares or nets.

The system was frighteningly simple and effective. Entire bands of caribou that began to move along the fence lines within the V could be directed into the corral and killed. As long as the caribou were on the barrens—and they would have been along the edges of the barrens year-round except during population lows—the Denésuliné were able to survive there with little chance of need or want. In the area north of Foxholm Lake out beyond the area now in use—on the highland tongue at the southern edge of the high tundra—the living should have been both comfortable and secure all year.

There is an interesting conflict between how the Western world has come to see the use of fences and drives by the Dené-suliné and how contemporary Denésuliné themselves see their use. Northern Athapaskan caribou drives, with their fences and pounds, seem to be seen by Western academics as a phenomenon similar to the drives of historic and prehistoric buffalo hunters on the Great Plains. This image of prehistoric hunters driving buffalo off a cliff to produce a mass kill seems to underlie academic interpretation of Northern Athapaskan caribou drives. The conflicting element in this interpretation is the size of the human population involved and the amount of human labor required. These past hunts on the Great Plains, which are solidly established, tend to be seen as activities carried out by relatively large groups of people and designed to feed a relatively large population.

The Denésuliné understanding of the use of drives in their own past is quite different. They talk about drives as a labor-saving device used by small groups of people rather than as a large-scale activity. The implied size of the groups conducting the drives is about that of the camps considered here: fifteen to twenty-five people of all ages with a maximum of three to four adult male hunters. There is little question that a successful drive could provide the basis for a temporary large-scale aggregation of Denésuliné, but this is not the way contemporary Denésuliné talk about them.

Considerable circumstantial evidence supports the Denésuliné view that drives were labor-saving devices designed for use by small camps. The pillars of the fences were made of stone rather than wood. Stone construction sounds impressive, but again our images are drawn from our own cultural experience rather than Denésuliné cultural experience. The posts of the fence are stone piles. They have the advantage that once constructed, they last for generations. Building a stone pile high enough to deflect caribou is not a daunting task. Eddy, brother-in-law to George and Wellington, had a curious habit: he liked to build stone piles. He made them during breaks when he was working, driving earth-moving equipment, and he made them by hand whenever we stopped for lunch or tea in the bush. He ate faster than anyone else, and as soon as he finished, he would move off a few yards and start to build a stone pile. (It would be neater to call them cairns, but that invokes a different culture—although it was entertaining to show pictures of his stone piles to archaeologists and ask them what they were.) It took him about twenty minutes to build a waist-high stone pile more than two feet in diameter. His stone piles would have served well as posts in a stone fence to be used in a caribou drive.

The key point is that the time and labor involved in building each post in a stone fence for a caribou drive was not excessive. Three or four active men could easily have constructed fences of a mile or longer with just a few days of labor. Once the fences were built they would last for generations with minimal maintenance. The corral, which was made from temporary materials, likely took more time, work, and maintenance than did the fences. It might well have been possible to recycle or reuse entire fences or parts of fences, directing them toward different angles of approach to reflect the changing directions of caribou travel.

The labor involved in operating a fence and corral again seems to fit with Denésuliné images better than it does with Western images. Most of the labor other than the heaviest construction could be done by individuals of school age on up. A small camp would normally have had a more than adequate labor force to build a set of V-shaped walls and a corral. Presumably snares and nets, which would have required caribou hide to make, would have been prepared in earlier seasons. The actual staffing of the fences and corral again is well within the labor capacity of a small camp. Children old enough to run and listen to their elders—again, those of school age—would have been capable of manning the fence walls to shoo caribou toward the corral after they had passed where the children had hidden. Women and older children of the camp would have been an adequate labor force to handle the areas around the corral walls to keep the caribou inside as well as providing enough large, noisy people to scare the caribou through the corral opening as they approached it.

As with the use of water crossings, the Denésuliné image of drives and fences being the activities of small camps has the advantage of better fitting the scarcity of resources and the huge scale of distances in this land. No matter how effective a V-shaped fence and corral set up was, animal life was still widely distributed on the land and erratic in when it appeared at any given spot. A series of small camps dispersed over the land, each operating its own V-shaped fence and corral, is a far better match to the resources and ecology of this place than is the image of occasional large-scale, labor-intensive drives and pounds designed to produce mass kills to feed large numbers of people.

Text 13

Shadows of the Past

The consequences of the geological history of the Dené-suliné homeland affect the movement of caribou within it and how the Denésuliné exploit that movement. Their country is peculiar in a number of respects. The ground—Precambrian granite—is among the oldest rock in North America. As of the time of this writing, not too far away were known surface rock exposures that were over 2 billion years old, the oldest exposed rock known on the surface of the earth (http://www.natureconservancy.ca/en/where-we-work/ontario/our-work/canadian-shield.html). At the same time the area's land surface is among the youngest surfaces on the planet. Foxholm Lake and Smalltree Lake lie but a few hundred miles west of the core area where the Laurentide Ice Sheet and its predecessors formed. The Precambrian granite buried as bedrock over much of the continent has here been scoured of its covering rock and exposed at the surface by the repeated advances and retreats of the ice sheets since the Pliocene. Ice sheets in this area frequently exceeded two miles in depth: mountains of ice more than 10,000 feet thick covering the land.

Because the climate within a glaciation varies radically through time, ice sheets are not fixed. They come and go with considerable regularity. Denésuliné land has seen ice sheets advance and retreat many dozens of times. Each time an ice sheet passes over the area, it scours the land beneath it. Each pass can tear away the ground surface to depths up to three hundred feet, even when that ground surface is solid granite.

It is no particular surprise that the land of the Denésuliné has virtually no topsoil as the last of the glaciations did not vanish from their homeland until within the last 10,000 years, and nearby areas to the east were under ice until 6,000 years ago. The land is so newly emerged from beneath the ice that it was never part of the Mammoth-Steppe tundra (Guthrie 1990: 200–72) and was never inhabited by the Pleistocene megafauna. During those times the ground surface was not buried beneath ice, it was covered by reindeer moss.

Ice is heavy. More than 10,000 feet of ice is a very heavy load. The weight of the ice sheet caused the land surface of the Canadian Shield to sink into the mantle of the earth. This sinking was a substantial process. Hudson Bay was a highland area before the ice ages began. When the ice melted from the surface of the land, the ground began to float higher on the mantle. The ground surface began to rise. The land continues to rise today. Hillsides along lakes often show a series of old shorelines, not because the lakes were higher but because the land has risen—rebounded. The land is so newly emerged from glaciation that drainage patterns have not had time to mature and form fully. The meltwater from the glaciers, trapped at the surface by the permafrost, is still draining away. It seems as though the water level has been the constant, with the land rising through it.

The action of ice is diminished without ice sheets, but it is not entirely absent. Its presence is still marked by the permafrost. Permafrost impedes vegetation growth—particularly tree growth—and keeps the land full of water although in terms of precipitation the region would qualify as near desert. Frost heave in inactive bogs can sunder the covered ground, making green mossy meadows look as though dinosaurs have been playing football there.

The ice that forms on the lakes each winter may be a poor substitute for an ice sheet but it is still a powerful force in shaping the land. During break-up each spring, the fractured ice covering the lakes is driven around by the wind. These sheets grind against the shores, reshaping and re-creating them. Boulders are moved about. Vegetation is crushed and carried away. Inlets may have their connections to the lake sealed, becoming isolated ponds, only to be rejoined to the lake again by movement of the ice in a subsequent year. Connections between lakes are opened and closed. Narrow rocky junctions between lakes can be purged of the rocks and boulders that fill them, turning two separate lakes into a single entity.

The land of the Denésuliné is one of constant change; change that is observable within the span of a human lifetime. The passage of but a few human generations can bring radical change to the lives of all who live here. This applies as much for the animals and the forest and tundra as for humans. The relationships that exist among the large animals that inhabit this land are new ones. Because the land was ice covered, no megafauna trod here. The caribou that are the basis of life for both wolves and humans are recent immigrants. They arrived as the glaciers vanished and the reindeer moss tundra established itself. The wolves came with the caribou. Humans entered the mix but a short time later.

The Denésuliné hunt this land. Their lives and the lives of their families come from their understanding of the land and the animals that live within it. Their success as hunters or trappers often depends upon the skill with which they can read the land and make use of its layout at a very local level to exploit the resources that live within it. The land and its conjunctions with the water that is so abundant change so frequently at a locally observable scale that it is impossible for people not to notice the changes as they walk the land. Changes can often be seen from year to year, sometimes from season to season. Over the course of a lifetime they are inescapable. Whatever the land is, it is not static and is not seen by the Denésuliné as a static entity. Although it has diffused into the culture in the last few decades, "Mother Earth" is not a traditional Denésuliné concept. Nevertheless, the Denésuliné see the earth as it is: an active, dynamic being that shapes their presence and provides for their existence.

Each kind of hunt now missing from Denésuliné life was an adaptation of the available technology to the then current environmental conditions and their expression in the state of the caribou herds. Like all humans, the Denésuliné experiment—knowingly or unknowingly—with technology and adapt its use to the circumstances and conditions that surround their lives. Each kind of hunt represents an adaptation of technology to a particular set of circumstances; each missing hunt carried with it its own particular patterns of thought and social practice. A missing hunt is a reflection not merely of a change in technology but of a change in how and where people lived and how they related to their environment.

Thinking about those types of hunts that have vanished from Denésuliné culture, as well as the social and ecological relationships that vanished with them, leads to an interesting question:

How Long Is The Memory Of Unused Technology?

It would be nice if we had an answer for this question but about all we can do is raise it and note that in our understanding of human history, it is one of those areas where presumption has substituted for knowledge.

Part of what we are reacting to is essentially a perceptual problem in the understanding of past human hunting cultures; one that transforms the continuously varying process of living with and adjusting to changing conditions into a stable and almost static state. This comes partly from being unable to think about things that occur through deep time in increments measured by the human life span. The transitions between human generations are rarely well marked in time and are almost never marked by physical remains. Neither is the variability in environmental or climatic conditions that routinely occurs within the space of a human life span. Technology leaves more traces in the fossil record than do the mechanisms humans use to pass knowledge of that technology through the generations.

The question is perhaps most acute when it comes to dealing with Neanderthal hunters. There the operating presumption seems to be that technology is never lost. We know Neanderthal lasted through a series of glacial advances and retreats. What gets lost is the variety of conditions that can exist within a glacial episode and the speed with which those changes can occur. Conditions within a North American ice age can vary from those of a full glacial grip to conditions warmer than those found today. Within that variation in conditions is the shortness of a human life span and the constant problem of transmitting knowledge from generation to generation.

Consider, as an example, making clothing. The kind of clothing needed during the height of glacial conditions and the technology to make that clothing are very different from the kind of clothing needed when the local climate is much warmer. Since the harsh conditions of a full glacial episode are repetitive over the course of an ice age, we can be certain that Neanderthal was able to make clothing capable of functioning in full glacial conditions. But what about the thousands or tens of thousands of years-that can intervene between those episodes of full glacial conditions? How are we to presume that that knowledge endured during those thousands of years in which it was not needed? An equivalent point is making the full winter caribou hide coats, pants, mittens, and footgear used regularly by the Denésuliné until the 1930s and occasionally made and used until the 1970s. How long does the knowledge of how to make them last once women cease teaching their daughters how to make them? Similarly, how long would the knowledge of how to make full winter gear suitable for being out and functional in full glacial conditions last once Neanderthal mothers no longer made them and their daughters could not grow up watching them being made?

The mechanisms by which long-term cultural knowledge is transmitted from generation to generation quickly move into the areas of myth and folklore. Well beyond the issues we intend to focus upon here. By the same token, when we consider the long-term transmission of that knowledge over tens of generations or more, that knowledge quickly reaches a level of abstraction in its transmission that we do not understand. Because of the lack of depth in our own understanding of our own history and how it works on the ground to transmit knowledge from generation to generation, we have not studied it to a degree sufficient to give us any real understanding of how these processes work.

If we return to the issue of Neanderthal clothes making, we can get to the crux of the problem. When climatic conditions changed and warmer times prevailed, which could last for many generations, such that Neanderthals did not need that full winter clothing capable of standing up to full glacial conditions, what do we presume about their behavior? Did they continue sometimes for thousands of years to make that unneeded clothing they would never need or use? Or did they cease making it? If they ceased making it, how many generations of Neanderthal daughters growing up without seeing their mothers make that full winter clothing would it take to lose the knowledge of how to make it?

We could avoid the implications raised by this discussion of Neanderthal sewing by referring the issue to the use of myth and folklore as the means by which the knowledge of how to make full winter clothing was passed from generation to generation. Unfortunately, as we have no idea how this kind of knowledge could be encoded to last through so much time in such specific detail, avoidance is all it is. It is like using human nature as a way to explain human behavior. Human nature might well be the reason humans behave the way they do in certain circumstances and thus the true explanation for their behavior. However, since we have no idea what human nature is and what range of behavior is encompassed by the term, any use of it as an explanation of human behavior is invalid.

Contemporary Denésuliné do not make stone tools. In any practical sense, they do not know how to make them, and we have never seen or heard of anyone trying to make them. They frequently find stone tools and know what they are. They know these tools were made by ancestral Denésuliné before the fur trade brought metal tools among them. Their explanation of how their ancestors made the tools has shifted from a mechanical explanation of the process of making them to other grounds of explanation. Denésuliné believed the world in which they lived was constructed by *inkoze* (Smith 1973; Sharp 2001). Inkoze is what Westerners would call supernatural power. Denésuliné explain the presence of stone tools, particularly arrowheads and knives, as the ancestors using their inkoze to shape the stone by using a flicking motion of their fingernails to make the grooves in the stone. They will demonstrate how this was done as a means of illustrating just how much inkoze the ancestors had.

Contemporary archaeologists and paleoanthropologists know that making stone tools is a complex process involving visualization, planning, a variety of tools, and a great deal of understanding of materials and processes. The question here is about the Denésuliné explanation—which has now passed into folklore—of how stone tools are made. It obviously does not transmit sufficiently detailed knowledge of how to make stone tools to allow someone to sit down and make them. It does, however, transmit an essential point about stone tool making: that the stone is shaped by exerting force upon it in such a manner as to groove the stone away from its centerline to achieve the desired shape. This is an extremely abstract representation of making stone tools. The question becomes: does this abstract representation of the process of making stone tools provide a sufficient guide for future Denésuliné to reinvent the process of making stone tools should they ever need to return to making them?

Did knowledge of how to make full winter clothing get transmitted over dozens of generations of Neanderthals in an equally abstract manner?

The only sure way to transmit a technological process through time in detail sufficient to allow it to be practiced is by using the technology, thus allowing children to grow up observing it and participating in its use. The key seems to be the recognition that knowledge of past technology is not transmitted through time in detail or in its specifics but through some sort of verbal or other symbolic form that encodes a guide that allows descendants of future generations to experiment and reinvent that past technology. Technologies get lost because they are no longer relevant to the circumstances of contemporary life, but they can be reinvented. Indeed, in the case of Neanderthal clothing, it was routinely reinvented. Culture, as we understand it from our contemporary experience of it, is capable of providing that kind of guide to a future recreation of lost technologies. The key, however, is not a dataless debate about the nature of past culture but the recognition that technology itself is not blindly transmitted through time in an unchanging manner but is invented and reinvented as part of the processes by which generations of individuals adapt to the constantly changing conditions of the environments in which they find themselves living.

Interlude 2

Wolves, Caribou, and Approaching Prey

If you walk this land in the company of a dog and happen to encounter caribou, the caribou will detect you before they detect your dog. The moment they detect your dog, their attention will be directed toward it and their actions will be determined by what your dog does rather than by what you do. The relationship between wolves and caribou is far older than is the relationship between humans and caribou.

Caribou are a wide-ranging species. They had recently ranged as far south as what were to become the Middle Atlantic states. When they colonized this land as it emerged from the glaciers, they came to it as a species that had had a long relationship with the predators of the ice age. Throughout their vast and ever-changing range they had survived not only competition with a host of other browsers and grazers but also the pressures of a plethora of predators, including the short faced bear (*Arctos simus*), dire wolf (*Canis dirus*), and large cats such as the American lion (*Panthera leo atrix*) and scimitar cat (*Homotherium serum*).

The wolf was the only large predator to follow the caribou into this new land after the megafaunal extinction. The relationship that exists between the two of them is far simpler than were the myriad of relationships each had had with other species in the far more diverse and complicated times of the ice age. The relationship that has been established here between wolf and caribou is now well established. It has been stable for more millennia than civilization has existed. In the absence of interference by Western Civilization and its market forces, wolves pose no threat to the caribou—something that it seems it is impossible for government agencies and sport hunters to understand.

The First Nations inserted themselves into the relationship between wolves and caribou several thousand years after it had formed. Unlike the Western Civilization that followed them, the First Nations cultures quickly understood the relationship between the wolf and the caribou. When the ancestral Denésuliné took occupancy of this land from the First Nations' cultures that had preceded them, they inserted themselves into that relationship as equal participants whose values and practices were geared to its preservation.

As co-predators of the caribou who are each equally equally dependent upon their individual relationships with the caribou, First Nations peoples and wolves have developed different strategies for exploiting the caribou. These differences in strategies of exploitation are reflected in differences in the way they are exposed to the caribou and in the different tactics humans and wolves use to prey upon them.

The relationship between the wolf and the Denésuliné as co-predators of caribou had a certain complementarity to it. Wolves hold the role of pursuit and endurance hunters. Humans are unable to compete with them at this type of predation. There are times of the year when wolves have to disperse their population while they are raising their young. Each pack has to be localized around a den within a specific geographic territory. During this period of localization the wolf population is forced to rely for sustenance mostly upon rodents and small game. The localization period lasts until the young are old enough to be fully mobile and live without the protection of a den. Once this occurs, and throughout the rest of the year, wolves become far more mobile animals. They are capable of routinely covering distances of up to fifty miles in a single day.

The territorial nature of the wolf pack is one of the cultural variables that exist among wolves. In this region of the world, at least during the times of the year when they are not tied to dens, territoriality is relaxed. What remains of it is centered upon the moving pack rather than upon fixed boundaries on the land. Now freed from the den area, wolf packs travel widely. Their incursion into the forest is readily apparent on the ground when caribou begin their winter movement into the forest. When the wolves come, packs seem able to mix comfortably and move freely over the land even though they are in the presence of other packs. Whether this relaxation of territoriality is cause or effect, it reflects their life as pursuit and endurance hunters of caribou.

The tundra and the subarctic cover an immense area of land. There are alternative means for wolves to survive within it other than by depending upon the caribou. Nevertheless, caribou are the primary food source within the land, and the bulk of the wolf population will attempt to survive by exploiting it. For our concerns here with the complementarity between wolves and humans as predators of caribou, this means that those wolves that have committed their survival to the pursuit of caribou have to move over the landscape to stay within effective predation range of the caribou.

This need to stay within effective hunting distance of the caribou reflects one of the major differences between the Denésuliné and the wolf as predators of caribou. It requires of wolves a much greater degree of mobility than is needed by their human counterparts. Think of all the times when in describing the situation at a camp before a hunt began, it was mentioned that caribou had been moving into or out of the area around the camp; all those times when the Denésuliné were on the land without the presence of caribou. For the Denésuliné, these times were bridged by their ability to store meat. The presence of their stored meat allowed them to remain where they were until the caribou returned. The situation was quite different for the wolves sharing the area around those camps. A wolf-killed caribou is good for about a maximum of one week before it has been so thoroughly consumed (or been scavenged by other animals or deteriorated past the point that it can no longer be eaten) that it is useless for further consumption. At this point, the wolves have to move on in search of more caribou; they have to find the caribou wherever they have moved. Humans who lacked the ability to store meat would be forced into a far more mobile kind of existence than it would be possible for them to sustain over time.

The instructive "Herd-following" debate between Bryan Gordon and the late "Tiger" Burch (Burch 1972, 1991; Gordon 1975, 1990) has effectively demonstrated that, at the level of the aboriginal Denésuliné population, they were dependent upon herd following. This in the sense that they had developed a subsistence system dependent upon exploiting caribou throughout its entire annual range. As a people, the aboriginal Denésuliné followed the caribou. Perhaps more accurately: as a people, the aboriginal Denésuliné exploited the caribou throughout its entire annual migration, no matter where the caribou were in the course of that migration.

This is an important point and the basis of the complementarity in the way that humans and wolves serve as co-predators upon the caribou. Humans exploit the caribou throughout their entire range (save in recent times far out on the tundra during the summer), but they do so by moving to intercept the caribou during their migrations. While as a people the Denésuliné follow the herds, at the local level of their camps and hunting units (Sharp 1977; J.G.E Smith 1970, 1976), the Denésuliné move to intercept the caribou within the range of territory utilized by each regional band. Humans are not physically capable of keeping up with caribou when caribou are on the move. No camp of humans can move quickly enough or sustain the constant movement that would be necessary to follow the caribou. Wolves can do this except at those times of the year when they are tied to a den or caring for small pups.

These differences have consequences. From the standpoint of the caribou, it means that the presence of wolves is an almost constant throughout their lives. It does not mean wolves are always where caribou happen to be at any given moment, but it does mean that the presence of wolves is an ordinary feature of the life of a caribou. As a consequence, caribou—like with that dog on the tundra—are always alert to the possible presence of wolves. A human presence is not an ordinary feature of caribou life. Contact between humans and caribou is far less frequent than is contact between wolves and caribou. As a consequence, caribou are not always on the alert for the presence of humans.

If wolves have taken the role of pursuit and endurance hunters of caribou, aboriginal humans seemed to have taken over the big cat role as ambush hunters. Some forms of human hunting, such as the use of drives, pounds, nets, and snares, have no nonhuman analog at the size scale of these species. All of these however, share a rough similarity in that they involve preparing a place on the ground and waiting for the caribou to try and move through that place on the ground. We suspect that in aboriginal times the pattern of accidental contact with caribou that forms the basis of contemporary Denésuliné hunting played a lesser role in their subsistence hunting. In effect, subsistence in these environmental circumstances that depends upon accidental contact with the prey is a product of the usage of the modern repeating rifle. We think that in earlier times, when there were no repeating rifles, the Denésuliné would have had to rely upon ambush hunting to a far greater extent than do the contemporary Denésuliné. Their pattern of land usage would have been far different from that displayed by the contemporary Denésuliné. How the contemporary Denésuliné place themselves upon the ground represents a change away from an earlier placement pattern designed to exploit more fully those localities where the topography and vegetation cover would have allowed the ancestral Denésuliné to establish ambush points that enabled them to get physically closer to caribou.

Curiously, this means that in a sense, the subsistence hunting pattern (reliance upon accidental contact with caribou) by Denésuliné of the recent era (i.e., post-modern repeating rifle period) has begun to converge upon the caribou hunting pattern displayed by wolves.

The land the Denésuliné inhabit is vast and largely unsettled, which has consequences for both the caribou and the Denésuliné. Contact with humans is always dangerous to wild animals. It always disrupts and disturbs their pursuit of the activities that make up their lives. Unlike wild animals that live in more settled regions, caribou do not have to face the constant contact with humans or their machinery that comes from commercial activities or agriculture. The land is not constantly wandered by prowling humans. There are no fishermen, hikers, bicyclists, birders, campers, or tourists. This lack of contact with humans affects how caribou respond when they do face a human presence. They do not automatically flee at their first detection of a human presence, as do so many wild animals that must endure a greater human presence. They do not know how to vanish unseen into cover routinely at their first detection of a human presence. In spite of thousands of years of human predation upon them, they are sufficiently undisturbed still to rely upon their speed and ability to run away from danger as an adequate protection from a human presence. Although at times of the year this can make them seem almost oblivious to what surrounds them and indifferent to a human presence, they are not unaware of what else is in their environment. They are merely confident of their ability to outrun what else is out there and they carefully control the distance to which they will allow individuals of other species to approach them.

Approaching caribou is not about sneaking up on them. It is about approaching them in such a way that they are not so disturbed by the hunter's presence as to break into flight. The vision and hearing of caribou are acute. Their sensory range is considerable, and their preference to live as herd animals means many sets of eyes and ears monitor the vicinity where they happen to be at any moment in time. The caribou will know the hunters are approaching; the caribou encountered in most of the hunts examined in this book knew the hunters were there. The art of an approach—and it is an art that calls for great skill and experience—comes from managing the approach in such a way that it does not cross that line of disturbing the caribou so greatly that they break into flight before hunters can place themselves so that they can engage them with their weapons.

An approach requires silence, and it involves careful control of the hunter's motion; use of the word "deliberate" and the phrase "carefully controlled" is itself quite deliberate. Movement can be steady, but it must not be threatening. The concentration displayed by a wolf that is approaching a prey animal it intends to attack can be present in the hunter. Hunters approaching prey do concentrate intensely upon the animals they are approaching, but they must not communicate that concentration to the caribou. Caribou find that intense focus threatening and are liable to flee from it. The Wolf animal/spirit has the speed and agility to communicate its focus and concentration to its potential prey and still effectively carry off its attack. A human hunter does not. What Wolf can communicate, and may use as part of its hunting technique, the human hunter must hide.

The deliberateness of the motion of the hunter determines how cover is used in an approach. The hunter moves toward the prey, often by angling the approach, and uses cover to break up the caribou view of his approach—as well as his silhouette and the linearity of the weapons and implements he is carrying—but he does not sneak from cover to cover. The pattern of his movement must remain fluid and nonthreatening, obvious to the caribou but not worthy of attention. Moving from cover to cover—bush to bush, tree to tree, rock to rock—is not fluid. Erratic motion becomes an enemy of the approach. It disturbs the caribou far more than does walking an open path behind incomplete cover so that the hunter's passage behind the cover places it between him and the caribou without creating an erratic course of travel.

The approach of a single predator is less disturbing to caribou than is the approach of several predators. An approach by a single hunter is often easier than are approaches by multiple hunters. If there are multiple hunters, each hunter must pay constant attention to the movement of the other hunters. Each hunter has to pace his own movements and judge his own place on the ground in accordance with what everyone else is doing and how they are moving. A solitary hunt also has the advantage of removing nuances of social relations among the group of hunters from the individual hunter's focus. These concerns are not conscious issues debated by hunters as they approach their prey, but they are part of the continuing mental activities—we do not wish to use the words "unconscious" or "subconscious" as they carry too much cultural baggage—that are a normal and continuous aspect of life as a social being. Denésuliné hunters concentrate intensely upon their hunts. Any reduction in the level of their other concerns aids that concentration.

Hunt 14

Caribou

Caching in the Fall

B y early October the conditions in our camp had changed dramatically. What had been a good year for caribou that had seen the camp well supplied with meat for the winter was on the edge of becoming a season of concern and privation. Making dry meat for the fall-winter season, which had dominated the late summer hunting, is largely an August into September activity. The women of the camp had already made and stored what they thought to be an adequate supply of dry meat to last until Christmas. Food was generally in reasonable supply, but there had been sporadic episodes of hunger. Store-bought supplies were worryingly low. Prospects for the upcoming trapping season were becoming uncertain. Caribou had been abundant when they were in the area, but their appearance had been erratic. They would appear in numbers and flood the area, only to vanish a few days later, sometimes to stay gone for weeks. The Denésuliné are familiar with this pattern of behavior and the men had adjusted their hunting to account for it. When caribou were present, the men quickly began to hunt and took them in numbers sufficient to meet camp needs. When caribou were absent, the hunters did not search for them but devoted their time to other tasks. Still, the weather was unseasonably warm and freeze up was not progressing as rapidly as was desirable. There had been some discussion among the men as to whether we had adequate supplies to last until Christmas or if the trapping season might have to be cut short by an early return to the village.

In September, when hunters from the village had stopped flying in to hunt, planes had ceased to arrive from the south and the camp lost any chance of resupplying. It was too early to bring meat into the camp and store it on open-air stages, as the meat would not yet freeze. With George's father-in-law and his family in the camp for the winter, the camp was larger and had greater needs than in previous years. There were still some caribou off the north end of the north-south bay, but they were not present in large numbers. George managed to kill twelve bulls there on October 12. They were a number of miles away, but he was not content to leave the meat piled in the bush, as he would normally have done at this time of the year. Due to the lack of snow cover and the small lakes and muskegs not yet being solidly frozen over, transporting the meat in by dog team was taxing. He had had to spend a difficult day out with his dog team to bring it in.

The root of everyone's concern was a small black bear that had discovered the meat caches the men had made out in the bush. Close to hibernation, the bear was on a feeding binge. Beyond the bear being hungry and eating considerable quantities of the meat, the way bears and some other animals behave when they find a meat cache was at issue. If wolves find the meat they can quickly consume large quantities of it; although once the meat has frozen together, it may be difficult for them to tear the pile apart to get all of it. Wolverines are destructive but are relatively small animals and are not common. The real problem is that besides eating the meat, some species also foul it, among them bears, gulls, and other birds.

Bears are enormously strong animals that can easily tear apart even a frozen meat pile. They rip the pile apart and scatter around what they have found. They also mark some of the meat by defecating upon it. While this may scent mark the meat and protect it for the bear's purposes, it fouls the meat past the point that the Denésuliné can use it. When large birds get access to the meat they also foul it with their excretions. Sea gulls are more destructive this way than are ravens. We are not sure one can say individual sea gulls are more destructive than individual ravens, but gulls far outnumber ravens. Fortunately for the Denésuliné, sea gulls do not overwinter in the area, and by September they are close to departing.

By late September the bear had begun to feed upon and ruin meat caches stored in the bush; this was first mentioned in field notes on September 27, 1975, as a recurring event. Denésuliné men like to have meat caches on or near their trap lines. Aside from providing an immediate source of food for use on the trap line, they are perceived as safe places to cache food for the camp. The men had begun to lay in a winter meat supply as they were out exploring their projected trap lines. They did this individually—trap lines are run individually—and their preliminary explorations often took them considerable distances away from camp. These individual explorations created a greater chance to encounter the scattered caribou bands that were still in the area.

It was these isolated meat caches that the bear first discovered. By late September the bear had to have had hibernation on its mind and should have been engaged in a serious attempt to pack on as many calories as it possibly could. Caches of up to twenty butchered and stacked caribou, not to mention the nearby surviving remnants of the gut piles and other offal from butchering the caribou, were something no sane bear would pass up.

At first the loss of stacked meat was noted as an irritation, an unfortunate loss that would have to be compensated for by taking more caribou and making more meat piles. However, the bear proved clever as well as hungry. It began systematically searching out other meat piles and ate, marked, and scattered their contents. It was not possible to record exactly how many meat piles there were or their exact locations. All the meat piles that had been cached in the bush were on the west side of the camp. They were located from up on the flat highland alongside the east-west bay of Foxholm Lake (J on map

1) down to out along the creek along which George's father-in-law was planning to run his trap line (M on map 1).

Over the next few weeks until it vanished, presumably to a well-nourished hibernation, the bear found and destroyed every meat cache the men of the camp had been able to establish to carry them through the upcoming season. The entire meat supply of the camp, save what had been brought into the camp itself, was gone. The men of the camp were not happy. They made a number of attempts to find the bear. Individually they went out at night or in the early morning to check the piles and try to locate what they determined was a quite small, probably female bear. George's father-in-law was particularly irritated by the depredations the bear had perpetrated upon him and put the most effort into trying to find it.

Caribou had passed some distance to the west of us during the week of October 12, when George shot his bulls, but the effect of the bear was so substantial that the men were unwilling to make the trip out to shoot any. They felt the caribou were so far away from camp that the bear would get the meat before they could transport it into camp, and it was not worth the effort.

The effect of all of this was to make the camp somewhat edgy about prospects for the upcoming pre-Christmas hunting and trapping season. Fresh meat was now in short supply and the situation, while not threatening, was far from satisfactory. Freeze up was delayed. The small lakes were not yet frozen over, and the muskegs were still soft. The overnight snows were only quarter- to half-inch amounts that melted off during the day. The ground itself was largely bare, with only spotty snow cover in shaded or sheltered places. Travel was difficult. It was in this context that George devoted a significant amount of time and energy to hunting. He took time away from helping his father-in-law finish the new cabin to go out on foot and hunt.

Overnight between October 12 and 13, the small lake facing the cabins finally froze over, but the weather was still so warm that the ice was not strong enough to use. There was still no usable snow cover on the ground.

On October 17, 1975, a day that was mild but breezy and overcast, George was out on foot hunting. He had walked west of the camp up onto the highland flats above the heavy scrub timber growth just past the last beach at the south end of the north-south bay of Foxholm Lake. He was about one and a half miles from camp when he saw a large bunch of caribou. They were on the north shore of Foxholm Lake heading to the point at the narrows (between D and K on map 1) where they could cross to the south shore of Foxholm Lake without having to swim more than a short distance. They were roughly two miles away from where he stood on the highland.

Once he saw the caribou and determined that they were heading for the narrows, he broke into a run for the camp. He had a difficult mile and a half to cover, skirting heavy brush and wet areas in an effort to cover the distance in as short a time as possible. He ran into the camp from the west. Out of breath from his sprint, he shouted to his father that there were caribou coming down the east side of the north-south bay, and he snatched up some equipment from his cabin before he took off through the woods. His father grabbed his rifle and some shells and took off after him. I took my rifle and followed.

The best point to intercept the caribou, if they moved down through the muskegs and wet areas inland of the rocky shore and timber of the north-south bay, would have been just past the north shore of the small lake. Rough ground and the undergrowth along parts of the shore, especially the heavy growth of blueberry bushes on its north shore, made that route impractical for rapid movement. George instead headed into the woods up the portage route between the small lake and Foxholm Lake but after a few hundred yards began to diverge to the right. His course would bring him out past the crest of the hill some two hundred feet before the point where the southernmost part of the granite outcrop was buried under the sand of the hill. Most of this route was through the widely spaced climax timber of the sand hill. It was only as we approached the place where the end of the granite outcrop was buried in the sand that there was enough moisture in the ground to support vegetation thick enough to call undergrowth.

Moving through this undergrowth was noisy and somewhat cumbersome. Beyond it the ground became rocky and the footing difficult for someone in a hurry. We had to cover only forty or fifty yards over this rough ground before we came near the break where the ground dropped down to overlook a large area of mixed wet ground and muskeg (H-14 on map 1). In line abreast, George on the north, Paul in the middle, and myself on the south, we carefully crossed the rough ground to what was in effect a platform elevated above the lower ground. To everyone's surprise, I think, the caribou had crossed at the narrows and moved up through the forest on the south shore of Foxholm Lake and into the inland meadows of the eastern shore of the north-south bay. We found ourselves standing on the bench just above the head height of the caribou.

These caribou had followed the meadows directly south from the narrows, paralleling the shore of the north-south bay. They had arrived from where George had first seen them just moments before we arrived. This was one of the largest bunches of caribou we ever saw in the area. There were still thirty-five to forty caribou in the bunch. They were mostly bulls but there were a number of yearling animals mixed in with them. They were standing directly in front of and slightly below us in a large wet meadow and were closely grouped together, feeding.

The three of us watched the caribou for a few seconds, each determining which animal to shoot first, and without a word we simultaneously opened fire. When caribou are grouped like this, they do not form a single line. Even though they stay in close company, the animals are scattered as they feed. Some were standing in front of others between where we were and where they were. As soon as the first shot is fired, caribou in such a context begin to move rapidly. They are startled by the noise of the rifle fire and the hollow booming noise bullets make as they hit the chest cavities of animals that have been shot. They see other animals falling to the ground if well shot or making the noises and movements of pain if not well shot. They almost instantly begin to run, but the problem is where to run and in which direction to head. Caribou are herd animals. They seek one another's company and desperately try to stay together in a group. They try to run away in a group, but the animals at the ends of the bunch, those that could set a direction of flight, are often the ones hunters single out to shoot. The caribou turn away from the noise. They turn away from animals falling in front of and among them. They try to turn and follow others that are fleeing. The confusion and carnage leave them with no clear direction in which to turn or flee. They turn and head one way, only to turn and flee in another direction, always seeking to stay close to the others of their kind. Skilled hunters work this confusion, seeking out animals that are most exposed and provide the clearest shot yet also display the features that make a caribou worth shooting.

By the time the caribou had sorted out their confusion and begun to head away from us, there were twenty bull caribou lying on the ground. For the Denésuliné, to be among the bodies of caribou they have killed—caribou that have chosen to die for them—is fraught with meaning. The presence of caribou dead on the ground, with all the potential for the continuation of human life that their bodies represent, is a culmination of the symbolic and emotional relationship between Denésuliné and Caribou and all the other animal/spirits that form the core of the Denésuliné universe; an embodiment of meaning that reaffirms the order of their universe and their place within that universe (Sharp 2001: 65–73; 117–24; D. M. Smith 1973).

If the killing of a large animal is an emotionally charged experience, it is also the source of a series of pragmatic tasks that involve a considerable amount of work and effort. The animal has to be field butchered quickly. It does not aid the preservation of the meat or improve its quality if the carcass is left intact for any substantial period of time. The intestines and other internal organs have to be removed from the carcass in order to prevent contamination and spoilage.

Caribou that are knocked down are not always dead. The wound that has knocked them down is usually severe enough to put them into shock, but this is not always the case. Wounded caribou are much more placid than are wounded moose or bear. When large numbers of animals have been knocked down, as here, the approaching hunters find themselves facing downed animals displaying various degrees of quiescence. Caribou that are not in shock sometimes attempt to kick or gore hunters who approach them.

Hunters approaching the downed animals quickly assess their state. By preference, they turn their attention to those that are dead, allowing the remaining animals to expire quietly while the dead are butchered. Those that do not die have to be dispatched. Animals that have gone into shock are grasped by the antlers. The head is raised and turned downward with the nostrils directed toward the ground to expose the back of the animal's neck. A small cut of an inch or so is made in the skin by the second cervical vertebra. The point of a knife is pushed between the vertebrae to sever the spinal cord, instantly killing the animal.

Animals that do not become passive by going into shock and cannot be handled have to be killed. The Denésuliné do not like to waste a rifle shell by shooting a downed animal, both because of scarcity of shells and because of the damage another shot inflicts upon the carcass. Denésuliné belief about animal abuse prohibits them from killing the animal by blunt force trauma. The most common means of dispatching an animal under these circumstances is by throwing the largest available knife underhand into the rib cage.

It was too late in the season and their hair was too long for the hides of these animals to be of value for clothing. There was no need of caribou hide leather, but the hides were useful as ground cloths and tarps. They were taken back to the camp when the remains of the animals were transported back. The parts of the animals that were left behind uncovered—some of the heads, the guts and lungs, and any offal that had spilled out of the intestines—are far more attractive to passing scavengers than was the meat piled and covered for overnight storage.

The twenty caribou that went down represented enough food to last until Christmas for the six adults, one teenager, and five small children who directly depended upon the three of us. They also represented a substantial task for the three of us. It is normal practice for Denésuliné hunters to butcher only game they themselves have killed (Sharp 1988a). To do otherwise could be interpreted as making a claim of ownership to the downed carcass. Because relations among the three of us were smooth enough and because Paul was suffering from ill health, we were able to butcher the animals without worrying about that convention and finished the field butchering within a few hours.

Where the caribou fell was fairly close to our winter camp. The small lake had now frozen over. The smaller lakes, ponds, and muskegs were freezing. The ground was hardening with the cold. Snow was about to begin to cover the ground in depth. This meant that the caribou could be transported back to the winter camp by dog team the following day and would be exposed only for a single night to possible scavenging by the bear. As we had had no contact with the bear for some time, it seemed already likely to have gone to its den. We were willing to gamble on this. The meat was left stacked overnight. It went undisturbed and was transported to camp the following day. The food crisis that had troubled the camp was ended. The coming season would be plagued with other kinds of shortages and difficulties, but at least everyone would have food.

Text 14

Hunting from High Ground

This hunt is an almost perfect exemplar of the features that figure into the paleoanthropological understanding of the hunting behavior of our ancestors and related species. The hunt began from high ground and relied upon the human ability to see game from long distances. The hunter was able to judge the behavior of the prey animals and estimate their numbers. He was able to anticipate their probable future direction of travel as well as determine the most probable location at which they could be intercepted. He used the human ability to run long distances to run back to the camp, where he used human vocal communication to gather allies rapidly to convert a solitary hunt into a collective one. The killing itself involved a further long distance run and occurred as a collective activity. The butchering and transporting of the meat also became a collective activity.

What is perhaps most unusual about this hunt, with its classic combination of features, is the rarity with which hunts like this occur. This hunt was the only one of its kind we observed. The features may all be real and significant aspects of the way our ancestors and related species hunted game, but their combination in a single hunt is not common.

Relying upon this combination of features is not a very effective way to hunt caribou. Other simpler methods of hunting produce better results and a higher probability of kills. George later stated that at the time of his original sighting of the caribou band, it had contained roughly one hundred animals. By the time they had moved to where we ambushed them, more than half of the animals had left the band to go elsewhere. Wherever they had gone, they were not visible from the ambush point. This is one of the great problems with relying upon hunting from a distance with fast-moving prey. Unless there is some terrain feature, such as a gully or a near vertical face, to channel the movement of the prey, even a distance of a mile and a half or two miles provides too great an opportunity for the prey to disperse to allow it to be hunted effectively. The caribou had several square miles of terrain over which they could disperse once they crossed the narrows of Foxholm Lake. That any of them arrived at the ambush point had more to do with the barrier created by the shore of the north-south bay than with any skill of the hunters or any human capacity to estimate their movement. It was at least as likely that we would have arrived at the ambush point to find no caribou as to have found the thirty-five to forty we did find.

Hunts that start from a closer distance and allow greater use of the local topography during the approach are simply far more effective than are hunts that begin from long distances away and rely upon long distance running to close with the prey.

All acts, even the most solitary acts of lunatics and madmen, are social acts. Every hunt, even a solitary hunt conducted miles from any other human being, is a social act existing within a cultural context that determines its purpose and the means by which it will be carried out. Every hunter is a social being embedded within a cultural matrix that has created him and ordered his experience of the world within which he lives. Culture creates personalities. Personalities do not create culture. This matrix has provided him with a detailed belief system about what animals are and how humans are supposed to act in their presence. It has taught him how they are to be approached and treated as well as the uses that can be made of their bodies. It has taught him how they are to be killed and butchered and how their remains are to be treated as well as how, when, and why it is appropriate to kill them. All this is brought to the hunt, as are the lifelong individual experience of the hunter and the stories and tales he has heard from others throughout his life (Brody 1981; Cruikshank 1998; Legat 2012).

Within the social field of meaning that is culture (Sharp 2001: 117–24), some acts occur within a context so nuanced and complex that they are essentially impossible to explain to other humans who lack familiarity with the context. One of these acts is prey selection: the act of choosing the specific animal toward which a hunter will direct the fire of his weapon. It would probably be stretching things to call prey selection a "total social phenomenon" (Mauss 1967: 1), but it is one of those pivotal acts around which the social and the individual coalesce in dramatic fashion.

When a hunter faces his prey, he is intensely aware of the state of, and history of, his own individual relationship with the animal/spirit he is attempting to kill. The hunter is not just abstractly aware of this moral/spiritual context; he is specifically aware of the recent history of his own previous attempts to kill animal/spirits of the kind of the prey. He is aware of his own individual skill level as a hunter and his proficiency with his weapons as well as his fatigue level and his immediate physical condition and how they could affect his performance.

Because animals are beings that are simultaneously mortal creatures with bodies that can be used and consumed by human beings as well as immortal spiritual beings in communication with the other spiritual beings temporarily embodied in the form of other animals of their kind, there is always the possibility that any animal encountered will choose to display the power of its spiritual aspect through a refusal to die for the hunter or through other actions asserting the spiritual power of the animal/spirit. If the animal/spirit is observed and pursued by the hunter, the choice to display this power rests solely with the animal/spirit. It is only knowable to the hunter through the actions of the animal/spirit once their encounter has begun. Any encounter with an animal/spirit has this potential (Sharp 1988b, 1994a, 2001).

When a man hunts, even if by himself, he does so in a social context. That social context is normally related to his membership in a particular group. The needs of the group come into play in how he approaches the animals he encounters and which ones he chooses to pursue. Obvious examples are whether the group is in need of hides or meat or if the group has other specific needs that will direct his actions either during the encounter or in deciding whether to pursue any encounter that occurs. Relations between the hunter and other members of the group come into play in determining the hunter's actions and the choices he makes. Issues of seniority or respect can add to tensions and rivalries within the group and may lead an individual hunter to make either more or less aggressive choices about the pursuit of prey than he might make if those tensions and rivalries did not exist (Sharp 1988a). There is the simple question of need. Does the camp have enough food? Are specific types of food (e.g., fat) or other resources (e.g., sinew) in short supply? It can be as simple as that people are tired of eating one kind of meat and would like a change in their diet by eating the flesh of a different species.

Consideration of what to do with the flesh of any animal that is killed comes into play. How many animals can the hunter butcher and process if he kills them? How is the meat to be put into storage or transported back to camp? How will or must the meat he kills be distributed once it has been killed? Is it, say, worth the effort to kill a moose if the hide of that moose is committed to a distant female relative?

If the hunt involves more than one hunter all these issues are intensified by the presence of others. The state of social relations within the hunting party comes into play with considerable force and with infinite variation. Do you assist the cousin who is hunting with you even if you cannot stand him? Is it better to back off on your own efforts if the product of the hunt is liable to go mostly to aiding relatives you do not respect or like? Has another member of the hunting party been trying to assert some measure of authority over you? Even a slight reduction in effort—one shot not taken or one animal ignored—can have consequences within the web of social relations that binds every group and hunting party together.

Hunting can be a risky business. This was especially so when the spear was the primary weapon or when dangerous animals were hunted with bow and arrow. How much risk does one take and what circumstances make additional risk worth taking?

During the months when there is no snow cover, caribou prefer to spend their time in places not very similar to the places where humans prefer to spend their time. Much of their food is found in places that are wet underfoot, and they are easily able to negotiate those surfaces. Because of the way their hooves spread out, they exert far less pressure upon the ground than humans do. This allows them to walk and run easily over wet surfaces into which humans sink or bog down. The same low ground pressure and spreading of their hooves allows them to move over snow surfaces into which a human would sink and provides them with traction on surfaces on which humans risk slipping and falling. Caribou are vulnerable to breaking or otherwise damaging their legs, but they seem better able than we are to move comfortably over ground surfaces that are rough and uneven or covered with cobble-sized stones.

During the months of the year when snow covers the ground, the advantage in movement caribou have over humans only increases. They can move quickly through snow that is deep enough to seriously impede human movement. The snow pack that forms each winter is generally deep enough to remove the problems to mobility that come from cobbles and rough surfaces. The caribou walk on the snow. Conditions are rarely such that they walk on the surface of the snow, but neither do they sink deeply enough into the snow to break through it and walk on the underlying ground surface.

Caribou do move over the solid surface provided by eskers and sand hills, particularly during periods when there is no snow cover, but they mostly move over those surfaces, using these places as routes of travel rather than as destinations.

These things have consequences for human hunters. Given that the Denésuliné prefer to shoot from close range, a great many of their hunts involve the hunters seeing caribou in locations where they are feeding or resting and then carefully approaching them. This almost always involves deliberate and carefully controlled movement through whatever cover is available rather than a mad rush toward the prey. There are occasions involving lovely spring or summer days on dry ground with plentiful cover when approaching caribou is a sheer delight. However, those occasions are rare. Almost inevitably, an approach requires the hunter to cross stretches of ground where the footing is wet, soggy, uncertain, or just plain bad—often without cover—until he is close enough to engage the animals. A normal hunt involves quiet, careful slogging over wet or rocky ground into places where humans rarely choose to go and in weather conditions that are usually cold, windy, uncomfortable, and often wet. If conditions are not cold, windy, and wet, they may be hot, bug-infested, and wet. The uncomfortable remains a constant.

It is sometimes impossible to approach the animals quite as closely as the hunter desires, so it becomes necessary to end an approach with a rapid walk or short sprint over difficult ground while in the open and fully exposed to the view of the caribou. This rapid motion by hunters is generally disturbing to caribou and may precipitate immediate flight. Making that rapid motion to close into a firing position has to be a carefully calculated—if almost instantaneous—decision.

Ultimately, there comes the moment when the hunters find themselves as close to the prey as they can get. What follows is one of the most intense acts in Denésuliné culture. Weapons have to be prepared to fire. The hunters have been carefully watching the prey as they approach it, trying to judge what kinds of animals are there as well as their size, age, sex, and condition, but it is not until they assume their final firing positions that they can complete their evaluations. In no more than two to three seconds—to take as long as five seconds would be an anomaly disturbing to the hunters and liable to produce a reaction from the caribou—the hunters judge the size, condition, age, and sex of the caribou. They sort out the placement of the animals on the ground, determining which animals are standing in front of others, at which animals they have a clear and unblocked shot, and whether they should shoot for the head or body of any animal that attracts their interest. If there are multiple hunters, they will segment the herd, deciding where to place their first shots. Normally each hunter shoots at an animal in the segment of the herd directly to his front, but this is not always the case. They try to determine which animals are leaders within the herd or likely to take the lead once the firing begins. Their interest is in the caribou most likely to lead the herd in flight. Some hunters may well identify the animal they think most likely to assume the lead after the first shot has been fired and note it as the target for their second shot, so that it cannot lead the herd away. While this is going on, the hunters are continuing their visual examination of the herd, seeking out individual caribou that are injured or diseased, show cancerous growths, skin infections, or hair loss, or are otherwise physically marked in such a way as to eliminate them as targets.

All this occurs without a word being spoken. The moment the hunters open fire is a moment of continuity with Dené-suliné hunters that stretches back through the generations of their forebears and the use of muskets, bows, and both thrusting and throwing spears. It is a moment hunters will know until and unless semi-automatic or automatic weapons come into use. Each hunter faces the band of caribou with a weapon that fires one shot at a time. In spite of the speed of fire of a modern repeating rifle and the collective volume of fire several modern repeating rifles can generate, the hunter has one shot. One choice. One caribou to select. One opportunity to take.

As soon as the first shot is fired, the caribou begin to move. Each hunter has to keep track of the effect of his initial shot. Which animal has he hit—or has he missed? What happened to the animal he has shot? Did it go down and is it dead? Is it still on its feet? If so, where is it going? He must make note of the shots fired by others in the hunting party and the animals other hunters have hit. Bullet strikes do not leave discernible sign on the caribou they strike—as do arrows—that indicate ownership of the downed animal. Each hunter has to be aware of the shots fired by other hunters and the effects of those shots if conflict and dissension are to be prevented when it is time to butcher what has been killed.

The movement of the animals as the hunters prepare for a second shot needs observation and response. Where is the band going? Is it trying to escape in the same direction or has it been disrupted so that individuals are milling around? Animals that are attempting to flee and are being followed by others have to be singled out and brought down. The confusion, shock, and noise cause the animals to move around. The animal that is most desired as a target may well have others standing between it and the hunter. Is there a clear shot at it? If a desired caribou can be shot, where can it be shot? Shooting at the neck or head introduces a greater risk of missing the animal entirely. If only the abdomen is exposed, is it worth making a shot knowing that an abdominal shot will rupture the intestines and risk fouling the meat? Should the next shot be fired at a less desirable animal at which there is the opportunity for a clear shot that will drop it? If the surviving members of the caribou band are starting to follow a less desirable animal, should a shot be taken at that animal to try and turn the herd back so that more can be killed?

The calculations continue, the judgments are made, and the firing continues until either the caribou band together and escape to a distance such that the Denésuliné choose not to fire or enough animals have gone down that the hunters have no need for more.

The nature of the approach varies with the weapon used. Rifles and muskets are fired from a standing position; only a minimum of motions is needed to prepare the weapon to aim and fire it at the chosen target. This is not the case with bows and spears. We do not know if there was a pre-contact trade in wooden blanks that could have been used to construct bows. If there was, it is unlikely—given the ongoing hostilities between the Denésuliné and the Cree—that they would have ever been anything but rare. As it is, hardwoods are scarce in Denésuliné territory. Along the tundra, they are extremely limited in variety and numbers.

We know of no indication that the Denésuliné ever used other than a simple, straight bow made from a single piece of wood: a bow that was easy to make and could be made very quickly (see Hearne 1958: plate 5, figure 1, for a drawing of a Denésuliné bow from the 1770s). The Denésuliné have chosen willow (various *Salix* spp.) as the preferential wood from which to make their bows. Willow has both advantages and disadvantages (Frison 2004: 202–4). Although flexible, it is not a very strong wood. In the form of a straight bow that is not even recurved, it does not make for a bow with a heavy draw weight. Since Denésuliné bows have a low draw weight, arrows fired from them deliver less force and cover a shorter distance than do those fired from better made bows constructed of more suitable woods found elsewhere in North America. If the power of the willow bow is weak, willow does have off-setting advantages. Willow of the size the Denésuliné used in their bows is an almost ubiquitous growth along the northern lakes south of the tundra. It is a readily available material that can quickly be found should it be necessary to construct a bow while out in the bush. Besides its flexibility, willow is a wood that stands up well to the extreme temperatures encountered in the subarctic. Tolerance for the cold is a critical factor, given the temperatures the Denésuliné routinely encounter. Choosing a wood for its ability to work in the intense cold of winter is no small thing. It is a factor that works its way into the design and construction of all the wooden tools that have to be used in cold weather, notably ax handles. A tool made from a weaker but more flexible wood that can stand up to the extremes of winter weather is often a superior choice to a stronger wood that is liable to break or shatter in the extreme cold.

The Denésuliné bow was not more than chest height. The Denésuliné did not fire their bows from a vertical position. The bow was held parallel to the ground (90° from the vertical) and roughly waist high. The arrow was held by four fingers. The bow was rarely fired from a standing position. The archer held the bow horizontal and moved forward at a walk or quick run as he aimed and shot. The manner in which the bow was released meant the hunter had to be moving forward toward his prey when he engaged it. This would have altered the nature of Denésuliné prey selection, as the forward motion of the archer to discharge the bow would have been another alert to the caribou that they were under threat and would have given them another moment's warning to initiate flight.

This was also true with the use of a throwing spear. In order to achieve the distance and force required, the hunter had to be moving forward to throw the spear. In each case the continuity of choice remained. Arrows must be fired one arrow at a time, as spears must be thrown one spear at a time.

With the rifle, throwing spear, and bow and arrow, the targeted part of the caribou was and is the chest cavity. This is where the weapon is most likely to deliver a fatal blow without being turned aside by the bone structure of the animal. The abdomen remains the most easily penetrated and vulnerable part of the animal, but it is also the part where a lethal blow is liable to take the longest time to kill—with the concomitant risk of the animal fleeing a greater distance before it lies down. The accuracy and shock effect of the modern rifle have made the head and neck more attractive targets. It is unlikely that they were favored parts of the animal for shots with either the spear or the bow and arrow.

With the thrusting spear the continuity of the approach and prey selection begin to break down. The thrusting spear has one great advantage and one great disadvantage. If use of thrusting spears to kill swimming caribou from canoes is any guide to how the ancestral Denésuliné used thrusting spears to kill caribou on land, they preferred to strike the killing blow in much the same way they held a canoe paddle. The left hand (on a right-handed hunter) would be placed high on the shaft or at its top, with the right hand low on the shaft. The blow would be delivered from left to right with as much of a downward component as could be managed. The right hand would be used to deliver the force needed to penetrate the animal and deliver a fatal blow, while the left hand would be used to guide the stroke.

The great advantage to the use of the thrusting spear was that the killing stroke was short and downward: a stroke whereby the spear could be quickly thrust and then quickly withdrawn to be available for another stroke. The thrusting spear is, in essence, a repeating weapon. This poses a curious question that we cannot answer, since neither of us has much background in analysis of lithic tools. If the spear is intended for use as a repeating weapon, then the design of the base of the spear point and the manner in which it is hafted to the shaft should reflect that use. One would expect the appearance of designs allowing the spear to be quickly withdrawn with minimal chances of the weapon getting hung up in the prey animal after a thrust had been delivered.

When hunting from a boat, the kidneys were the favored target, but this is not likely to have been the case when hunting on land. The kidneys are a small target, and a slight miss in the placement of the stroke risked driving the spear point into the vertebral column with its attendant risk of breaking the point or lodging the weapon in the animal. It would also have required carrying the spear above the head rather than chest high.

The great disadvantage to the thrusting spear is that the hunter has to close fully with the animal in order to strike. This necessity would have altered the kinds of locations where the Denésuliné were able to hunt, placing a premium on those places where concealment was greater and the caribou were more vulnerable to being approached. When the thrusting spear was the primary weapon, it is reasonable to assume that the areas around water crossings played a more central role in pre-freeze-up Denésuliné caribou hunting than they did once firearms became the primary hunting weapons.

The need to close completely with the animal obviously reduced ancestral Denésuliné chances to obtain a kill. Certain things about closing with the prey deserve consideration. Approaching a caribou from the front is more dangerous than approaching one from the back or side. The antlers are far more dangerous head on. A kick from the front legs can be delivered far more accurately. Even a simple sideways head butt by an unantlered animal can deliver a serious injury. Closing with the caribou most likely involved moving into the herd from an ambush position and trying to move among fleeing animals in order to deliver short downward and slightly forward thrusts into the abdomen. Ideally the thrust would penetrate the diaphragm and strike the lungs or another internal organ. If not, the blow needed only to sever enough abdominal tissue to cause the animal to die from blood loss or infection while allowing the spear to be quickly and cleanly withdrawn for another blow.

These were not modern times operating under a view of time usage dictated by a clock. Time was used in accordance with the demands of the task at hand rather than being imposed upon the task by some external measure. Killing by wounding and taking the time to follow up was quite an effective way to accomplish the task at hand.

Consideration of use of the thrusting spear leads brings to mind the Clovis points used as weapon tips for spears. Life as a subsistence hunter now requires each hunter to spend much of his time out in the bush by himself. This was likely also the case for hunting peoples during the last stages of survival of the megafauna. The bush is a dangerous place. The Denésuliné male insistence on going armed into the bush is not just because they are hunters; it is also because it is potentially dangerous out there, and they never know what they might encounter. If that is true for the contemporary Canadian subarctic, it certainly applied during the time of Clovis points. If your primary weapon is a spear, the presence of a large, sharp, well-crafted Clovis point on the end of that spear would have been a comfort. Even if the point did not work any better than did other types of spear points, its very presence must have provided a degree of assurance that improved the functionality and ability to travel evinced by those who risked unexpected contact with creatures of a size and disposition we can only imagine.

Discussing prey selection with paleoanthropologists and others specialized in examining hunting among ancestral humans and related species has proven an interesting experience over the years. The phenomenon is so nuanced and complex that discussing it has proven a quick and effective method for determining whether someone's knowledge of the subject has any basis in experience. Any personal knowledge of hunting makes a difference. I (Henry) have concluded that the central thrust of Frison's *Survival by Hunting* (2004) needs to be considerably amplified. Experience of hunting large game animals in the presence of aboriginal subsistence hunters is now extremely rare and destined only to become rarer. There is little point in suggesting that it be part of professional preparation for those who specialize in understanding the hunting behavior and subsistence patterns of ancestral human and related species. However, if part of the professional education of those specialists included time spent walking in the bush during the cold and snow of a subarctic winter, or the chance to try to approach wild animals in the relevant habitat, I suspect it would induce a greater alteration in the interpretation of the hunting behavior of ancestral humans and related species than anything else that has occurred in the last half century.

Hunt 15

Caribou

Failed Hunt

AUGUST 1992

FOXHOLM LAKE, NORTHWEST TERRITORIES

During the late 1970s George decided to build a winter camp on the north shore of Foxholm Lake (H-15 on map 1). He had in mind a location several hundred yards east of the sand hill at the narrows. The sand hill, where we had camped several times over the years, was shaped like an isosceles triangle with its point to the south. It stretched northward some 250 yards and was some 100 yards wide at its base. At this point the land rose ten to fifteen feet up a moderate slope that ran (east to west) across the entire width of its base and overlooked to the north a large, rocky bay off the north-south bay of Foxholm Lake. This small incline at the back of the sand hill (K on map 1) offered a puzzle that it took more than twenty years to figure out.

There was a small patch of timber at the top of the slope leading down to the lake. Another small patch surrounded a small pond along its eastern shore. The sand hill itself was covered by reindeer moss, but the moss did not extend all the way to the rear of the sand hill. Part way up the incline at the back of the sand hill, the reindeer moss gave way to low, creeping vegetation that extended onto the incline. Above this creeping growth the incline was bare stone for some fifteen or twenty feet. Reindeer moss again covered the ground at the top of the incline and continued, mixed with other low growth, down the back (north) side of the sand hill. At the eastern and western sides of the incline, where the ground dropped away toward the north-south bay (west) and the narrow north shore of Fox-holm Lake (east), the ground was again covered by reindeer moss. The steeper parts of these two drops were exposed glacial till of stony gravel that supported no vegetation.

The exposed bare stone that covered the incline was of a peculiar character. Bare surfaces are not unusual in this country, but what made the patch of exposed stone on the incline stand out was the nature of the stone that was exposed. Instead of being bedrock or a sheet of exposed granite, the exposed surface of the incline was covered entirely by lithic debris; worked fragments left behind from the manufacture of stone tools. We never noticed finished material lying on the ground, but every fragment of rock that we examined there showed signs of having been worked by human hands.

Patches of lithic debris are common in this country, but this was by far the largest one we ever encountered. It may have been considerably larger than the dimensions given here, as the worked material extended right to the start of the plant growth, and we did not remove or disturb any growth to see how far the lithic debris extended beneath it.

We have no idea how long it would have taken ancestral hunters using the area to create such an extensive patch of lithic debris. The debris we saw was so extensive that given the small size of the population occupying this area, we presumed what we were seeing was a debris field that must have taken a considerable period of time to build up. It could well have represented the efforts of generations.

From the time we first noticed it in 1970, we assumed it was a work area for making tools and further presumed it was mostly used for making projectile points. It was intriguing to think that what we saw on the ground represented the time and work of generations of hunters over hundreds of years making projectile points as they hunted from the incline. The cobbles and rounded stones of the ridge and shoreline provided a plentiful supply of raw material, and the ridge itself gave some shelter from the north wind. It is possible that the side of the incline was simply a work area for ancestral Denésuliné camped nearby, but given the way contemporary Denésuliné conduct their work and activities, that seemed implausible. Such an extensive work area away from a place where they could also hunt and engage in both activities at the same time did not seem reasonable. If it was an odd but not unreasonable place for a work area, it seemed a most peculiar place from which to hunt.

The bay behind the ridge was so rocky that we never even attempted to take a boat into it. George rejected out of hand the idea of making his camp near it as a float plane would never be able to come to shore through the bay. From the top of the hill toward the bay was a very steep slope. The opposite shore of the bay led into a rather wet mature spruce forest, but there were no large animal trails through it. The steep slope up the back of the sand hill had no animal paths on it either and never showed tracks from animals attempting to climb up or down it. The ridge would not have had caribou swimming across the bay at its back or moving around its eastern shore and then up the steep slope of the ridge.

It seemed an unlikely place for hunters to work on stone points while they were hunting the sand hill. There was so much open ground between the incline and the front of the sand hill where the caribou trails and crossing were that it would not have been possible to move from the work area on the incline to the front of the sand hill without alarming any passing caribou and risking their scattering. The view to the west of the ridge was across the expanse of the north-south bay and up to the highland beyond. It would have taken a boat trip and more than an hour of travel to reach any game that was seen there, so it did not seem like a plausible place to work while monitoring the west side of the north-south bay.

The bay behind the ridge extended eastward past the sand hill and cut into the north shore of Foxholm Lake. Northward along the (east) shore of the bay was a patch of nondescript mature spruce forest. The north shore of Foxholm Lake closest to the sand hill was no more than thirty yards wide (i.e., the triangular sand hill was the west end of a point of land projecting into Foxholm Lake). It was not easy to get off the back of the sand hill and down to the north shore of Foxholm Lake. There was a spot where it was possible to climb down off the back of the hill to the lake shore, but it was a steep and uncomfortable climb over bare sand and glacial till. At the base of the route down the sand hill, the ground was littered with large glacial erratics. The front of the triangular sand hill, rising some twenty-five feet above the north shore of the lake, was far easier to get up and down. The slope to the lake shore by the narrows provided steady footing and was easy to negotiate, if somewhat steep. Coming off the front of the sand hill to the north shore of the lake involved a descent into a small gully then a climb of a few steps up to the lake shore.

A large caribou trail ran along the north shore of Foxholm Lake. It ran from the narrows on the lake and went up the south end of the sand hill. From there it dropped down into the gully and then paralleled the shore of Foxholm Lake. The trail continued eastward along the north shore for several hundred yards. The ground surface along the shore was but four or five feet above the lake level. Along this narrow part of the shore, just past the sand hill and bordering the bay to its north, were the remains of a white trapper's cabin that had been built in the late 1930s or the early 1940s. The cabin was noteworthy only because there were a few tall spruce trees around it and because its owner, who was decades gone and unidentifiable, had collected the birch bark covering of abandoned Denésuliné canoes from all over the north end of Foxholm Lake and used them to cover the inside walls and roof of his cabin. Collapsed and decayed, the cabin was usable only for firewood and had vanished by 1992.

The shore just east of the sand hill was glacial till rather than sand. The actual shoreline was either rocks and boulders or small sand beaches that extended one or two yards inland from the water. Behind both lay the edge of the debrading bank, slowly collapsing from both internal and external action, at the top of which lay the actual land surface. The ground surface above the debrading edges of the shore was covered by reindeer moss. It was through this border area that the large caribou trail passed. Thirty feet inland from the lake, past the stretch of reindeer moss, the land would not support mature forest. For a hundred feet the land was instead covered with dense hardwood shrub growth —mostly willow—that stood eight to ten feet high. There was no obvious indication that this stretch had ever supported anything but scrub hardwood. When the hardwoods were in leaf, visibility within this patch of scrub timber was virtually nonexistent. A number of small caribou trails cut through the scrub and led back into the mature forest that began some fifty to one hundred feet beyond its northern edge.

George chose to place his camp about fifty yards northeast of the end of this stretch of willow scrub, where the ground was open and rose a good thirty feet above the lake surface. His camp sat on open ground, facing south across Foxholm Lake. To the north the open ground continued some 150 feet before it merged into mature spruce forest. Just inside the forest was a second large caribou trail. This one ran near a mile from west to east, paralleling the lake shore but under the cover of the trees, before feeding off to other trails that led around the small lakes to the north of Foxholm Lake and off to the north toward the tundra.

George built his first cabin there in the early 1980s. The nature of Denésuliné economic circumstances had changed dramatically over the prior twenty years. Bush construction now had a far greater permanence about it and was much more elaborate in nature. By 1992 George had had his camp at this spot for a decade, and it was far more complex than could have been imagined in the 1970s. The camp had two outbuildings and his cabin had grown to three rooms. It was not only far larger and more solidly constructed than those that had been built only two decades earlier—it even had glass windows. It was well furnished, both with furniture brought from the south and with furniture handmade at the cabin. He had installed a generator and had electrical service for lighting, a freezer, and a television for watching VCR tapes. His family's primary nighttime entertainment came from watching tapes made with the camcorder he carried with him when he went out into the bush or onto the lake.

When we came up to spend August 1992 in the bush, we chose to go to Foxholm Lake near the camp George had established. We set our tents in a cluster farther east along the lake shore, roughly a hundred yards from George's cabins. Throughout the month members of the extended family came up to spend time with us, both to visit and to make dry meat. It was in this area near our tents that the dry meat rack was constructed and the women made dry meat (Sharp 2001: 177–81).

During our stop in the village Karyn and her younger sister Catherine found themselves adopted by a small puppy. (This seemed to happen every time we visited the village.) A mix of German shepherd with the local dog population, the pup was less than three months old. She had largely recovered from a broken right foreleg and had been left by her owners without water or food when they went out of town. As they were not due back for more than a week, Karyn and Catherine decided her situation was intolerable and brought her along with us into the bush. The puppy took well to bush life. She soon developed a fondness for spending most of her days at George's cabin, where there were always people about, and her nights in the tents where our party was. A trail ran between the two areas, and she happily used it to wander back and forth between the two camps.

One August afternoon, when she was no more than three and a half months old, I wandered from our camp up to George's. As I approached George's cabin I could see Phil standing outside it. The puppy was near him, also outside the cabin. As I got closer a large bull caribou came out of the woods slightly west of and several hundred feet behind the cabin. The bull was walking toward the lake shore, apparently oblivious to— or unconcerned by—our presence.

The puppy was the first to see the caribou. She immediately barked and set off in pursuit of it. Phil, surprised by her bark, turned and saw the caribou. He immediately grabbed a rifle from George's cabin and set off in pursuit. I was some distance away from them but set off in pursuit of the puppy too. The caribou was startled to hear the puppy bark and immediately broke into a run. The bull changed his direction of movement from toward the lake shore to toward the patch of scrub hardwoods and quickly entered it by one of the small caribou trails. The puppy continued in pursuit of him. We could hear her barking as she moved through the patch of scrub timber attempting to catch him.

Phil reached the patch of scrub before I did and immediately entered it by the same trail the caribou had taken. As I approached I could hear the two of them, one barking the other crashing through the scrub, as they attempted to locate the caribou. As soon as I entered the scrub, I was lost. It was possible to see only a few feet down the caribou trail. Vision to the sides was completely blocked by the scrub and leaves. The patch of scrub proved to be crisscrossed by caribou trails, making its interior an absolute maze in which it was impossible to locate anything.

It did not take long for Phil to catch up with the puppy and take her out of the scrub. I heard them outside and headed as best I could toward them, emerging on the open part of the lake shore by the main caribou trail. The bull caribou had vanished. He could have jumped into Foxholm Lake and swum across, but it is more likely that he simply ran west on the trail to the sand hill and crossed at the narrows to the south shore.

Text 15
A Puzzle

It took some time to realize that the answer to the placement of the work area at the back of the sand hill lay in the puppy's chase of the caribou. Once the caribou ran into the scrub, it was safe from our pursuit (not that our quest was very serious). Searching through the scrub led to the recognition that this vegetation had characteristics that were the probable basis for so many ancestral Denésuliné spending so much time on that incline at the north end of the sand hill. They were there to hunt. Their manufacture of stone tools was not an end in itself but a means to keep busy while they waited.

From the incline on the sand hill where the tools were made, a hunter did have a good view of the narrow part of the north shore of Foxholm Lake, where the large caribou trail led to the sand hill and the narrows at its south end. The area north and northeast of that narrow stretch of shore was timber covered, but to the north the timber opened onto the tundra. Caribou moving south off the tundra or through the timber would have encountered Foxholm Lake and would have been channeled along that trail to the narrows. It was possible for them to swim the lake from the north shore to its south side, and we often saw them do so. However, the vast majority of caribou preferred to stay on the shore and follow it to the narrows rather than swim across the lake.

A hunter sitting at the work site on the incline on the sand hill would have had ample time to see approaching animals and leave the sand hill to conceal himself along the shore of Foxholm Lake. Egress from the back of the sand hill was not easy, but it was fairly concealed, and the distance that had to be covered was at most two hundred yards. Given the preferences displayed by white trappers in their choice of ground on which to construct their cabins, it is most likely that the area where the abandoned trapper's cabin had previously stood had been open ground partially covered by scattered mature spruce trees. This type of growth does not provide ideal cover for ambushing caribou, but it would have provided enough cover for hunters to move through it without being particularly obvious to caribou moving west along the caribou trail. The scrub hardwood growth would have helped screen their movements from approaching caribou.

The scrub timber itself had a number of characteristics that would have been of use to hunters. It would have offered a place of concealment from which they could have ambushed caribou passing along the trail. It would have worked well for hunters armed with bows and would have been a reasonably good place for several hunters armed with thrusting spears to be able to come into the direct contact with the caribou that they needed in order to use their weapons. Because of the distance between the scrub and the caribou trail, this would not have worked well as an ambush point for a single hunter armed with a thrusting spear. It might also have been an awkward place for hunters armed with throwing spears to use, as it would have been difficult to find concealed places allowing the run necessary to throw the spear and yet not making the hunter immediately obvious to passing caribou, enabling them to escape.

The scrub had other possible uses. It was large enough and deep enough to allow a number of hunters to hide in it so that they could break from it as a band of caribou passed. This would have allowed them to send hunters to both the front and rear of the passing bunch of caribou. The caribou would have had few choices. They could have tried to run through the hunters, exposing themselves to the hunters' weapons, or they could have leapt from the ground over the shoreline and into the lake to swim to its south side. Given the tendency of startled caribou to mill about briefly before taking off in a single direction, and the short distances between the caribou trail, scrub timber, and lake shore, this could well have been a productive area from which to ambush passing caribou and close with them to make maximum use of the weapons available.

The caribou trails within the patch of scrub were narrow and twisty, affording running caribou little forward visibility. If caribou could be induced to enter the scrub patch, it would have been a very effective location in which to place snares to entangle them.

If canoes were to be used, the incline would have been usable as a watch point from which the hunters could spot and move to intercept caribou that chose to cross from the north shore to the south shore of Foxholm Lake. The west side of the sand hill is thirty to forty feet high, but it does have a small beach along its base on which canoes can be temporarily beached. There is too much open ground for hunters to move from the back of the sand hill where the incline is to the front of the sand hill where the narrows are. However, if caribou were seen coming along the trail to the narrows, hunters working on the ridge could slip down the west side of the sand hill and move along the beach to their canoes without being seen by the caribou. The narrows are but 100 to 125 feet wide and shoulder deep to bull caribou, but since most of the animals would wade rather than swim, it would take some time for them to cross. Canoes could be hidden within a hundred feet of the narrows so that the hunters would have had time to get to the canoes and paddle into the caribou as they made their crossing. If there were enough hunters available—or if there were women and teenagers available—it would have been possible to place people on the southern shore to frighten the caribou and turn them back into the water. This would have greatly increased the elapsed time before the caribou could escape, allowing the hunters more time among them.

We have emphasized that all hunting is local. The possible terrain usages considered here should give an indication of just how local is local. Success, especially with traditional weapons, is dependent upon careful use of local terrain features and vegetation over distances of meters and tens of meters. J. C. Crocker's point is key: hunting success depends not so much upon knowing where to find animals as upon knowing what to do when you do find animals.

With caribou, the key for the hunter is knowing how to use the terrain and control one's movements to allow closing with the animals to the point of being able to use weapons effectively. This demands a substantial knowledge of animal behavior and considerable experience of how they behave in different circumstances. Talent and physical ability certainly play a role in generating a successful hunter, but being a successful hunter owes far less to those factors than it does to a lifetime of learning and careful observation. Denésuliné hunters are students of the animals they hunt and the environment in which they live, and there is no substitute for experience and practice.

Hunting caribou with modern repeating rifles demands different skills and very different use of the terrain of the homeland in which the Denésuliné live than does hunting caribou with spears or bows. When, where, and how one hunts all change as a function of the weapons in use. That we will ever be able to understand the nature of these changes is uncertain. Perhaps all we can do is aim to understand that changes have occurred and to exhibit sensitivity to the fact that they have occurred.

If success in hunting is absolutely dependent upon skill at local terrain usage and knowledge of animal behavior, this does not mean that is all there is to it. Larger factors determine success, in both a geographical and a social sense. Frison's description of the hunting "revealed in bone beds" as "systematically opportunistic" (2004: 41) is particularly brilliant. Time and again we have seen how Denésuliné culture creates mechanisms—from gender roles to ideas of responsibility to stories and myth—that foster this systematically opportunistic approach to hunting.

The movements of caribou and other large animals are largely undeterminable. The landscape upon which Denésuliné and animals live their lives is so vast and unpopulated that individual encounters between humans and animals are almost always accidental and unpredictable. The opportunistic aspect comes from the Denésuliné ability to react to those accidental encounters: Crocker's "knowing what to do." This is the basic skill set that makes a hunter, and the mechanisms of Denésuliné culture have ensured the creation and re-creation of that skill set and that is always embodied in each generation.

The systematic quality comes into play at different levels of the cultural system. What culture can ensure, what has made the Denésuliné so successful at the business of survival, are the mechanisms that control the systematic. This means ensuring that Denésuliné hunters live lives that get them out into the bush and moving through it with sufficient frequency to generate opportunistic contacts. While on an event by event basis each contact between a hunter and an animal is accidental, Denésuliné culture ensures that hunters are the kind of people who are out and about often enough and over large enough areas to make those accidental contacts highly probable—indeed, probable enough to ensure survival and continuity through untold generations.

The way the field of meaning that is culture works is often extremely abstract. None of the Denésuliné discussed in this work understand their world in such a way that they would explain how they hunt caribou around Foxholm Lake in terms of the effects of a 5,000-square-mile dry upland stretch of tundra upon summer movements of caribou herds toward their wintering areas. They have walked, camped on, and hunted a very large part of those 5,000 square miles. Their worldview and means of expressing themselves are different, but they have that knowledge encoded in their life experiences, their family histories, the stories they and their ancestors have told, and the myths and legends that are part of their cultural heritage. That knowledge directs and determines not just the way they hunt caribou but the way they experience and live their lives.

Selected Bibliography

This bibliography has been selected not only to give the references cited but also to ensure adequate presentation of references to areas and topics addressed in this book that are beyond the normal range of anthropological consideration.

Acton, D. F., G. A. Padbury, and C. T. Stushnoff. *The Ecoregions of Saskatchewan*. Winnipeg: Canadian Plains Research Center, 1998.

Ardrey, Robert. *African Genesis: A Personal Investigation into Animal Origins and the Nature of Man*. Brooklyn: Delta, 1963.

———. *The Territorial Imperative*. New York: Fontana–Collins, 1969.

Atwood, Margaret. *Survival: A Thematic Guide to Canadian Literature*. Toronto: McClelland and Stewart, 1972.

Benton, Michael J. *When Life Nearly Died: The Greatest Mass Extinction of All Time*. London: Thames and Hudson, 2003.

Bonnicksen, Thomas M. *America's Ancient Forests: From the Ice Age to the Age of Discovery*. New York: John Wiley and Sons, 2000.

Brody, Hugh. *Maps and Dreams*. New York: Pantheon Books, 1981.

———. *The Other Side of Eden: The Hunters, Farmers and the Shaping of the World*. Douglas and McIntyre: Vancouver, 2000.

Burch, E. S., Jr. "The Caribou/Wild Reindeer as a Human Resource." *American Antiquity* 37 (1972): 339–68.

———. "Muskox and Man in the Central Canadian Subarctic 1689–1974." *Arctic* 30 (1977):132–54.

———. "Herd Following Reconsidered." *Current Anthropology* 32, no. 4 (1991): 439–44.

Chinsamy-Turan, Anusuya. *Forerunners of Mammals*. Bloomington: Indiana University Press, 2012.

Cohen, R., and J. W. VanStone. *Dependency and Self-sufficiency in Chipewyan Stories*. Bulletin 194. Ottawa: National Museum of Canada, 1963.

Cruikshank, Julie. *The Social Life of Stories: Narrative and Knowledge in the Yukon Territory*. Lincoln: University of Nebraska Press, 1998.

Curtin, P., G. Brush, and G. Fisher. *Discovering the Chesapeake*. Baltimore: Johns Hopkins University Press, 2001.

Frison, George. *Survival by Hunting: Prehistoric Human Predators and Animal Prey*. Berkeley: University of California Press, 2004.

Gamble, Clive. *The Paleolithic Settlement of Europe*. Cambridge: Cambridge University Press, 1986.

Gangloff, Roland A. *Dinosaurs under the Aurora*. Bloomington: Indiana University Press, 2012.

Gordon, Bryan C. *Of Men and Herds in Barrenland Prehistory*. Archaeological Survey of Canada, Mercury Series 28. Ottawa: National Museum of Man, 1975.

———. "More on the Herd Following Hypothesis." *Current Anthropology* 31, no. 4 (1990): 399–400.

———. *People of Sunlight: People of Starlight: Barrenland Archaeology in the Northwest Territories of Canada*. Archaeological Survey of Canada, Mercury Series 154. Ottawa: Canadian Museum of Civilization, 1996.

Gould, Stephen Jay. *The Structure of Evolutionary Theory*. Cambridge MA: Harvard University Press, 2002.

Guthrie, R. Dale. *Frozen Fauna of the Mammoth Steppe*. Chicago: University of Chicago Press, 1990.

Hawkes, F., J. F. O'Connell, and J. Coxworth. "Family Provisioning Is Not the Only Reason Men Hunt." *Current Anthropology* 51, no. 2 (2010): 259–64.

Hawkes, F., J. F. O'Connell, and N. G. Jones. "Hunting Income Patterns among the Hadza: Big Game, Common Goods, Foraging Goals and the Evolution of the Human Diet." *Philosophical Transactions of the Royal Society of London*, Series B: Biological Sciences, vol. 334, no. 1270 (1991): 243–50.

Hearne, Samuel. *A Journey to the Northern Ocean*. Toronto: Macmillan Company of Canada, 1958.

Helm, J., and D. Damas. "The Contact Traditional All-Native Community of the Canadian North: The Upper Mackenzie 'Bush' Athapaskans and the Igluligmiut." *Anthropologica n.s.* 5, no. 1 (1963): 9–22.

Hubert, H., and M. Mauss. *Sacrifice: Its Nature and Function.* Chicago: University of Chicago Press, 1964.

Jarvenpa, Robert. *The Trappers of Patuanak: Toward a Spatial Ecology of Modern Hunters.* Canadian Ethnology Service Paper no. 67, Mercury Series. Ottawa: National Museums of Canada, 1980.

Jarvenpa, R., and H. Brumbach. *Circumpolar Lives and Livelihood: A Comparative Ethnoarchaeology of Gender and Subsistence.* Lincoln: University of Nebraska Press, 2008.

Keith, Sir Arthur. *A New Theory of Human Evolution.* New York: Philosophical Library, 1949.

Kemp, Tom S. "The Origin and Radiation of Therapsid Mammal-like Reptiles: A Palaeobiological Hypothesis." *Journal of Evolutionary Biology* 19, no. 4 (July 2006): 1231–47. Quoted in *Forerunners of Mammals*, edited by Anusuya Chinsamy-Turan, 3–4. Bloomington: Indiana University Press, 2012.

Kendrick, A., P. O'B. Lyver, and Łutsël K'é Dene First Nation. "Denésoliné (Chipewyan) Knowledge of Barren-Ground Caribou (*Rangifer tarandus groenlandicus*) Movements. *Arctic* 58, no. 2 (2005): 175–91.

Lee, R. B., and I. DeVore. *Man the Hunter.* Chicago: Aldine, 1969.

Legat, Alice. *Walking the Land, Feeding the Fire: Knowledge and Stewardship among the Tlicho Dene.* Tucson: University of Arizona Press, 2012.

Lorenz, Konrad. *On Aggression.* New York: Mariner Books, 1974.

Mauss, Marcel. *The Gift.* New York: W. W. Norton, 1967.

Morgan, Elaine. *The Descent of Woman.* London: Souvenir Press, 1972.

Needham, Rodney. *Belief, Language, and Experience.* Oxford: Basil Blackwell, 1972.

Osgood, C. B. *The Ethnography of the Great Bear Lake Indians.* Ottawa: F. A. Acland, 1933.

Petch, Virginia. "Relocation and Loss of Homeland: The Story of the Sayisi Dene of Northern Manitoba." PhD diss., University of Manitoba, 1998. Collections Canada.

Pielou, E. C. *After the Ice Age: The Return of Life to Glaciated North America.* Chicago: University of Chicago Press, 1991.

Ray, S., J. Botha-Brink, and A. Chinsamy-Turan. "Dicymodont Growth Dynamics and Lifestyle Adaptations." In *Forerunners of Mammals,* edited by Anusuya Chinsamy-Turan, 120–22. Bloomington: Indiana University Press, 2012.

Robertson Smith, W. *The Religion of the Semites.* London: Adam and Charles Black, 1901.

Seton, Ernest T. *The Arctic Prairies.* New York: Harper Colophon Books, 1981.

Sharp, Henry S. "Trapping and Welfare: The Economics of Trapping in a Northern Saskatchewan Chipewyan Village." *Anthropologica* 17, no. 2 (1975): 29–44.

———. "Man:Wolf::Woman:Dog." *Arctic Anthropology* 13, no. 1 (1976): 25–34.

———. "The Chipewyan Hunting Unit." *American Ethnologist* 4, no. 2 (1977a): 377–93.

———. "Bilaterality and Strategies of Caribou Hunting among the Chipewyan." *Arctic Anthropology* 14, no. 2 (1977b): 35–40.

———. "Comparative Ethnology of the Wolf and the Chipewyan." In *Wolf and Man: Evolution in Parallel,* edited by Roberta Hall and Henry S. Sharp, 61–64. New York: Academic Press, 1978.

———. "The Null Case: The Chipewyan." In *Woman the Gatherer,* edited by F. Dahlberg, 221–24. New Haven: Yale University Press, 1981.

———. "Some Problems in Wolf Sociology." In *Wolves of the World,* edited by F. Harrington and P. Paquet, 423–33. Park Ridge NJ: Noyes Publishing, 1982.

———. "Giant Otters, Giant Fish, and Dinosaurs: 'Apparently Irrational' Beliefs in a Chipewyan Community." *American Ethnologist* 14, no. 2 (1987): 226–35.

———. *The Transformation of Bigfoot: Maleness, Power, and Belief among the Chipewyan.* Washington DC: Smithsonian Institution Press, 1988a.

———. "Dry Meat and Gender: The Absence of Ritual for the Regulation of Animal Numbers and Hunting in Chipewyan Society." In *Hunters and Gatherers,.* Vol. 2: *Property, Power and Ideology,* edited by T. Ingold, D. Riches, and James Woodburn, 183–91. London: Berg Publishers, 1988b.

———. "Memory, Meaning, and Imaginary Time: The Construction of Knowledge in White and Chipewyan Cultures." *Ethnohistory* 38, no. 2 (1991): 149–75.

———. "Inverted Sacrifice." In *Circumpolar Religion and Ecology: An Anthropology of the North*, edited by T. Irimoto and T. Yamada, 253–71. Tokyo: University of Tokyo Press, 1994a.

———. "The Power of Weakness." In *Key Issues in Hunter-Gatherer Research*, edited by E. Burch Jr. and L. Ellana, 35–58. London: Berg Publishers, 1994b.

———. "Asymmetric Equals: Gender Equality among the Chipewyan." In *Power and Gender in Native North America*, edited by L. Klein and N. Ackerman, 46–74. Norman: University of Oklahoma Press, 1995.

———. "Experiencing Meaning," *Anthropology and Humanism* 21, no. 2 (1996): 171–86.

———. "Non-Directional Time and the Dene Life-Cycle." In *Circumpolar Animism and Shamanism*, edited by T. Irimoto and T. Yamada, 93–104. Sapporo: Hokkaido University, 1997.

———. "A la recherche du caribou." *Recherches Amérindiennes au Québec* 38, no. 3 (1998): 63–70.

———. *Loon: Memory, Meaning, and Reality in a Northern Dene Community*. Lincoln: University of Nebraska Press, 2001.

Slobodin, Richard. "Some Social Functions of Kutchin Anxiety." *American Anthropologist* 62, no. 1 (1960): 122–33.

———. *Band Organization of the Peel River Kutchin*. Bulletin no. 55. Ottawa: National Museum of Canada, 1962.

Smith, David M. *Inkonze: Magico-religious Beliefs of Contact Traditional Chipewyan Trading at Fort Resolution, NWT*. Canadian Ethnology Service Paper no. 6, Mercury Series. Ottawa: National Museums of Canada, 1973.

———. *Moose-Deer Island House People: A History of the Native People of Fort Resolution*. Canadian Ethnology Service Paper no. 81. Mercury Series. Ottawa: National Museums of Canada, 1982.

Smith, James G. E. "The Chipewyan Hunting Group in a Village Context." *Western Canadian Journal of Anthropology* 2, no. 1 (1970): 60–66.

———. "The Ecological Basis of Chipewyan Socio-Territorial Organization." In *Proceedings: Northern Athapaskan Conference*, edited by A. McFadyen Clark, 389–461. Canadian Ethnology Service Paper no. 27, Mercury Series. Ottawa: National Museums of Canada, 1975.

———. "Local Band Organization of the Caribou Eater Chipewyan." *Arctic Anthropology* 13, no. 2 (1976): 12–24.

Steyer, Sebastien. *Earth Before the Dinosaurs*. Bloomington: Indiana University Press, 2012.

Stringer, C., and C. Gamble. *In Search of Neanderthals*. New York: Thames and Hudson, 1993.

Irimoto, Takashi, and Takako Yamada. *Circumpolar Religion and Ecology: An Anthropology of the North*. Tokyo: University of Tokyo Press, 1994.

Tanner, Adrian. *Bringing Home Animals*. New York: St. Martin's Press, 1979.

Thomas, Keith. *Man and the Natural World: Changing Attitudes in England 1500–1800*. New York: Penguin Books, 1984.

VanStone, James W. *The Changing Culture of the Snowdrift Chipewyan*. Bulletin no. 209. Ottawa: National Museum of Canada, 1965.

Washburn, S. L. *The Social Life of Early Man*. Chicago: Aldine, 1961.

Wessels, Tom. *Reading the Forested Landscape: A Natural History of New England*. Vermont: Countryman Press, 1997.

Wilson, John, and Ron Clowes. *Ghost Mountains and Vanished Oceans: North America from Birth to Middle Age*. Toronto: Key Porter Books, 2009.

Index

accuracy, 79, 80
Acton, D. F., et al., xxxvii
Adam, Ben, xiv, 74–75
African model, 19, 95–100
aim point, 266
air clarity, 65
Alexander, Herb, xxxiii
"All Native Communities" (Helm and Damas), 150
ambush hunting. *See* hunting
American attitudes toward guns. *See* firearms
American lion, 240
ammunition pouch, 203
animals: abuse of, 255; dried for storage, 42; food locations of, 57–58; killing of, 25; sentience, 26, 71
animal/spirits, 23–24, 56–57, 211–12, 259–60
approaching caribou. *See* caribou
Ardrey, Robert, 99
area of exploitation, 124–25
Artchie, Abraham, xiv, xvi, 28, 29, 30, 32
Atwood, Margaret, 26
automatic weapons. *See* weapons

bannock, 49

beauty, xxxvi–xxxvii, 138
beaver, 14–15
belief, 24
berries, 50, 132
black bear, 13, 103, 185, 202–3, 249–51
Blue Babe, 103
boats, 59–60; landings, 118
boiling bones, 50
boreal forest, full, 29
bow and arrow, 264–66
Brody, Hugh (*Maps and Dreams*), xxvii
Brumbach, H., 12, 134
buffalo, 14
bulldogs, 129–30
Burch, E. S., Jr., 13, 243
butchering: moose and caribou, 5, 30–31, 130–131. *See also* caribou, butchering

cabins, log, 181
caliber. *See* firearms
camps, 114; formation, 108, 115–18; Joe's Camp, 2, 3, 155, 202; large, 115–26, 127; selection, 51, 90, 113–14, 156–57
Canadian Archaeological Service, 144

canoes, 279
caribou, xxxvii, 1–2, 3, 12, 15, 81,
135; approaching, 245–47, 268;
behavior, 53–54, 79–80, 81, 214–15,
217–18, 221–22, 223, 225–26, 227,
234, 244–47, 253–54, 257, 261–
64, 263–65; butchering, 5–9, 254;
calving grounds, 225–26; dispatching wounded, 255; fat, 6–7, 185–86;
fetus, 111; hair, 178–80; head, 5;
holding area, xxxiv, 2–3; killing, 4;
leaving hide on, 36; migration, 15;
milling, 54, 254; mobility, 15; rut,
185; spearing, 223–25; spring migration of, 64–65; and summer on tundra, 150–51, 225–27, tongue, 6;
trails, 222; vision, 66; winter range
of, 213; winter trails of, 214; and
wolf, xxxi, 19–80, 109–10, 240–
47; and wolf and human triad, 80,
241–47
Caribou Eaters, xxxviii, 150; finding
caribou, 62–63
caribou hide, 6, 174–75, 178–79, 180,
182–86; dried and worked, 177–
78; as ground cloths, 179; leather
from, 175, 180, 181–82; parka and
pants from, 180; as sleeping bags,
178; storing caribou hide clothing,
178–80; tanning, 175; winter clothing from, 178–80, 236–39; winter
hides, 178–79, 180
change, 234–35
choke points, 169
choosing where to live, 137–38
Christian attitudes toward animals,
23
Clovis points, 268–69
commercial value, 205
concentration, xxviii, 245–47; and
persistence while hunting, 51–56,
246
conical hill, 164
cooking outside, 40
cordage, 182–83
cougar, 14

Cree, 73, 176, 225, 265
Crocker, J. Christopher, 61–62, 280,
281
Curtin, Bush, and Fisher, 17

Dakelh (Carrier), 20
dangers of the bush, 21, 57–58, 119,
143–44
day trips, 122
deadfalls, 219–20
death rattle, 129
deer, 14
deliberate pursuits, 210
Denésuliné, 11–12; conceptualizations
of animals, 23–24
Department of Natural Resources
(DNR), xi
dire wolf, 240
Discha, xiii, xiv, xxxix, 28, 42
dispatching wounded caribou, 255
division of labor, xxix, 193–95
dog, 195, 197; beds, 116–18; food, 7,
10, 136; packs, 183; teams, 54, 55,
58, 116–17, 122–23, 212–13; walking a, 240
drives, pounds, and fences, 21–22,
225–31
drunken forest, xxxv
dry fish, 42, 43, 135
dry meat, 41–42, 186, 248; caribou
as, 41, 43–49, 85–86; cleanliness of
making dry meat, 33; fat in, 41; fly
blown, 134; making, 43–49, 132–35;
moose as, 33; preference for caribou,
133–34; smoking, 47–49; spoilage
of, 132; storage of, 45–46, 132, 242–
43; racks, 43–44, 108–9
duck hunting, 206

the Earth, 235
Echinococcus granulosis, 7
economic explanation, 120–21, 122,
137–38, 205–7
Eddy's stone piles, 229–30
effort, 166–67
eggs, 136
English River, xvi, 42

establishing independence, 83–84

fair fight, 18
fences, 112–13, 227–28; and pounds, 86–87
firearms: .243 caliber, 73; .30-.30 caliber, 77, 78; access to, 17–18, 73; American attitudes toward, 16–18; flintlock muskets, 73–76; modern repeating rifle, 77–86, 225; percussion cap rifle, 76–77; rifled muskets, 76. See also weapons
fish net, 135, 183
flintlock muskets. See firearms
Fond du Lac people, 160
food storage: in the bush, 34–38, 38–40; cooking and, 39–40; of fat, 35–36, 186; in water, 38, 39, 146–47; of western foods, 40
forest fire, xxxv–xxxvi, 143
freezer, community, 33–34
Frison, George, 16, 60, 269, 280–81

Gamble, Clive, 98, 105
gasoline, 122
gender, xxx, 19–21, 98–100, 119–20, 194–95, 230–31; gender and hunting, xxv, 78–79, 119, 230–31; rifles, animal/spirits, 78–79. See also women
geological history, 232
glacial action, xxxiii–xl
goose hunting, 205–6
Gordon, Bryan, 243
governmental control, xxxix–xl
grass, 29
grizzly bear, 13–14, 204
growth and decay, xxxiv–xxxvi
guns, 17. See also firearms; weapons; women
gunsmith, 78
Guthrie, Dale, 103, 233
gut piles, 8–9, 109, 110, 126, 255–56

Hearne, Samuel, 19–20
herbivory, 15–16
herd following, 243

hides, 170, 187–88; and fat, 170, 204; calf, 171–73; and hunting, 184–87
highland, 160–61
How Long Is The Memory Of Unused Technology, 235–39
hunters, female. See women
hunting, 16, 17–19, 21, 22, 62–63, 75–76, 77–78, 80–86, 170–71, 185–86, 210; as an adaptation, 80–86, 235; ambush, 224, 244; causality in hunting, 205–7; as a chaotic process, 61; as a contest between human and animal, 18; dangers of, 56–57, 81; deliberate, 60–61; endurance, 87–88, 216–219; from high ground, 108–11, 112, 167–69, 252–54, 257–58; on lake ice, 65–67, 67–69, 110–12; as a male activity, 19–21, 97–100; nature of subsistence, 11–13, 18, 26, 56; opportunistic, 60, 280–81; and scavenging debate, 16, 98–101; snowmobile, 53–54, 66–67, 110–11, 112, 216; social context of, 260–61; solitary, 209–12; sustained yield, 82; tactics, 15, 18, 79–80, 81, 93, 128–29, 202–4, 207–8, 211, 214–15, 248, 254, 262–64, 277–82; tactics in water, 223–25; of yearlings, 186
Hudson Bay, 253
Hudson's Bay Company, 73, 84, 225
human nature, 237

ice sheets, 232–33
inactivity, 190–91
inkoze, 237–38
insects, xxx–xxxi, 51, 91, 94, 117–18, 129–30, 135, 179, 187, 201, 226; blood loss to bites of, 117, 129; warble flies, 179–180

jackfish, 191–92
Jarvenpa, R., 12, 134, 213

keeping busy, 137
Keith, Sir Arthur, 99

"knowing the land," 60–61

lake ice, 52–53, 67–69, 233–34; break-up of, 234; candling (chandling) of, 52; pancaking of, 52
the land, xxxiii–xxxiv, xxxvi, 3–4
learning to shoot, 82–83
linearity, 227, 246
lithic debris bed, 271–72
Lorenz, Konrad, 99
lowlands, 161
lynx, 28–29

machete, 131
Mammoth Steppe, xxxvii, 233
Man the Hunter Conference, 98
marrow, 49–50, 104; and grease, 49
meat: caches, 71–72, 247–50; distribution of, 32–33, 34, 111; dragging, 91; freezing, 34, 38, 41; lost, 55, 131; permafrost food storage for, 34–35; piles, 8–9, 36–37; preparing, for storage, 41, 71–72; sale of moose, 32; spoilage, 91; transportation of, 8, 9, 22–23, 91, 145, 147–48, 204; transportation of, by dog team, 148, 215; transportation of, by snowmobile, 215
megafauna, 39, 187–88, 233
microenvironments, xxxvi–xxxviii
military weapons. See weapons
mission, xiii, xiv, xxxviii, xxxix, 11, 28
mobility and transportation, xxxii, 3, 12, 22–23, 26–27, 57–60, 85–86, 88–89, 91–92, 120, 121–22, 131, 142–43, 145, 148–50, 183, 211–12, 214–16, 247–49, 256, 261
moose, 13, 205; hide, 175–77
Morgan, Elaine, 99–100
Mother Earth, 234–35
moving meat or moving people, 148
muskeg, 38–39, 159–60
muskets and bear, 75
musk ox, 13, 43

Neanderthal, 16, 19, 167, 186, 236–37, 238–39
need for clothing, 187
Needham, Rodney, 24
nets, 182–83, 221; small game, 213–14
the noble hunter, 25
not hunting, 136

O'Connell, J. F., 100
opportunistic hunting/accidental contact, 60, 63, 211–12, 244–45

pace of animal life, 97–98
pack frames, 91
parkland tundra, 11, 13
participant observation, xxiv, xxv–xxvi
pemmican, 14, 42–43; buffalo, 14, 42; musk ox, 42
percussion cap rifle. See firearms
permafrost, xxxiv, 11, 38–39, 69, 233
physical demands of bush life, 84
Pleistocene Europe, xxxvii
Pliocene, 232
Precambrian Shield, 232–33
predation, 15–16, 26, 103
prey: approaching, 79–82; choice, 11–12, 70, 206; selection, 70, 262–65
the puppy, 275–76

radius of activity, 123–24
rainfall, xxxiv, 11
rate of fire, 82–83
registered traplines, xl, 137
reindeer moss, xxxvi–xxxvii, 29, 140, 222, 234
Riddle, Fred, xiv, 38, 155
rifle, modern repeating. See firearms
rifle cases, 78
rifled muskets. See firearms
ring of stones, 164
Riou Lake Road, 28
rock sled, 91
Royal Canadian Mounted Police (RCMP), xl

Sanderson Lake, 143, 155
sand hill, 270–71, 273
Sayisi, 106
scale, xxxi–xxxii, xxxvii, 12, 21–22, 24–25, 97, 98, 102–7, 148–51, 187–88, 189, 193–95; and microenvironments, 135
scale of human presence, 115, 120, 125
scavengers, 31, 95–98; large, 36, 37, 249–51; loss to, 55; small, 36, 37; and storage, 8–10, 35–36, 249–51
scavenging 16, 98–104; finding dead animals, 101–7
scimitar cat, 240
self-sufficiency, xxix
semiautomatic weapons. See weapons
sewing, 198, 236–37
sexual division of labor, 193–200
short-faced bear, 240
silence, xxxvii
small game, 12–13, 136
Smith, D. M., 238, 254
smoke tents, village, 33
smoking small animals, 49
snares, 219–20; and nets, 182–83, 219–21
snow, 57, 59, 69–70
snowmobiles, xli, 70
snow probes, 105–6
snowshoe hare, 12, 13, 219
snowshoes, 218
social acts, 258–59
social context of a hunt. See hunting
solitary hunts. See hunting
sparseness of animal populations, 97–98
spearing caribou. See caribou
spear points, 267
stages, 34–35
stone tools, 237–39
summer inactivity, 132

Tanner, Adrian, 134
temperament, 199–200

temperatures and rainfall, xxxiv, 11, 91
themes, xxx–xxxii
Thomas, Keith, 17
throwing spear, 266
thrusting spear, 266–67
time, 268
tipis, 180–81
toilets, 115, 119
topsoil, 233
Total Social Phenomenon (Mauss), 259
tracking: bear, 28; moose, 28–30
traditional diet, 85
trails, 86–87, 121; networks, 57, 58
transmission of knowledge, 235–39
trash and debris, 116
travois, 91

unscavenged carcass, 93, 94–95

vegetation, xxxiv–xxxv

walking a dog. See dog
warble flies. See insects
water: crossings, 221–25; danger of, 59–60; drinking, 113
weapons: automatic, 73; military, 73; modern repeating rifle, 77–86, 225; percussion cap rifle 76–77; semiautomatic, 73. See also firearms
white birch, 162
willow, 53–54, 265–66
wolf, 14, 22, 37, 101, 109–10, 112, 192, 205, 216, 219, 221, 234, 240–47, 249; and caribou, xxxi, 19–80, 109–10, 240–47; and caribou and human triad, 80, 241–47; concentration, 246
wolverine, 38, 249
women: as hunters, 19–20, 21, 194–95; labor of, xxx, 26–27, 178, 188, 193–99; physical limitations on, as hunters, 20–21; and rifles, 119–20. See also gender

yarding, 60–61

Other works by Henry S. Sharp

The Transformation of Bigfoot: Maleness, Power, and Belief among the Chipewyan

Loon: Memory, Meaning, and Reality in a Northern Dene Community

CPSIA information can be obtained at www.ICGtesting.com
Printed in the USA
BVOW04*1426030515

398341BV00006B/29/P